RADICAL PHILOSOPHY

2.04
Series 2 / Spring 2019

Laboratories of gender
D-M Withers 3

'By contraries execute all things'
Alberto Toscano 9

Is logos a proper noun?
Yijing Zhang 23

Dossier: Social reproduction theory 33

    On the value of social reproduction
    Alessandra Mezzadri 33

    After the housewife
    Kalindi Vora 42

    Social reproduction and empire in an Egyptian century
    Mai Taha and Sara Salem 47

    Social reproduction theory
    Silvia Federici 55

Late style and contrapuntal histories
Alex Fletcher 59

Critical Theory's contexts of cooperation
Oskar Negt in conversation with Johan F. Hartle 73

Reviews 86

    Pascal Chabot, *Global Burnout*
    Hannah Proctor 86

    Asad Haider, *Mistaken Identity*
    Samir Gandesha 89

    Giorgio Agamben, *What is Philosophy?*
    Giorgio Agamben, *Taste*
    Jae Emerling 93

    Nathan Brown, *The Limits of Fabrication*
    Daniel Katz 97

    Janina Wellman, *The Form of Becoming*
    Nick Lambrianou 101

    Jeff Love, *The Black Circle: A Life of Alexandre Kojève*
    Jorge Varela 104

    David Sosa, ed., *Bad Words*
    Heather Stewart 107

    Stefanie R. Fishel, *The Microbial State*
    Chris Wilbert 110

    Alfie Bown, *The Playstation Dreamworld*
    Mike Watson 112

    Cohen and Duckert, eds., *Veer Ecology*
    Alice Gibson 114

Editorial collective
Claudia Aradau
Brenna Bhandar
Victoria Browne
David Cunningham
Peter Hallward
Stewart Martin
Lucie Mercier
Daniel Nemenyi
Hannah Proctor
Rahul Rao
Martina Tazzioli
Chris Wilbert

Engineers
Daniel Nemenyi
Alex Sassmanshausen

Creative Commons BY-NC-ND
Radical Philosophy, Spring 2019

ISSN 0300-211X
ISBN 978-1-9999793-3-1

Laboratories of gender
Women's liberation and the transfeminist present
D-M Withers

In 2018, the Feminist Archive South received funding from the UK Government Equalities Office to run events in community locations across the South West. This programme enabled cross-generational engagements with inspiring histories of the recent feminist past.[1] Activities were open to self-identified women and non-binary people – a point that enraged so-called 'gender-critical feminists' who reject the idea that 'sex' can be subsumed by 'gender' while claiming it is fundamentally not possible to change the sex one is assigned at birth. Posie Parker – a proudly anti-trans agent provocateur who recently gained international notoriety[2] – attended one of the workshops run in partnership with TIGER (Teaching Individuals Gender Equality & Respect), a Bristol-based not-for-profit co-operative who work with schools and youth organisations to address gender inequality.[3] Parker signed up under a pseudonym and, when she arrived, shouted aggressively at the workshop facilitators, accusing them of being misogynists. She continued to interrogate those present throughout, and upon leaving, tore down creative work made by participants. That evening a video appeared on YouTube in which Parker recounted her version of events. Over 27 thousand people have now seen it, and an extensive comment thread reveals many people who find delight in her actions and perceive her hate speech as entertainment.

How do we make sense of such displays of anti-trans feeling, especially among those who self-describe as feminists? Transgender has occupied a fraught place within feminism since the 1970s, which is often expressed through anxious policing of the boundaries determining what and who women are. Yet transgender is woven in diverse ways into the fabric of all feminist interventions that seek to rework the material constitution of bodies, institutions, imaginaries, laws, culture, times and spaces. My contention here is that the activist, epistemic and ontological legacies of the British Women's Liberation Movement (WLM)[4] are woefully – and irresponsibly – absent from how 'gender-critical' feminists in the UK have articulated their arguments about what feminism is, and who its constituents are. In their fervent and often cruel expressions, they ventriloquize the building blocks of feminist knowledge upon which they stand, but simultaneously disavow. Transgender activists and their allies also frequently overlook potential alliances with the activist struggles of the WLM. This is perhaps understandable given the persistent characterisation of the WLM as irreducibly distant from and inherently hostile to trans experiences, of all kinds. Even so, this is an injustice to the radicalism of the WLM – a social movement that must be credited for creating conceptual and lived resources for much of the feminism, including transfeminist discourse, we can speak and think with today.

A different public understanding of feminism's theoretical and activist history is therefore required: one that gives proper place to its activist foundations in the WLM and demonstrates how this movement has been entangled with a kind-of transgender politics from its inception. I say *kind-of* here with some caution, knowing the dangers of bringing different historical periods into conversation when it might not always be possible to situate alliance through obviously shared conceptual or political languages. The WLM's gender politics cannot be mapped seamlessly onto contemporary trans struggles, this much is true. Nevertheless, contemporary trans politics are in part a legacy of the WLM, and in particular, the way the movement created meaningful and supportive contexts for those designated 'female' at birth to re-invent their embodied and psychic existences. Through expanding what 'woman' could be, the experimental social contexts the movement created transformed what it meant to be a woman or a man, a girl or a boy, in everyday life.[5] In this arena, the WLM has contributed substantially to the *trans-formation* of sex by making gender legible as a social practice. So whilst there has been a drive to uncover and understand the historical legacies of trans exclusionary or anti-trans feminism, it is also important to ask other questions about the histories of feminist activism and knowledge. How has women's liberation conditioned the transfeminist present, and how did medicalised ideas about transsexuality and intersex influence the development of feminist knowledge in the early 70s?

Gender and transformation

The WLM created social contexts that re-made women's nature. As a social movement it staged a sustained revolt '*against* natural laws'.[6] Its ontological and political legacies are an example of what Dimitris Papadopoulos calls 'activist materialism' that 'mixes ontology and practice through and through'. In *Experimental Practice*, Papadopoulos describes the history of activist materialism as 'unstable [and] full of discontinuities and breaks'. Within this understanding, 'matter itself cannot be conceived outside or as a mere object of human practice but *as a process of change*.'[7] What is fundamentally missing from our understanding of the WLM – whether invoked within the paywalls of academic feminist theory or the rabid annals of twitter – is *how* the WLM contributed to the substantial transformation of the female sex's *material* existence. This transformative activity gave form to the social apparatus and enduringly tricky playground we now call 'gender'. It opened up sociolegal, cultural and psychic fields to the exploration of potential alternatives in which a woman could deviate from her 'nature' and 'change the ontological conditions of everyday existence'.[8]

Such social engineering was possible because the movement was informed by a new kind of conceptual, as well as technoscientific, freedom to experiment across the boundaries of 'nature' and 'nurture.' British sociologist Ann Oakley's 1972 book *Sex, Gender and Society* is credited in the English Oxford Dictionary as introducing the modern usage of the word 'gender', and it is here we find the history of women's liberation and transgender lives braided in the most intimate tangle. In an oral history interview conducted in 2012, Oakley reflects on how she adapted 'gender' from psychiatric concepts used to explain the psychic and embodied experiences of transsexual and intersex people:

> [I adapted the term 'gender'] from American psychiatry, psychiatrists who were working with people with various degrees of, I mean, you know, women who thought they were actually men and men who thought they were actually women, and people born with various degrees of physical intersexual conditions. They, those psychiatrists had realised that you have to make a distinction between what biology provides in the way of a body, and what the culture provides in the form of ideas about how men and women ought to behave.[9]

Oakley's appropriation of a particular historical and medicalised construction that sought to grapple with transsexual experience is often overlooked. Studying the socio-medical phenomenon of intersex and transsexuality can, she wrote in 1972, 'tell us a great deal about the relative parts played by biology and social rearing: there are a multitude of ways in which it can illuminate the debate about the origin of sex differences. To start with what is perhaps the most striking finding, boys without penises may become "normal" males: girls with penises and without uteruses may become "normal" females.'[10] By the late 1970s, other feminist sociologists echoed her conceptual move, claiming transsexual women 'as striking examples of processes that affected all women's lives,' material evidence of the 'plasticity of gender, giving credibility to agendas of social change.'[11]

To understand the epistemological evolution of contemporary feminism, the centrality of transgender must be taken seriously. The WLM was informed by a medicalised understanding of transgender. Such logic lay at the root of the movement's investigation into how everyday life could be different for women and men, girls and boys; it demonstrated the dissonance between ascription and lived experience, that biology need not be destiny and existence could, through cultivation, be made – and re-made – otherwise. The WLM spread transgender through its social bodies. While it did not explicitly define activist claims, this form of politics was nonetheless 'forcefully present' in a historical opening that questioned and practically overcame the limitations of sex.[12]

It is certainly true that women's liberationists used 'gender' to emphasise the repressive aspects of social conditioning, rather than foreground gender's liberatory potential. Gay Preston's illustration, published in 1974, presents a striking critique of the violence of gender socialisation.[13] It starts with a boy and girl inside open boxes that gradually close up into coffins as the children grow up. Commonplace statements declaring the rigidity of gender stereotypes accompany the illustrations: 'only sissies play with dolls' and 'girls don't climb trees'. The coffins are too small for adult bodies, figures are squashed into spaces they could never fit: 'your hair's too long you look like a girl', 'you'll end up an old maid'. The final nail in the coffin is marriage: the grand institution of what Adrienne Rich would later call 'compulsory heterosexuality'; a social death represented by the blank, boarded up coffins. For many women's liberationists, it was this kind of gender that had to be destroyed. Gender stereotypes were – and remain – maddeningly stultifying. So if 'gender-critical' feminists express antipathy toward 'gender', this could be a hangover from a historical moment when gender was equated wholesale with negative conditioning. 'We wanted to get *rid of* gender', they argue, not give it social substance. Yet this is to overlook an important fact: the WLM gave new life and meaning to 'gender'. 'Gender', in the context of the movement, became a malleable property. It was no longer simply restrictive; it also became expansive. This socialised enlargement pulled 'sex' into a dialogical process that reconfigured its shape and substance too.

Practices of women's liberation

The British WLM was grounded in experimental, prefigurative 'lifestyle' politics that questioned what it meant to be a 'woman' outside of patriarchal conditioning. One of the many tendencies that informed the WLM's political frameworks was 'cultural feminism': a kind of feminism imported from the US that sought to create a 'women's culture.' In the US, 'women's culture' was associated with women-only activities such as music festivals, record labels, bands, credit unions and publishing houses, as well as aesthetic theories about language, film, fashion, music and spirituality.[14] These ideas travelled to the UK via musical products and other kinds of 'merchandise' produced within the US WLM, but also, crucially, through individual activists who visited the US and were inspired by the example of women-only organisation, autonomy and empowerment.[15]

Sophie Lewis has recently argued, following historian Alice Echols, that 'cultural feminism' represented a 'paranoid faction' of US radical feminism that gave rise to transphobic feminist ideology in the US. Lewis also implies this influence was reproduced, homogenously, in the UK.[16] She writes that trans exclusionary feminism 'crossed over to Britain in the 1980s, when cultural feminism was among the lesbian-separatist elements of antinuclear protest groups who saw themselves as part of a "feminist resistance" to patriarchal science, taking a stand against nuclear weapons, test-tube babies and male-to-female transsexual surgery alike.'[17] This periodisation and location of trans exclusionary feminism does not, however, adequately reflect the historical conditions that gave rise to the phenomenon in Britain. In the British WLM, cultural feminism was more practical than ideological, pragmatic rather than paranoid. It was the means through which women would build 'an alternative society where women are not oppressed; housing networks, farms, businesses, busic [sic], art & therapy are all steps in the direction of women taking power.'[18]

Ideas about 'women's culture' helped create new kinds of contexts – experimental social laboratories – in which the female sex was bent into new, irreversible shapes. As women learnt how to fix PA systems, repair faulty car engines, explore the contours of a drum kit, or mend the plumbing, their sex was not – and never could be – insulated from 'gender': each force field fed into and modulated the other, expanding what the female sex could 'be' through exposure to techniques and *practice*. Such activities were central to constructing a material power of women's liberation, to paraphrase Cynthia Cockburn, which utilised women-only networks, spatial politics and technique to change women's position in society on an individual and collective basis.[19] The ex-*pressions* of bodily life that flowed from the movement's gender laboratories were acts of social sculpting[20] which became 'materially ingrained into the affects, the muscles, the sociability, the desires, the lifeworlds'[21] of feminism – and across wider society – in decades to come. Re-educating and re-training the female body – enabling the exploration of alternative forms of existence – happened *within* the WLM, *inside* its material politics. The construction of women-only spaces – unmarked by the categorical differentiations that characterise contemporary feminism such as 'cis-gender women' and 'trans women' – intensified experimentation. Women-only spaces enabled participants to cultivate and transform their potential; the female sex began to walk, talk and make life in new ways. This ontological transformation of the female sex deposited lasting material residues in social space which potential subsequent generations have fed off, picked up and lived with, often without realising it: an accumulation of feminist debt[22] that furnishes the possibility for thinking and acting in the world in feminist ways.

The theoretical roots of trans-exclusionary feminism in the British WLM were, in contrast, laid down in 1977 when a renegade faction – 'revolutionary feminism' – came to prominence.[23] Revolutionary feminism modified Shulamith Firestone's ideas about sex class – dislocating Firestone's emphasis on technology as key to women's liberation – and arose, so its founders claimed, because women's liberation in Britain lacked a coherent political theory. Since the WLM had emerged in the late 60s, revolutionary feminists argued, the movement had been 'water[ed] down' and now 'ceas[ed] to be a threat' – a dilution which 'cultural feminism', they argued, was partly responsible for.[24] For revolutionary feminists, 'sex struggle is the struggle. All women are in the 'class' that is women, subsuming all minor differences – which anyway come from male supremacy.' As with contemporary 'gender-critical' feminists, revolutionary feminists placed great emphasis on biology and were peculiarly fixated on genitals: 'Possession of a penis, an external and visible singular organ which tumesces toward the ultimate orgasm and then collapses, *apparently with a will of its own*, will colour a man's experience of life.'[25] The penis, they claimed, was a 'physical disability or mutation' that marked a man as 'animal', and male violence against women was framed as a response to a traumatic realisation of an 'inability to bring forth life.' 'Yes we are angry, yes we do love women, yes we do hate men [...] yes all women are a class, yes all men are potential rapists [...] yes we are extremists'[26] they incanted. Revolutionary feminists, rather than 'cultural feminism', have pushed forward the trans-exclusionary agenda in Britain. Many of its adherents – the most well known being Sheila Jeffreys – are prominent voices in the resurgence of 'gender-critical' activism in the twenty-first century.[27]

Technics of sex and gender

From the late 60s onwards, feminist demands in the UK for female autonomy (articulated since the 1920s)[28] synthesised with a technoscientific context that enabled the concept of autonomy – once abstract and distant – to become a lived experimental practice. The WLM converged with a historical moment when the ontological ground opened up and swallowed any remaining fantasies of static and symmetrical sex roles: of man as 'the human' and woman as appendage, constructed from his excess bodily matter, that mythic 'spare rib'. Upon that ground, the reality of female autonomy was furnished with mobility and women tested and tore past limitations of their flesh. The freedoms to explore what the 'female' body could do in the 70s – how it could be substantially stylised and re-configured – were therefore *epochally unique*.[29] Wider availability of birth control meant this micro-generation could experiment intensively in everyday life, 'intoxicated and belligerent about their freedom not to have babies'.[30] Birth control technology enabled the 'female sex' to rigorously *practice* autonomy, even though such autonomy was by no means distributed evenly across divisions of race, class and geographical location.[31] Birth control technologies were not a panacea and for some women were deployed coercively to curtail or block their capacity and right *to* reproduce. Nonetheless, these technologies substantially 'modified [the] environment' in which women existed and opened up a radically 'new field of action, demanding a new adaptation and arousing new needs'.[32]

For revolutionary feminists, however, the female sex's increased proximity to technoscientific innovation did more to poison the possibility of women's liberation rather than support it. Lewis rightly points out that technophobia runs through the trans exclusionary feminist imaginary,[33] and such fear is clearly articulated in 'Some Plans Men Have for Our Future,' a document written by revolutionary feminists in the late 70s.[34] Revolutionary feminists flipped women's increased access to birth control to highlight the possibility of 'sex choice'; they discussed the introduction of 'gels' that would 'enable you to choose the sex of your child' while in 'the future embryo feminists would be adjusted by counseling at gender-identity clinics or turned into "men."'[35] Transsexuality, along with male homosexuality, was presented as the logical outcome of a world where girls and women were fated for elimination under the rubric of scientific progress with 'transsexual surgery [being] a creation of men, initially developed for men.' Transsexualism, they speculated, was the means 'to replace women preparatory to reducing their numbers. The women that men create are far closer to their ideal than a "natural" woman could ever be.' The paper concludes with cautionary words about the development of mini computers and 'chip' technology. Worries about automation and unemployment haunt each wave of technological change and in the late 70s 'it will not have elapsed your attention that it is in the main "women's jobs" that are being eliminated' through rapid computerisation. This created, they argued, an 'obvious' need for 'capitalism and male supremacy to reduce the numbers of women, and hence people in the future.' The connections for revolutionary feminists were abundantly clear: '"sex choice" will do it for them.' Women were, the revolutionary feminists insisted, 'an endangered species'.[36]

But the simple fact is that human society, always already conditioned by technics, cannot move back to a mythical and unsullied 'state of nature'. Such a pure state never existed and experiments in the gendered realm do not leave sex untouched[37]. Of course technoscience is not inherently liberatory and can be oppressive in the wrong hands. Yet women's liberation – the rapid and dramatic change in many women's lives over the past 50 or so years – would not have been possible without technoscience that supported bodily experimentation. No matter what the 'gender critics' may say, in the world today you can indeed transform your sex, and such a process can occur in many different ways, through surgery, hormonal change, fantasy, aesthetic presentation and more. It is not the case that one is born a woman and can never become a man, or whatever else there is to become.

D-M Withers' work engages with feminist heritage; they are currently researching the history of feminist publishing as part of the Leverhulme-funded project 'The Business of Women's Words'.

Notes

1. See Hatpins to Hashtags, 'Feminist Futures,' accessed 7 April 2019, https://h2h.feministarchivesouth.org.uk/feminist-futures.
2. Cockburn, 'Terfs take America...: what happened when British female rights activists went to Washington?, *Spectator USA*, 31 January 2019, https://spectator.us/terfs-take-america/.
3. See 'Teaching Individuals Gender Equality & Respect' (TIGER) website, http://www.tigerbristol.co.uk/about.html.
4. The Women's Liberation Movement (WLM) was the largest women-centred social movement active in 1970s Britain. White majority and middle-class in cities, its regional, de-centralised structure meant its class reach was complex and broader. The politics of the movement extended to 'ordinary' women through magazine publications like *Spare Rib* and books published by Virago Press and the Women's Press. From 1971, the WLM was autonomous and women organised separately from men to support their 'liberation'. The WLM was ideologically heterogeneous and employed multiple political strategies to address women's exclusion from public life and oppression in the everyday. The Black Women's Movement (BWM) and Wages for Housework (WFH) are examples of other women-centred movements from the 70s. The BWM was black and working class majority while WFH was predominantly characterised by coalitional work between working class white and black women. The BWM and WFH were smaller than the WLM but were no less significant in terms of their contribution to feminist knowledge and activism. Of most relevance here is that the BWM and WFH did not share the same political contentions about transgender as were expressed by minority factions in the WLM. For more on the WLM's regionalism see Sue Bruley, 'Women's Liberation at the Grass Roots: a view from some English towns, c.1968–1990', *Women's History Review* 25:5 (2016), 723–740.

For an introduction to the history of the BWM in Britain see Diana Watt and Adele D. Jones, *Catching Hell and Doing Well: Black Women in the UK – the Abasindi Cooperative* (London: Trentham Books, 2015), and on WFH and coalitional working see Louise Toupin, *Wages for Housework: A History of an International Feminist Movement, 1972–77* (London: Pluto Press, 2018) and Wilmette Brown, *Black Women and the Peace Movement* (Bristol: Falling Wall, 1983). For a general introduction to the history of women-centred movements in Britain, see 'Sisterhood and After: The Women's Liberation Oral History Project, 2010–2013', British Library, accessed 7 April 2019, https://www.bl.uk/sisterhood.

5. For example, Pat VT West refers to 'real' trans women being present at the Acton conference in 1972, a conference that herself and Jackie Thrupp attended in male drag; the keyboard player for the Northern Women's Liberation Rock Band was a transsexual woman and performed with them at the 1974 Edinburgh National Women's Liberation conference. It would be a significant stretch to say that transsexual women and men were *welcomed* in the movement, but there is limited testimonial and archival evidence that they were *present*. Pat VT West interviewed by Viv Honeybourne, 'Personal Histories of Second-Wave Feminism, 2000-01', Feminist Archive South, University of Bristol Special Collections, DM2123/1/Archive Boxes 79.

6. Sally Fraser and Amanda Sebestyen, 'Going Orange' in *'68, '78, '88: From Women's Liberation to Feminism*, ed. Amanda Sebestyen (Bridport: Prism Press, 1988), 104–116, 107. Emphasis added.

7. Dimitris Papadopoulos, *Experimental Practice: Technoscience, Alterontologies and More-Than-Social Movements* (Durham: Duke University Press, 2018), 79–81.

8. Ibid., 79.

9. Ann Oakley interviewed by Margaretta Jolly, 'Sisterhood and After: The Women's Liberation Oral History Project, 2010-2013', British Library Sound & Moving Image Catalogue reference C1420/56/01, transcript p. 50/track 1. © The British Library and The University of Sussex.

10. Ann Oakley, *Sex, Gender and Society* (London: Maurice Temple Smith, 1972), 159.

11. Raewynn Connell, 'Transsexual Women and Feminist Thought: Toward New Understanding and New Politics,' *Signs*, 37: 4 (2012), 857-881, 861.

12. Papadopoulos, *Experimental Practice*, 6.

13. The illustration was first published in the collection *Conditions of Illusion: Papers from the Women's Movement* and later printed by the See Red Poster collective: https://seeredwomensworkshop.wordpress.com/.

14. See Gayle Kimball (ed.) *Women's Culture: Renaissance of the Seventies* (London: The Scarecrow Press, 1981).

15. For an example of how 'Women's Music' travelled across transnational borders, see D-M Withers, '"neither pure love nor imitating capitalism": Euro WILD and the invention of Women's Music distribution in Europe, 1980–1982', *Feminist Review*, 120:1 (2018), 85-100.

16. Sophie Lewis, 'How British Feminism Became Anti-Trans,' *New York Times*, 7 February 2019, https://www.nytimes.com/2019/02/07/opinion/terf-trans-women-britain.html.

17. Lewis, 'How British Feminism Became Anti-Trans'. Although Greenham Common was a women-only peace camp it is noted by scholars and camp attendees as a site of gender and sexual experimentation (Sasha Roseneil, *Common Women, Uncommon Practices: The Queer Feminisms of Greenham*, (London: Continuum, 2000)); inventive material politics (Anna Feigenbaum, 'From cyborg feminism to drone feminism: Remembering women's anti-nuclear activisms', *Feminist Theory*, 16:3 (2015), 265–288); a central node in the international women-centred peace movement of the 80s (Alison Bartlett, 'Sites of feminist activism: *Remembering Pine Gap*', *Continuum*, 30:3 (2016), 307–315, among others. It is worth remembering that Ann Pettitt, one of the founders of Women for Life on Earth who organised the walk to Greenham in 1981, did so because she was alienated by the specific kind of separatism promoted by revolutionary feminism. See Ann Pettitt, *Walking To Greenham: How the Peace Camp Began and the Cold War Ended* (Aberystwyth: Honno, 2006). See also http://www.yourgreenham.co.uk/.

18. Amanda Sebastyen, *Feminist Practice: Notes from the Tenth Year! (Theoretically Speaking)* (London: In Theory Press, 1979).

19. Cynthia Cockburn, 'The Material of Male Power,' *Feminist Review*, 9:1 (1981), 41–58.

20. Bernard Stiegler, *Symbolic Misery Vol. 2*, (Basingstoke: Policy, 2015).

21. Papadopoulos, *Experimental Practice*, 43.

22. Sumi Madhok has articulated a notion of feminist debt at 'Politics of Struggle', LSE, 12 February 2019.

23. For more on debates between revolutionary feminists and other factions in the WLM see the excellent Jeska Rees, 'A Look Back at Anger: the Women's Liberation Movement in 1978,' *Women's History Review*, 19:3 (2010), 337–356.

24. Revolutionary Feminists,'Statement from the First Year', British Library Add MS 89305/17 (1978).

25. Ibid., emphasis added.

26. Ibid.

27. 'Academics are being harassed over their research into trans issues', *The Guardian*, 16 October 2018, https://www.theguardian.com/society/2018/oct/16/academics-are-being-harassed-over-their-research-into-transgender-issues.

28. See for example, the activities and theory of the Family Endowment Society in Clare Debenham, *Birth Control and the Rights of Women. Post-Suffrage Feminism in the Early Twentieth Century* (London: I.B. Tauris, 2013).

29. Juliet Mitchell, 'Women: The Longest Revolution', *New Left Review*, 40 (1966).

30. Zoe Fairbairns, *Benefits* (London: Virago 1979), 14.

31. 'Depo-Provera: The Ignorance Injection,' Black Cultural Archives DADZIE 1/10.

32. Gilbert Simondon [1965] 'Culture and Technics', *Radical Philosophy* 189 (2015), 17–23.

33. Sophie Lewis, 'Serf and Terf: Some Notes on Some Bad Materialisms,' *Salvage*, 6 February 2017, http://salvage.zone/in-print/serf-n-terf-notes-on-some-bad-materialisms/.

34. Sheila Jeffreys, Sandra McNeil, Maria Katyachild and Siva Rosachild (n.d.) 'Some Plans Men Have for Our Future.' British Library Add MS 89305/17.

35. Ibid.

36. Ibid.

37. Bernard Stiegler, *Technics and Time, 1: The Fault of Epimetheus* (Stanford: Stanford University Press, 1998).

'By contraries execute all things'
Figures of the savage in European philosophy
Alberto Toscano

'Savages' were invented in the Old World but encountered in the New.

> J.G.A. Pocock, *Barbarism and Religion*

It is imperative to accept the idea that negation does not signify nothingness; that when the mirror does not reflect our own likeness, it does not prove there is nothing to perceive.

> Pierre Clastres, 'Copernicus and the Savages'

The savage Other

The call to decolonise philosophy demands, among other things, a preliminary assessment of the shaping power of the colonial relation across the discipline's history. Such an inquiry involves an excavation of how the European encounter with, and exploitation of, other peoples conditioned the different forms taken by the problem of *anthropological difference*.[1] My concern in this essay is to explore how philosophers adopted, adapted and transformed – and in a sense invented – the figure of the savage from the late sixteenth to the late eighteenth century. In particular, I want to examine the varying and sometimes contradictory ways in which the savage emerged as the living negation or inverted image of civilised Western humanity. I have been greatly inspired in this undertaking – of which this essay is but a preliminary sketch – by two still-untranslated landmark works of philosophical historiography by Italian scholars, Sergio Landucci's *Philosophers and Savages* and Giuliano Gliozzi's *Adam and the New World*.[2]

From Horkheimer and Adorno's location of anti-Semitism within the *Dialectic of Enlightenment* to Said's *Orientalism*, from Beauvoir's *The Second Sex* to Cedric Robinson's *Black Marxism*, the critical history of Western philosophy and rationality has abounded in explorations of the intimate if often obscured bonds between the speculative subjection of Otherness and its social, material counterparts. The blatant instrumentality of the idea of the savage to the colonial project, from the Spanish conquest to the ongoing dispossession of indigenous people across the globe, would appear to militate against any sustained or nuanced investigation. Surely, we are dealing with the bluntest of racist and legitimising myths, to be fought politically rather than ruminated academically? In what follows, I want to propose that contrary to this justifiable but reductive reflex, there is much to be gained from an investigation of the uses to which the idea of the savage was put by European thinkers in the crucible of colonial modernity – mainly, perhaps, for a historical understanding of the politics of philosophy itself, but also to gain some insight into the contradictory endurance of colonial imaginaries in the present.

The idea of the savage played a critical role in the emergence of modern political philosophy, and the subsequent unfolding of the ideologies of progress and the social sciences of development: classical political economy, anthropology, sociology. In the period of this intellectual ferment, in a Europe wracked by inner turmoil and external conquest – which is to say amid the throes of the colonial emergence of a capitalist world from the matrix of Christian feudalism – the savage was figured largely with reference to the encounter with the indigenous people of North America, albeit drawing, as the term's etymology suggests, on an intra-European imaginary of the *homo sylvaticus*, the man of the woods.[3] Though preceded by images of Otherness that drew on narratives of conquest and encounter in the Caribbean and Brazil (as we'll see below with Montaigne), it was with reference especially to so-called 'Canadians' that modern philosophy sought to draw speculative and normative lessons from what appeared as savage difference. As Pocock has observed, the Americas became 'a vast laboratory in which European speculative experimenters [tested] their hypotheses regarding the human mind'.[4]

The first philosophical appearance of European philosophy's 'Canadians' seems to have come with the debate among supporters and objectors to Descartes' account of the innateness of the idea of God's infinity. The engineer and physicist Pierre Petit argued that the absence of such an idea among the indigenous people encountered by French colonists offered empirical proof of the falsity of the Cartesian deduction. This view appeared in the 1641 'second objections' to the *Meditations*. 'Canadian philosophy' as a locution actually appears in the 1707 inaugural lecture of a German professor Jonas Conrad Schramm, responding to the writings of the Baron de Lahontan (to whom we'll return in the conclusion, and who instead referred to indigenous people as 'Americans') – where he speaks, paraphrasing Aristotle on the origins of Greek philosophy, of the 'stammering' philosophy of the native peoples of so-called 'New France'. Jacob Brucker's five-volume critical history of philosophy (1742-44) would also include a lengthy entry on the 'Philosophy of the Canadians', as would Diderot's *Encyclopaedia*, presenting their 'natural religion' as a kind of spontaneous deism.[5]

What kind of 'Other' is the savage? At first, and perhaps second and third glance too, the savage seems to differ from the Others that have so magnetised twentieth-century critical thought, lacking the unsettling, subversive qualities which reason's confrontation with alterity is often deemed to have. In his suppressed 1961 preface to *History of Madness*, Michel Foucault envisaged a *history of limits* that would interrogate a culture from the (in some sense *impossible*) vantage point of its exterior, a hollowed-out void or tear 'by means of which it isolates itself, [and which] identifies it as clearly as its values',[6] forming the hidden basis of its historicity. Foucault drew here on Nietzsche's identification of the origin of European metaphysics in the forgetting of the experience of the tragic. He presented not just madness (or unreason) as such a site of tragedy's foreclosure, but also dreams (or the unconscious), and the Orient. These were all 'limit-experiences of the Western world', each one of which, 'at the frontiers of our culture, traces a limit that is simultaneously an original division'.[7] Reflecting recently on the articulation of difference, otherness and exclusion in the phenomenon of racism, Étienne Balibar, in dialogue with Edward Said's *Orientalism*, presents the latter as a paradigmatic study of something like an 'essential' Otherness, an 'uncanny double', 'who is not only an adversary but embodies a negation of one's moral and aesthetic and intellectual values, an Other who, at the same time, in the most contradictory manner, has to be constructed as a passive "object" of representation, study, dissections, classifications, and an active "subject" of threats, or simply of an alternative path to civilisation and salvation'.[8] This is an immanent and constitutive alterity.

Does the savage represent such an alterity, such that, to continue with Balibar,

> the construction of the Other is the construction of an *alienated Self*, where all the properties attributed to the Other are inversions and distortions of those vindicated for oneself, where indeed the Self is nothing but *the Other's Other*, whose identity and stability is permanently asserted and secured (in the imaginary) through the representation of an essential Other, or an essentialised Other, whose identity in this respect *arrives from the Other in inverted form*?[9]

The answer is mixed. On the one hand, as I explore below, the savage is in some sense the 'perfect Other', the product of a matrix or accumulation of negations: he is *exactly what 'we' are not*. On the other, largely because of the simplistic formalism of this negation, the savage is rarely if at all the occasion for a limit-experience or an uncanny encounter, serving at best as the locus of ironic reversal and scepticism about the vaunted virtues of the 'civilised' – no doubt also an effect of the reliance of these philosophical texts on missionary literature already steeped in a classical and Christian image of Otherness, rather than on the encounters between settlers and First Nations.[10] As Sergio Landucci observes, perhaps the savage is really the *caput mortuum* of Western political philosophy.[11] This was the term – literally 'the dead head' – used by alchemists to describe the exhausted residue of their experiments. By analogy, the philosophical idea of the savage could be regarded as the sterile product of negating the distinctive and itemisable characteristics of Western political anthropology.

Antitypes

As Landucci has explored with daunting erudition, and as Ter Ellingson has amply corroborated in his compelling critique of anthropology's racial legacies, *The Myth of the Noble Savage* (2001),[12] the figure of the savage is a product of 'comparative negation', to use Ellingson's helpful formulation. Landucci starts his periodisation of philosophy's invention of the savage with Montaigne's famous essay 'Of the Cannibals', which, in John Florio's early seventeenth-century translation, includes the following lines referring to the native populations encountered by French colonists and missionaries in Brazil:

> It is a nation, would I answer *Plato*, that hath no kind of traffic, no knowledge of letters, no intelligence of numbers, no name of magistrate, nor of politic superiority; no use of service, or riches or of poverty; no contracts, no successions, no dividences, no occupation but idle; no respect of kindred, but common, no apparel but natural, no manuring of lands, no use of wine, corn, or metal.[13]

In Montaigne, this logic of negation, or privation, was intended to frame the radical diversity he regarded as consubstantial with human nature, and to sceptically puncture the superior pride of the civilised, both by relativising the very category of 'barbarism' and by proposing that the savage's greater closeness to nature condemned the 'bastardising' effects of our artificial customs. To paraphrase Foucault's treatment of Erasmus' *In Praise of Folly*, this was a critical-ironic rather than a tragic critique of Western polity and rationality.[14] Relying, by his telling, on a naïve and thus more reliable witness, Montaigne would then fill in the framework of otherness or difference-by-negation with the description of forms-of-life – anthropophagy, above all – which were incommensurable enough with our own to undermine the dominant doctrines that defined something like a universalising political anthropology of the Middle Ages: the Christian *consensum gentium* and Aristotle's vision of man as a *zoon politikon*. Though the uses and effects of Montaigne's savage, in which negation and difference heralded a sceptical and ironic suspension of Europe's divisive confidence in its own superiority, were *sui generis*, and though his attempt at a dispassionate description of indigenous forms of life was unique for his day, the logic of comparative negation was not.

In one of the very first travel narratives from the 'New World', a famous letter to his patron Lorenzo de Medici, the Florentine navigator Amerigo Vespucci declared:

> They have no cloth either of wool, linen or cotton, since they need it not; neither do they have goods of their own, but all things are held in common. They live together without king, without government, and each is his own master. They marry as many wives as they please; and son cohabits with mother, brother with sister, male cousin with female, and any man with the first woman he meets. They dissolve their marriages as often as they please, and observe no sort of law with respect to them. Beyond the fact that they have no church, no religion and are not idolaters, what more can I say? They live according to nature [*secundum naturae*], and may be called Epicureans rather than Stoics. There are no merchants among their number, nor is there barter. The nations wage war upon one another without art or order.[15]

In 1505, a version of Vespucci's privative description would caption one of the first visual representations of Amerindian peoples in Europe.[16]

Columbus' own 1493 letter, announcing his great 'discovery', spoke of the natives of 'Hispaniola' as having 'no iron and steel, nor any weapons, nor are they fit thereunto'. In 1511, Peter Martyr d'Angheria, in another landmark text for the European perception of the indigenous peoples of the Americas, would write in similar terms:

> Lande is as common as the sunne, and water; Myne and Thyne (the seedes of all mischeefe) have no place with them.... A fewe thinges contente them, havyng no delyght in suche superfluities, for the whiche in other places menne take infinite paynes, and commit manye

unlawfull actes.... But among these symple soules, a fewe clothes serve the naked: weightes and measures are not needeful to suche as can not skyl of crafte and deceyte, and have not the use of pestiferous money, the seede of innumerable mischeeves: so that yf we shall not be ashamed to confesse the trueth, they seeme to live in that golden worlde of the whiche olde wryters speake so muche, wherein menne lyved symplye and innocentlye without enforcement of lawes, without quarrelying, judges and libelles, content only to satisfie nature, without further vexation for knowledge of thynges to come.... They are content with so lytle, that in so large a countrey they have rather superfluitie than scarcenesse: so that (as we have sayde before) they seeme to lyve in the golden worlde without toyle, lyvynge in open gardens, not entrenched with dyches, divided with hedges, or defended with walles; they deale truely one with another without lawes, without bookes, and without judges...[17]

Francesco Guicciardini, in his *Storia d'Italia* (1537-1540) would say of native Americans that 'they had no knowledge (*scientia*) and no experience whatsoever of things'.

As Margaret T. Hodgen has shown, citing these and other examples from the early sixteenth century, such descriptions constituted 'conventionalised statements',[18] which were not unique to any one author, nor particularly philosophical in orientation. The barbarous or savage Other was defined by the privation of certain enumerable elements of European civilisation: law, property, sovereign power, the mechanical arts, agriculture, mathematics, writing, and so on and so forth. As Stephen Greenblatt remarked in his perceptive study of linguistic colonialism, 'The mention of the nakedness of the Indians is typical; to a ruling class obsessed with the symbolism of dress, the Indians' physical appearance was a token of a cultural void. *In the eyes of the Europeans, the Indians were culturally naked.* This illusion that the inhabitants of the New World are essentially without a culture of their own is both early and remarkably persistent, even in the face of overwhelming contradictory evidence.'[19] The framing division between *bios* and *zoe*, political life and 'bare' life, identified in Agamben's *Homo Sacer*, was manifest here in all its raw literalism (although, as we shall further detail below, the postulate of the cultural and political bareness of the Indians was not shared by all European philosophers).

Now, this particular convention, the negative itemising of difference, is nigh-on ubiquitous from the sixteenth century onwards, and can be registered across traveller's chronicles, and in Enlightenment encyclopaedias and dictionaries, and from Kant's anthropology to Darwin's voyages. To take just one striking example, from the Franciscan missionary Louis Hennepin's *Nouveau voyage d'un pais plus grand que l'Europe*:

> The Apostolick Man [missionary] ought much more to acknowledge this dependance upon the Soveraign Lord, in respect of those barbarous Nations who have not any regard of any Religion true or false, who live without Rule, without Order, without Law, without God, without Worship, where Reason is buried in Matter, and incapable of reasoning the most common things of Religion and Faith. Such are the people of Canada. ... They live without any subordination, without Laws or any form of Government or Policy. They are stupid in matters of Religion, subtle and crafty in their Worldly concerns; but excessively superstitious.[20]

Missing from Hennepin's list of negations is a leitmotiv found in many of the others, that the savages know neither thine nor mine, that they are peoples without property. Among innumerable examples (taken mainly from Landucci, Ellingson and Hodgen), we encounter it in:

- The Dutch geographer Joannes de Laet's 1633 *Novus Orbis*: '[they have] no laws, no political institutions, they act like animals'.

- The 1694 Dictionary of the Académie Française: '*Savage*, also said of peoples who usually live in the woods, without religion, fixed abode and rather more like beasts than animals'.

- In the soldier-explorer Baron de Lahontan's 1706 *Mémoires de l'Amérique Septentrionale*, in the chapter 'Moeurs et Manières des Sauvages' (Mores and Manners of the Savages): 'They have neither laws, nor judges, nor priests'; 'The Savages know neither yours nor mine'.

- In the naturalist Buffon's 1749 *Variétés dans l'Espece humaine*: 'no rule, no law, nor master, nor habitual society'.

- In Louis de Jacourt's entry *Sauvages* for Diderot's Encyclopaedia (1765): 'barbarian peoples who live without law, police or religion, and who have no fixed abode'.

- Leibniz in the same year, in the *New Essays Concerning Human Understanding*: 'Even with regard to the soul, their practical morality can be said to be in some respects better than ours, because *they have neither greed for the accumulation of goods nor ambition to dominate.*'

- Kant, in the lecture notes from his courses on philosophical anthropology of the 1770s: 'The American people are incapable of civilisation. They have no motive force; for they are without affection and passion'.[21]

- Charles Darwin on the inhabitants of Tierra del Fuego in 1839: '*The different tribes have no government or chief;* yet each is surrounded by other hostile tribes, speaking different dialects, and separated from each other only by a deserted border or neutral territory: the cause of their warfare appears to be the means of subsistence. ... They cannot know the feeling of having a home, and still less that of domestic affection; for the husband is to the wife a brutal master to a laborious slave. ... How little can the higher powers of the mind be brought into play: what is there for imagination to picture, for reason to compare, for judgment to decide upon?'[22]

If Europeans preoccupied with hierarchical codes of dress and appearance were culturally confounded by the savage's nakedness, viewing the indigenous populations of the Americas through the lens of law and property meant that where social and political relations were supposed to be, all that actually appeared was absence and lack. Yet, as Hodgen has noted, there is nothing particularly modern (or exclusively European) about this ethnocentric logic of contrast with the Other, who only exists as a negative or inversion of the Self. She encounters it in the twelfth-century Old French *Roman d'Alexandre*, where the Indian 'brahmin' were described as having 'no agriculture, no iron, no building, no fire, no bread, no wine, no clothing, nor anything pertaining to the productive arts or pleasure'.[23] She also finds it in Ancient Roman and Greek accounts of the nomadic Scythians (not by accident among the fantastic ancestors postulated by European writers for the Amerindian populations), who were said by Strabo in the first century BC to 'know nothing about the storing of food, or about the peddling of merchandise either, except for the exchange of wares [barter]', and whom Homer before him described as men 'who by no means spend their lives on contracts and money-getting, but actually possess all things in common... and above all things have their wives and their children in common'.

The sheer monotony of comparative negation is no surprise, if we reflect on the extent to which Renaissance and early modern thinkers interpreted the world through a framework compounded from Ancient Roman and Greek traditions, along with their Biblical hybrids. Particularly when it comes to their apparent ignorance of private property and its social consequences, the New World 'savage' is enduringly haunted both by ancient utopias of the Golden Age and by classical figures of barbarism. As Hayden White has suggested, in his suggestive study of the 'forms of wildness' that preceded the emergence of the modern figure of the savage, what we are dealing with in this pattern is a 'technique of ostensive self-definition by negation', in other words with the creation of *antitypes*.[24] From a certain angle, the modern 'savage' could be seen as the illusory realisation of the fantastic figure of the *wild man* which had menaced and enlivened the real and psychic margins of European cultures in antiquity and the middle ages. Did anything uncanny remain in the formalisation, projection and spatialisation of the pre-colonial *homo sylvaticus* onto the native peoples of the Americas, anything that would confront a colonising rationality with the experience of its limits?

We might be tempted to single out the 'noble savage' as one such obstacle to cognitive imperialism, but that identification would be mistaken. As Ter Ellingson, and before him Arthur Lovejoy,[25] Giuliano Gliozzi and Michèle Duchet have all detailed, the 'noble savage' is largely a retroactive and negative ideological construction; nineteenth-century pro-imperialist anthropological and philosophical polemicists attacked the 'myth of the noble savage' as a confected proxy for their assaults on the rather more imposing revolutionary legacies of Jean-Jacques Rousseau – who had himself never used that formulation, and who crucially differentiated the primitive state of nature from the social reality of North American populations. As Ellingson notes, the nexus between nobility and savagery was a short-lived and idiosyncratic product of Marc Lescarbot's experience in 'New France' in the early seventeenth century:

> Rather than an idealised equation of morality with nature, [the noble savage] was a technical concept based on legal theory, attempting to account for the problem of societies that could exist in the absence of anything Europeans might recognise as legal codes and institutions, by projecting a model drawn from European 'nobility' that could satisfactorily account for the absence of a wide range of European-style political and legal constructs. And rather than being associated with an idealisation of 'savage' peoples or promotion of them to the status of exemplars for revealing European corruption, it was instead offered in the context of a colonialist project that would promote European dominance, guided by a salvage ethnology that would show later generations how their forefathers had lived, once the inevitable destruction of their culture had been achieved.[26]

What comes to be misrecognised as a myth of the noble savage, as Ellingson concludes, is rather the sign of 'the lingering transformations of the Golden Age discourse of comparative negation and the dialectic of vices and virtues, playing itself out in oscillating interaction with the opposing energies and increasingly negativising forces of Enlightenment sociocultural evolutionary progressivism and nineteenth-century racism'.[27]

Building on a suggestion by Duchet, we could further argue that to the extent that the reality of the savage world is trapped in a 'network of negations' – negations that serve as screen and mirror for the 'Other's Other', the internally conflicted 'Self' of a Europe in cultural and political tumult – it is the very formalism of these negations which opens them up to a quasi-structuralist play of combinations and inversions of valence, as well as the emergence of various negative utopias.[28] As I will explore below, it matters to the historical mutation in the figure of the savage *which* negations take precedence. First and foremost, is the savage negatively the human without property (or else, positively, *with* common possessions), without religion (or *with* non-monotheistic spiritual practices), without government (or *with* equality), without industriousness (or *with* freedom)?

As I have just intimated, the negations can also be inverted, in either a critical or a utopian guise, namely in the form of what Anthony Pagden has termed the 'savage critic', the reversal of the savage as negative stereotype, the negation of the negation of the civilised.

> The savage was believed to live in a world of his own making, a world of extremes, of inexplicable and frequently repellent ritual behaviour, a world controlled by passion rather than reason. The literary image of what I shall call the savage critic is, in a number of crucial respects, an inversion of this stereotype. The fictitious Mexicans of Dryden, Sir William Davenant's Peruvians, the Huron and the Incas of Voltaire, Diderot's Tahitians, Denise Vairasse d'Alais's Australians, the Huron of the Baron de Lahontan (to take a random sample) all claim in their attacks upon the world of civil men that it is we, not they, who have failed to see what is written in the book of nature: that in the end it is we who have failed to grasp what it means to be human.[29]

As concerns utopia instead – and as White has aptly noted about the very idea of wildness – in moments of cultural, political and economic crisis, the *antitype* can become a positive type, even, we could add, a kind of *prototype*. Rather than a positive valuation of indigenous Amerindian societies (though this is not wholly absent, for instance from the writings of missionaries like the Jesuit Charlevoix) the 'nobility' (in the sense of affirmative value) of the savage lies in its negativity. By now, I imagine some readers may have already heard echoing, across the 'litanies of comparative negation', the libertarian communist slogan: *ni dieu, ni maître*, no Gods, no masters.

This negative dialectic of savage dystopia and colonial utopia is present in what is perhaps the most well-known literary instantiation of the savage as comparative negation of the civilised. This is Gonzalo's evocation, in Act 2 Scene I of Shakespeare's *Tempest*, of the anti-political 'commonwealth' he would impose, had he the chance, on Prospero's island:

> I' the commonwealth I would by contraries
> Execute all things; for no kind of traffic
> Would I admit; no name of magistrate;
> Letters should not be known; riches, poverty,
> And use of service, none; contract, succession,
> Bourn, bound of land, tilth, vineyard, none;
> No use of metal, corn, or wine, or oil;
> No occupation; all men idle, all;
> And women too, but innocent and pure;
> No sovereignty;--
>
> [...]
>
> All things in common nature should produce
> Without sweat or endeavour: treason, felony
> Would I not have; but nature should bring forth,
> Of its own kind, all foison, all abundance,
> To feed my innocent people.

As Shakespeare scholars began to notice in the late eighteenth century, and continue to discuss to this day, the speech appears as a *détournement* of Montaigne's 'Des Cannibales' – though Hodgen has argued powerfully for the position that if this is indeed the case, then Shakespeare borrowed from the least original, most conventional of Montaigne's musings on the ethico-political lessons of Brazilian anthropophagy. What is perhaps more telling in *The Tempest* is that this is *a European's utopia*, of the island as *tabula rasa* where one may elide or invert civilisation and its discontents; it is not a description of the 'natives', who receive in the figure of Caliban a far more pejorative, but also far more unsettling image.

We are in the presence here perhaps of a kind of *secondary or imaginary colonisation*, one that projects onto 'savage' colonised lands, spatialising it, a European desire for the negation of his own civilisation – a desire which, as White suggests, inverts the valence of the antitype in moments of cultural crisis. Shakespeare in a sense punctures the sureties of this colonial utopian imagination with the interjection of Antonio's *Realpolitik*: 'The latter end of his commonwealth forgets the beginning'. Gonzalo's withering away of the state in the colonies forgets that the birth of the commonwealth is a matter of 'treason, felony, sword, pike, knife, gun'. When in 1969 the Martinican anti-colonial poet and politician Aimé Césaire adapted Shakespeare's play in his own *A Tempest*, the words he put in Gonzalo's mouth also spoke to the limits of his negative and primitivist colonial utopia:

> I mean that if the island is inhabited, as I believe, and if we colonise it, as is my hope, then we have to take every precaution not to import our shortcomings, yes, what we call civilisation. They must stay as they are: savages, noble and good savages, free, without any complexes or complications. Something like a pool granting eternal youth where we periodically come to restore our aging, citified souls.[30]

Savage Warre, or, reading Thomas Hobbes in Virginia

I haven't forgotten about political philosophy, or its history, and it seems fitting now, having touched on the dialectic of political realism and anti-political idyll in *The Tempest*, to turn to that most fiercely anti-utopian of modern philosophers, Thomas Hobbes, a crucial author in Landucci's narrative. With Hobbes, we can briefly explore how notwithstanding the seemingly transhistorical invariance and portability of the savage as antitype, seemingly analogous negations can be the bearers of very different philosophical contents and projects. Four decades after Shakespeare's *Tempest*, Hobbes's *Leviathan* depicted the state of nature in the following well-known terms:

> during the time men live without a common Power to keep them all in awe, they are in a condition which is called Warre.... In such condition, there is no place for Industry; because the fruit thereof is uncertain: and consequently no Culture of the Earth; no Navigation, nor use of the commodities that may be imported by Sea; no commodious Building; no Instruments of moving, and removing such things as require much force; no Knowledge of the face of the Earth; no account of Time; no Arts; no Letters; no Society; and which is worst of all, continuall

feare, and danger of violent death; And the life of man solitary, poore, nasty, brutish, and short.³¹

Modern political philosophy is arguably born of a matrix of negations, juxtaposing an imaginary at once formalistic and terrifying of pure privation in the state of nature to the imperative necessity of the State, that *artificial man*. Though Hobbes, who was personally involved in the colonial enterprise as a stockholder of the Virginia Company,³² spoke of the 'savages of America' sparingly, he did so at crucial points in his oeuvre, and, as Landucci forcefully argues, the role of ethnological accounts of North American forms-of-life in shoring up or verifying Hobbes's political anthropology should not be underestimated. *Homo homini lupus est*, was, after all, an expression first used in a colonial travel narrative. Two paragraphs after his famous formulation 'solitary, poore, nasty, brutish, and short', anticipating the response of a sceptical reader, he notes:

> It may peradventure be thought there was never such a time nor condition of warre as this; and I believe it was never generally so, over all the world: but there are many places where they live so now. For the savage people in many places of *America*, except the government of small Families, the concord whereof dependeth on naturall lust, have no government at all; and live at this day in that brutish manner, as I said before. Howsoever, it may be perceived what manner of life there would be, where there were no common Power to feare; by the manner of life which men that have formerly lived under a peacefull government use to degenerate, into a civill Warre.³³

A number of elements of Hobbes' use of the savage antitype are worth pausing on. Hobbes firmly rejected Aristotle's political anthropology and psychology – the one that had served as a bulwark for the Spanish humanist and theologian Sepúlveda's juridical arguments about the Indians as 'natural slaves'.³⁴ He did so by affirming the thoroughly artificial character of politics: human beings are *not* 'political animals'. The state, like property itself, is a thoroughly artificial institution, whereas if we can speak of a 'natural' state among human beings this will be a state of *civil war*. In Hobbesian political philosophy the rejection of a natural political disposition is accompanied by the assertion of an instituted identity, both artificial and ineluctable, between social life and life under a state.

Hobbes's first important work had been a remarkable translation of Thucydides's *History of the Peloponnesian War*, a text in which armed strife within the city, *stásis*, is a pervasive theme.³⁵ He would project the spectre of internecine war *within the horizon of the European city or state*, be it ancient Athens or contemporary England, into his selective sampling of travel narratives of the Americas. Hobbes depicted the life of the 'savages of the Americas' as one of permanent warfare and insecurity, discouraging all productive and propertied activity. One may wonder whether Hobbes's fearsome images of North American warfare were more a function of the frightened reports of anti-colonial resistance, as manifested in the Virginia Company's own Jamestown settlement in 1622, than any account of indigenous practices of conflict and warfare. Though he certainly situated the savage of the Americas on an inferior rung in the hierarchy of the civilised 'arts', Hobbes, like his seventeenth-century rationalist contemporaries, maintained an ultimately homogeneous and paradoxically egalitarian philosophical anthropology. Social and political differences were *necessary* and salutary, but they were not *natural*.

Such an approach also implied that one could read the past of European countries themselves in the contemporary savage condition. The perception of the Other as 'allochronic', living in an other time, and in a space other than time, which Johannes Fabian juxtaposed to the notion of non-Western cultures as 'coeval', was later constitutive of the anthropological gaze.³⁶ It is painfully manifest in the widespread figure of the savage as a kind of 'living fossil'. Pierre Clastres identifies this perspective as the 'ancient Western conviction … that history is a one-way street, that societies without power are the image of what we have ceased to be, and that for them our culture is the image of what they have to become'.³⁷ This theme, later crystallised in Locke's dictum 'In the beginning, the whole world was America', makes an important appearance in the 1642 *Elements of Law*, where Hobbes writes of 'the experience of savage nations that live at this day, and by the histories of our ancestors, the old inhabitants of Germany and other now civil countries, where we find the people few and short lived, and without the ornaments and comforts of life'.³⁸

This European introjection of the 'savagery' projected onto the Americas is iconographically evident in the frontispiece to Hobbes's *De Cive*, which visually quotes De Bry's engravings for Thomas Hariot's 1588 *A Briefe*

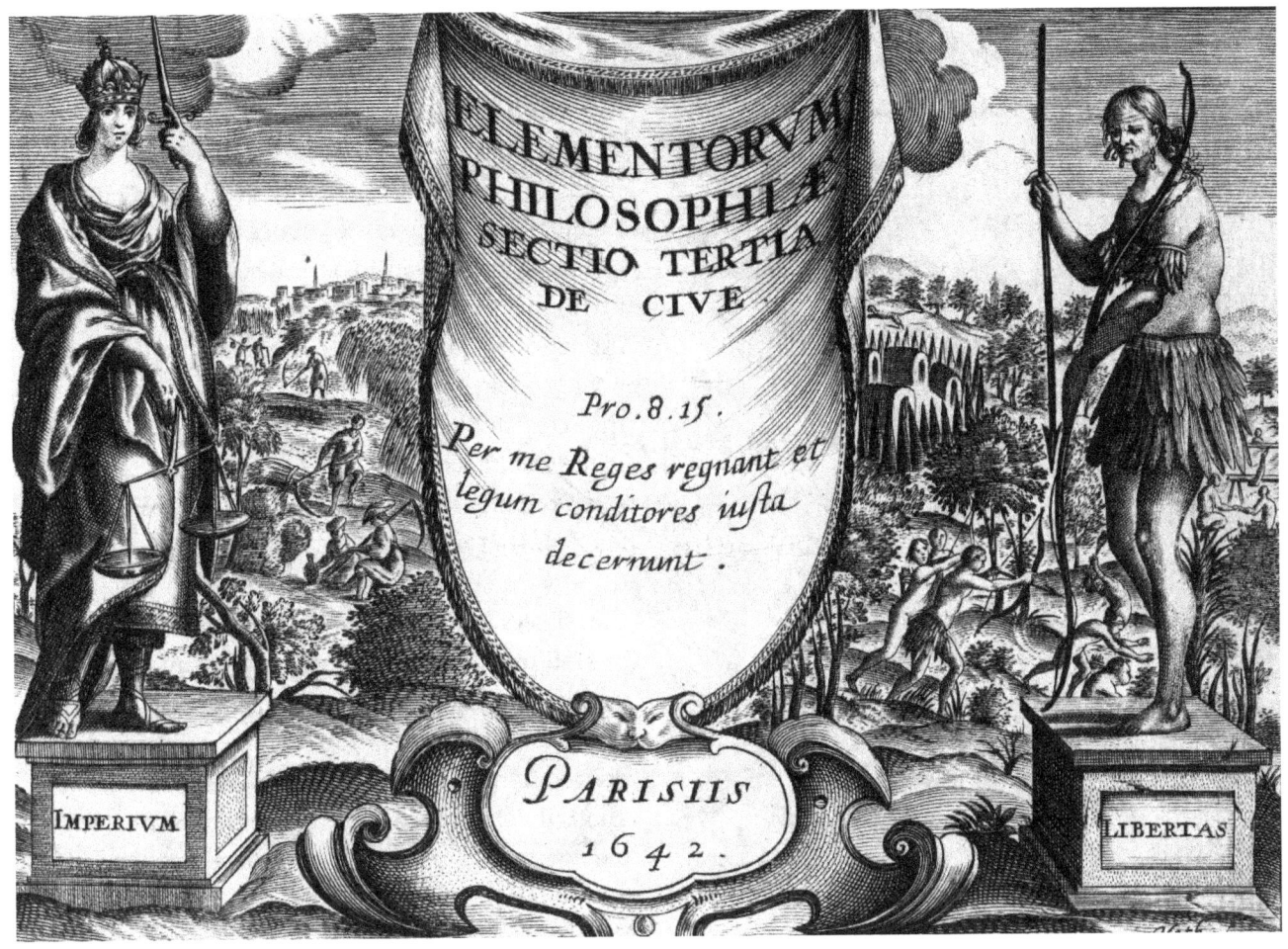

Fig. 1

and True Report of the New Found Land of Virginia (Fig. 1).³⁹ The juxtaposition of sovereign *Imperium* on the left, with its accoutrements of production, science and law to savage *Libertas* on the right (the two capped by the religious sphere, depicted as a sphere of political domination and judgment) could not be a pithier counterpart to the practice of comparative negation, while at the same time indicating the openly repressed utopian dimension of modern political philosophy, which, in Hobbes but also Locke and Adam Smith after him, recognises that order, law and production can only be secured at the cost of *freedom*. The iconography also shows us how much European imaginings of the Americas were steeped in a classical visual and political culture, one which, in the case of De Bry's compendium, made graphic the link between New World and Old World 'savagery' in a way that matched Hobbes's reflection in the *Elements*, by including a series of plates of ancient inhabitants of the British isles, the Picts, in their own 'state of nature' (Fig. 2; see over).⁴⁰

At a more theoretical level, attention to Hobbes's own use of the savage antitype suggests that, rather than operating an ethnocentric invariant across Western history, the figure of the savage shifted in historically and politically significant ways, and that these shifts were articulated, at least in part, in terms of a *hierarchy of negations*. In other words, though Hobbes's list largely matches Montaigne, and indeed echoes the Ancient and Mediaeval examples adduced by Hodgen, one negation reigns supreme: *the negation of the state*. It is from this, the savage absence of sovereign government, that stem all the other apparent privations: laws, property, security, agricultural development, productive labour, the arts, and so on. Contrast the dislocation of this hierarchy by Locke, for whom it is the absence of property in land which is the dominant negation, from which the others, especially that of government, then follow.

Fig. 2

This recombination of comparative negation, from the problem of *political order* to that of *productive development*, will be crucial in moving beyond the moral axiomatics of comparative negation, flipping between dystopian denigration and deromanticised utopia, towards a historical and materialist problematic of social development, in which means of subsistence serve as the basis on which the superstructure of laws, property, government, the arts and religion rests.[41] This paradigm, grounded in the Lockean ideology of property, and contradictorily presaged in Rousseau's anthropological speculations, will be fundamental to the development of classical political economy and its attendant philosophical anthropology, above all in the work of the Scottish Enlightenment, from Robertson's *History of America* to Adam Smith's writings on law, history and economics.

For Landucci (as for Ronald Meek, in his largely congruent study[42]), and notwithstanding all of its shortcomings, the bourgeois social science in which the savage is a figure of 'development' will mark a crucial step beyond the formalistic inversion of civilised type and barbar-

ous antitype, in the direction of a positive knowledge of social and cultural change and conflict. This 'progressive' history, in which the Scottish Enlightenment stands as Marxism's scientific precursor, has to incorporate a little too quickly and smoothly the acknowledged fact that modern racism is a key function of the shift from a rationalist to a socio-historical conception of the 'savage'. But it must also, to my mind, underplay how a framework of comparative negation is transmuted but not abandoned in the proto-ethnological philosophy of the Scottish Enlightenment. This is manifest above all in the endurance of the Lockean axiom that from the absence of property derive all of the other absences, lacks and lags that pertain to the savage condition. It is also demonstrated in the extremely selective way in which the writers of the Scottish Enlightenment assimilated and 'edited' the travel narratives of Jesuit missionaries in North America, for instance to minimise agricultural practices or marginalise the record of collective political deliberation, in order to underwrite the hierarchy of negations that Locke had put in place. These are some of the ideological devices that have enforced a settler-colonial relation in which, to Audra Simpson, 'to be Indigenous is to be structured into [a] position of scarcity'.[43]

A political miracle?

We should thus question the postulate, undergirding Landucci's research, according to which historicism or developmentalism, even if laced with the propertied ideologies of racial capitalism, is to be preferred to rationalism or scepticism, if only as a precursor of historical materialism. Or at the very least, we might take the prevalence of such a view in critical historiographies of the philosophical savage to impel a more self-critical perception of the survivals within Marxism of a stageism built on the implicit negation of indigenous forms of life. We can nevertheless draw an important lesson from Landucci's text, where he identifies the key turning point in the history of European philosophy's conceptualisation of the savage in the thesis – made with reference to missionary travel narratives originating from Jesuits in so-called 'New France' – that *there can be societies without a state*. The sharpest statement of this anti-Hobbesian argument, which seeks to counter the identification of social life with governed life that dominates European political thought from Aristotle's *zoon politikon* onwards, is to be found in a text of Leibniz from 1711, a response to the writings of the Baron de Lahontan, where the author of the *Monadology* writes that:

> The Iroquois and the Huron ... have reversed the excessively universal political maxims of Aristotle and Hobbes. They have shown ... that entire Peoples can live without magistrates and without quarrels. ... But the rudeness of these Savages shows that it is not so much necessity but the inclination to go towards the good and approach happiness, by mutual assistance, that is the foundation of Societies and States.[44]

A year earlier, in a letter also engaging with his reading of Lahontan, Leibniz had subverted the logic of comparative negation even more thoroughly, writing that

> It is entirely truthful ... that the Americans of these regions live together without any government but in peace; they know no fights, nor hatreds, nor battles, or not many, except against men of different nations and languages. I would almost say that we are dealing with a political miracle, unknown by Aristotle and ignored by Hobbes.[45]

Whatever the 'truthfulness' of such claims, Leibniz's mention of a *political miracle* opens up a possibility distant from most European and philosophical responses to the encounter with the indigenous populations of the Americas. Rather than a *negation* of Europe and its notions of the political – a negation that may have utopian or subversive valences, but ones that belong to an imaginary repertoire immanent to Greco-Roman and Judeo-Christian sources – the encounter with North American societies may require thinking of a different, unprecedented *politics*. As many commentators have detailed, the colonial encounter with the indigenous populations of the Americas was marked, in the intellectual sphere, by assimilation to the models, myths, conceptual imaginaries and formal taxonomies that populated the European mind in the sixteenth to eighteenth centuries and beyond, an encounter in which comparativism was laced with the violence of an imperialist instrumental rationality. In this sense, the idea of the savage largely served as a screen on which to project the reflection of a Europe wracked by the emergence of capitalism and its contradictions, as well as by the crisis of Christian political theology. The 'savage' was a kind of inverted mirror in which European intellectuals could pose the enigmas of the age: What is politics? What is law? What is religion? What is property?

Very rarely was there a sense, as in Leibniz's 'political miracle', that the people of the Americas could actually impel Europe to dislocate or expatriate its political philosophy. In a sense, European intellectual life would have to wait until the second half of the twentieth century, with the emergence of radical and anti-statist trends in anthropology, to give the 'savage' pride of place in a critique of the dominant image of the political. In this regard, Pierre Clastres's 1974 *Society Against the State* could be read as an extended elaboration of the anti-Aristotelian and anti-Hobbesian effects of the encounter with Amerindian people glimpsed by Leibniz.[46] From his field work among the Guayaki Indians in Paraguay, and the observations of so much anthropological work across the Americas, Clastres would draw a drastic challenge to the political anthropology of the West. This challenge stemmed from the ubiquity, in both North and South America, of societies where political power was not synonymous with the dialectic of obedience and command, with the monopolisation of violence and the separation of a distinct, state-bound political sphere. Clastres would even go so far as portraying Amerindian forms of chiefdom as collective stratagems to *prevent* the emergence of politics *as* sovereign domination. As he commented: 'One is confronted, then, by a vast constellation of societies in which the holders of what elsewhere would be called power are actually without power; where the political is determined as a domain beyond coercion and violence, beyond hierarchical subordination; where, in a word, no relationship of command-obedience is in force. This is the major difference of the Indian world.'[47]

Yet it would also be erroneous to treat the modern philosophical discourse on the savage as mere ventriloquism or monologue. Balibar's comments on the othering of the Orient are apropos here, especially in his reminder that an encounter at the level of the imaginary is an encounter nonetheless:

> Does imaginary mean that the Other is a pure fiction, a pure projection of the Western mind upon 'Orientals' who can't help it, who are entirely left outside of the picture that is supposed to picture them, or is it the case that within this imaginary frame an actual encounter does take place, conflictual to be sure, but also in a sense 'real', which would imply that the 'real others' also somehow

contribute to the construction of the idea of Otherness, albeit in a 'subaltern' place, but which can involve irreducible difference? ... The imaginary of which the idea of 'Orient' is the product, contradictorily combines a real encounter (if only an encounter with real texts, with the writing of the Other) and a denial of the reality of the encounter, indeed of its very possibility. Or, to put it in Althusserian terms, that it combines recognition with a misrecognition, each taking place within the limits and in the language of the other.[48]

As Giuliano Gliozzi noted in his methodological critique of Landucci's book,[49] while a history of ideas may lead us to suppose that, at least until the full deployment of colonial anthropology, the debate about the 'savage' was largely an intra-European discussion about the nature of humanity, a critical history of ideology shows us that European ideas and philosophies were deeply affected by the shifting demands of the *colonial relations* that Europe forced on so many other parts of the world. In Gliozzi's monumental study of the seemingly bizarre Biblical and counterfeit genealogies that European powers projected onto Amerindian populations to shore up the justificatory and juridical demands of their colonial policies – genealogies that sought the ancestors of the peoples of the Americas in the Tribes of Israel, pre-Adamite creation, the inhabitants of Atlantis, Jews, Tartars, Norwegians, the Dutch or the Welsh ...[50] – we see how unintelligible the colonial history of anthropology and philosophy would be if we fail to investigate its articulations in relation to very unique conjunctures of dispossession and resistance.

For example, the Spanish conquistadors in conflict with their crown could argue that the Aztecs were a properly political society, rather than a savage one, in order to ground the transfer of sovereignty that they'd supposedly agreed to. By the same token, the Spanish state could support the critique of Aristotle's natural slavery or refute the conquistadors' tale of the natives as sinful descendants of Jews – not out of a humanitarian concern with historical or anthropological truth, but because they needed wage-labourers to pay taxes to their metropolitan sovereign. Or, to return to our starting point, attentiveness to ideological conjunctures can reveal that behind Montaigne's redeployment of the logic of comparative negation, and his seemingly anti-colonial scepticism regarding claims of American barbarism and European superiority, lay a French Huguenot tradition of opposition to, and competition with, the hegemony of *Spanish* colonialism – whence the vociferous attacks on the genocidal nature of the *conquista*. But also that Montaigne's philosophy implied its own 'civilising' project, one in which recognition of difference remained the prelude to an *apologia* for the supposedly 'gentle' virtues of an emergent *French* colonial project. As Pocock has noted, the 'Enlightenment could deny history to others even as it asserted their humanity ... writing a *histoire philosophique* in which Europe was denounced for its imposition of history on a world of nature, but a *histoire politique* in which Europeans alone are actors.'[51]

In the end, the injunction to decolonise philosophy cannot be reduced to the goal of producing a philosophy shorn of its colonial sediments. Rather, it demands the unrelenting practice of working through that inexorably imaginary and ideological space – occupied by philosophy's many and mostly monotonous savages – in which a real encounter and the denial of that encounter remain inseparable from one another. This is a project that requires both the kind of historical archaeologies and genealogies that Sergio Landucci and Giuliano Gliozzi (along with Olive Dickason,[52] Michèle Duchet, Ter Ellingson and others) have contributed to, and a critical openness to the kind of 'political miracles' that Leibniz spoke of, the ones that can help dislocate a European and state-centred monopoly over the meaning of collective political life – a monopoly that remains among the most enduring legacies and present determinants of the colonial relation.[53]

Alberto Toscano is Reader in Critical Theory at Goldsmiths, University of London. The second edition of his book Fanaticism: On the Uses of an Idea *was published in 2017.*

Notes

1. See Étienne Balibar, '"Rights of Man" and "Rights of the Citizen": The Modern Dialectic of Equality and Freedom', in *Masses, Classes, Ideas: Studies on Politics and Philosophy Before and After Marx*, trans. James Swenson (London: Routledge, 1994), 39–60; *Citizen Subject: Foundations for Philosophical Anthropology*, trans. Steven Miller (New York: Fordham University Press, 2016).
2. Sergio Landucci, *I filosofi e i selvaggi, 1580–1780*, new ed. (: Einaudi, 2014) (this is a considerably revised version of the more explicitly Marxist first edition, published by Laterza in 1972); Giuliano Gliozzi, *Adamo e il nuovo mondo. La nascita dell'antropologia come ideologia coloniale: dalle genealogie bibliche alle teorie razziali (1500-1700)* (Florence: La nuova Italia, 1976).

Gliozzi's book has been translated into French: *Adam et le Nouveau Monde: la naissance de l'anthropologie comme idéologie coloniale: des généalogies bibliques aux théories raciales, 1500-1700*, preface by Frank Lestringant, trans. Arlette Estève and Pascal Gabellone (Lecques: Théétète, 2000).

3. See Roger Bartra, *Wild Men in the Looking Glass: The Mythic Origins of European Otherness*, trans. Carl T. Berrisford (Ann Arbor: University of Michigan, 1994). In his 1972 course on Rousseau, Louis Althusser suggests that the forest, conceived as a place of inexhaustible natural abundance, plays a critical role in the French philosopher's narrative and critique of origins, namely of figuring the savage as inhabiting a space without determinate 'places' (*lieux*). See Louis Althusser, *Cours sur Rousseau*, ed. Yves Vargas (: Les Temps des Cérises, 2015); translation forthcoming as *Lessons on Rousseau*, trans. G.M. Goshgarian (: Verso, 2019).

4. J.G.A. Pocock, *Barbarism and Religion, Volume 4: Barbarians, Savages and Empires* (: Press, 2005), 189.

5. See Landucci, *I filosofi e i selvaggi*; also Raymond Klibansky, 'Introduction', in *La Pensée philosophique d'expression française au . Le Rayonnement du Québec* (ed. Raymond Klibansky and Josiane Boulad-Ayoub) (Saint-Nicolas: Les Presses de l'Université Laval, 1998), 14–18.

6. Michel Foucault, *History of Madness*, ed. Jean Khalfa, trans. Jonathan Murphy and Jean Khalfa (London: Routledge, 2006), xxix.

7. Ibid., xxx.

8. Étienne Balibar, 'Difference, Otherness, Exclusion', *Parallax* 11: 1 (2005), 30.

9. Ibid., 30.

10. On the shaping role of Ancient and Biblical figures of Otherness in the colonial encounter, see Gliozzi, *Adamo e il Nuovo mondo*, and Pocock, *Barbarism and Religion, Volume 4*. For an iconographic reflection on this pattern of the preformation of the savage, inspired by Aby Warburg, see Carlo Ginzburg, 'Memory and Distance: On a Gilded Silver Vase (Antwerp, c. 1530)', in *Fear Reverence Terror: Five Essays in Political Iconography* (Calcutta: Seagull Books, 2017), especially pages 4–8 on the 'New World'.

11. Sergio Landucci, *I filosofi e i selvaggi, 1580–1780* (Bari: Laterza, 1972), 338.

12. Ter Ellingson, *The Myth of the Noble Savage* (Berkeley: University of California Press, 2001).

13. Michel de Montaigne, 'Of the Cannibals', in *Shakespeare's Montaigne: The Florio Translation of the Essays – A Selection*, ed. Stephen Greenblatt and Peter G. Platt (New York: New York Review of Books, 2014), 61. The question of the savage is also (differently) articulated by Montaigne in the essay 'Des Coches' (Of Coaches). For a thorough exploration of Montaigne's speculations on Amerindian life and their wide-ranging intellectual impact see Frank Lestringant (ed.), *Le Brésil de Montaigne. Le Nouveau Monde des «Essais» (1580–1592)* (Paris: Éditions Chandeigne, 2005).

14. Foucault, *History of Madness*, 165.

15. Amerigo Vespucci, *Mundus Novus: Letter to Lorenzo Pietro di Medici*, trans. George Tyler Northup (Princeton: Princeton University Press, 1916), 6.

16. Wilberforce Eames, *Description of a Wood Engraving Illustrating the South American Indians* [1505] (New York: The New York Public Library, 1922).

17. Margaret T. Hodgen, 'Montaigne and Shakespeare Again', *Huntington Library Quarterly* 16:1 (November, 1952), 33.

18. Hodgen, 'Montaigne and Shakespeare Again', 28.

19. Stephen Greenblatt, 'Learning to Curse: Aspects of Linguistic Colonialism in the Sixteenth Century', in *Learning to Curse: Essays in early modern culture* [1990] (London: Routledge, 2007), 24.

20. Quoted in Ellingson, *The Myth of the Noble Savage*, 57.

21. Elsewhere, Kant was not incapable of a (politically) romantic idealisation of 'Canadians', which seems to unsettle his certainty about the uncivilised character of the indigenous people of North America: 'Among all the savages there is no people which demonstrates such a sublime character of mind ... They have a strong feeling for honour, and as in hunt of it they will seek wild adventures hundreds of miles away, they are also extremely careful to avoid the least injury to it where their ever so harsh enemy, after he has captured them, tries to force a cowardly sigh from them by dreadful tortures. The Canadian savage is moreover truthful and honest. ... He is extremely proud, sensitive to the complete worth of freedom, and even in education tolerates no encounter that would make him feel a lowly subjugation. Lycurgus probably gave laws to such savages, and if a law-giver were to arise among the six nations, one would see a Spartan republic arise in the new world ... Among all the savages there are none among whom the female sex stands in greater real regard than those of Canada. In this perhaps they even surpass our civilised part of the world. Not as if they pay the women their humble respects; that would be mere compliments. No, they actually get to command. They meet and take council about the most important affairs of the nation, about war and peace. They send their delegates to the male council, and commonly it is their vote that decides. But they pay dearly enough for this preference. They have all the domestic concerns on their shoulders and share all of the hardships with the men.' It is worth noting that the passage about 'Canadian' women is immediately preceded by one of the infamous statements of Kant's persistent anti-black racism: 'There might be something here worth considering, except for the fact that this scoundrel was completely black from head to foot, a distinct proof that what he said was stupid.' See Immanuel Kant, *Observations on the Feeling of the Beautiful and the Sublime* [1764], in Kant, *Anthropology, History, Education*, ed. Günter Zöller and Robert B. Louden (Cambridge: Cambridge University Press, 2007), 60.

22. Quoted in Ellingson, *The Myth of the Noble Savage*, 141.

23. Hodgen, 'Montaigne and Shakespeare Again', 37.

24. Hayden White, 'Forms of Wildness: Archaeology of an Idea', in *Tropics of Discourse: Essays in Cultural Criticism* (Baltimore: Johns Hopkins University, 1978), 151–2. See also 'The Noble Savage Theme as Fetish', in the same collection.

25. Arthur O. Lovejoy, 'The Supposed Primitivism of Rousseau's "Discourse on Inequality"', *Modern Philology*, Vol. 21, No. 2 (Nov., 1923): 165–86.

26. Ellingson, *The Myth of the Noble Savage*, 32.

27. Ibid., 375.

28. On this 'network of negations', see Michèle Duchet, *Anthropologie et histoire au siècle des lumières* (Paris: Albin Michel, 1995 [1971]).
29. Anthony Pagden, 'The Savage Critic: Some European Images of the Primitive', *The Yearbook of English Studies* 13 (1983), 33.
30. Aimé Césaire, *A Tempest*, trans. Richard Miller (New York: Theatre Communications Group, 2002), 29.
31. Thomas Hobbes, *Leviathan*, ed. C.B. Macpherson (London: Penguin, 1985), 185-6.
32. Noel Malcolm, 'Hobbes, Sandys, and the Virginia Company', *The Historical Journal* 24: 2 (1981): 297-321.
33. Hobbes, *Leviathan*, 187.
34. Anthony Pagden, *The Fall of Natural Man: The American Indian and the Origins of Comparative Ethnology* (Cambridge: Cambridge University Press, 1987).
35. See Giorgio Agamben, 'Leviathan and Behemoth', in *Stasis: Civil War as a Political Paradigm (Homo Sacer II, 2)*, trans. Nicholas Heron (Stanford, CA: Stanford University Press, 2015), 25-69.
36. Johannes Fabian, *Time and the Other: How Anthropology Makes its Object* (New York: Columbia University Press, 1983).
37. Pierre Clastres, 'Copernicus and the Savages', in *Society Against the State*, trans. Robert Hurley with Abe Stein (Oxford: Basil Blackwell/Mole Editions, 1977), 11.
38. Thomas Hobbes, *The Elements of Law, Natural and Politic*, ed. J.C.A. Gaskin (Oxford: Oxford University Press, 2008), 80.
39. For a fascinating structuralist inquiry into the gendered iconography of the savage in De Bry, see Bernadette Bucher, *La Sauvage aux seins pendants* (Paris: Hermann, 1977). See also, more recently, Michael Gaudio, *Engraving the Savage: The New World and Techniques of Civilisation* (Minneapolis: University of Minnesota Press, 2008).
40. The iconographic and ideological survivals of archaic Britain in the imaginary of the savage projected onto the Americas is insightfully explored in Ioannis D. Evrigenis, *Images of Anarchy: The Rhetoric and Science in Hobbes's State of Nature* (Cambridge: Cambridge University Press, 2014), esp. chapter 8 'America', 202ff.
41. This momentous displacement from morality and normativity to development and social science is at the heart of Landucci's landmark study.
42. Ronald L. Meek, *Social Science and the Ignoble Savage* (Cambridge: Cambridge University Press, 1976).
43. Audra Simpson, 'The Ruse of Consent and the Anatomy of "Refusal": Cases From Indigenous North America and Australia', *Postcolonial Studies* 20 (2017), 25.
44. Gottfried Wilhelm Leibniz, quoted in Réal Ouellet, 'Introduction', in Lahontan, *Dialogues avec un Sauvage*, ed. Réal Ouellet (Montréal: Lux, 2010), 18.
45. Ibid., 18. See also §256 of the *Theodicy*: 'But even to-day entire tribes, such as the Hurons, the Iroquois, the Galibis and other peoples of America teach us a great lesson on this matter: one cannot read without astonishment of the intrepidity and well-nigh insensibility wherewith they brave their enemies, who roast them over a slow fire and eat them by slices. If such people could retain their physical superiority and their courage, and combine them with our acquirements, they would surpass us in every way. ... They would be, in comparison with us, as a giant to a dwarf, a mountain to a hill.' (Leibniz, *Theodicy: Essays on the Goodness of God, the Freedom of Man and the Origin of Evil*, ed. Austin Farrer, trans. E.M. Huggard [Eugene, OR: Wipf and Stock, 2001], 283).
46. Pierre Clastres's argument could also – along with the writings of Robert Jaulin, Jacques Lizot, and others – be legitimately read as an instrumentalisation of the anthropology of 'primitive societies' for the sake of an anti-Marxist polemic. For a trenchant critique of this libertarian anti-Marxist trend in anthropology, see Jean-Loup Amselle (ed.), *Le Sauvage à la mode* (Paris: Le Sycomore, 1979). While I cannot address this polemic in this forum (nor indeed the fascinating relation between Clastres's work and Deleuze & Guattari's speculations on the *Urstaat*, the war machine, and related themes), tackling it is crucial for any serious appraisal of the afterlives of European philosophy's savages.
47. Clastres, 'Copernicus and the Savages', 5. Clastres also tackled head-on the ethnocentric monotony of the discourse of comparative negation: 'the encounter between the West and the Savages has always been an occasion for repeating the same discourse concerning them' (8). To transcend this is it necessary to leave behind all *exotic* conceptions of the 'savages'. Clastres's critique of the supposition whereby 'the absence of any command-obedience relationship *ipso facto* entails the absence of political power' (9) prevents him from articulating his critique in terms of a notion of the *non-political*, such as we may encounter in the partially congruent views advanced in Cedric J. Robinson's *Terms of Order*.
48. Balibar, 'Difference, Otherness, Exclusion', 30.
49. Giuliano Gliozzi, 'I filosofi e I selvaggi', in *Differenze e uguaglianza nella cultura europea moderna. Scritti 1966-1991*, ed. Anna Strumia (Napoli: Vivarium, 1993). This collection also includes several illuminating essays on the place of 'savages' and the 'New World' in European thought and culture.
50. Gliozzi, *Adamo e il nuovo mondo*; see also in English his 'The Apostles in the New World: Monotheism and Idolatry Between Revelation and Fetishism', *History and Anthropology* 3:1 (1987): 123-48.
51. Pocock, *Barbarism and Religion*, Volume 4, 223.
52. Olive Patricia Dickason, *The Myth of the Savage and the Beginnings of French Colonialism in the Americas* (Edmonton: University of Alberta Press, 1984).
53. While my focus here has been almost exclusively on matters of historiography and intellectual history, any further elaboration of the speculative figure of a non-statist 'political miracle' will perforce need to engage with contemporary developments in indigenous political thought. See Audra Simpson, 'The Ruse of Consent and the Anatomy of "Refusal"', and *Mohawk Interruptus: Political Life Across the Borders of Settler States* (Durham, NC: Duke University Press, 2014); Glen Sean Coulthard, *Red Skin, White Masks: Rejecting the Colonial Politics of Recognition* (Minneapolis: University of Minnesota Press, 2014).

Is logos a proper noun?
Or, is Aristotelian Logic translatable into Chinese?
Yijing Zhang

During Jacques Derrida's visit to China in 2001, he held a meeting with the Chinese philosopher Wang Yuanhua.* Derrida opened their dialogue with a sentence that had the effect, no doubt involuntary, of aggravating his interlocutor and all of those Chinese listeners present: 'China doesn't have philosophy, but/only thought [中国没有哲学，但/只有思想, Zhongguo meiyou zhexue dan/zhi you lixiang]'. This was not actually the original form of the sentence as the French philosopher had pronounced it, but my own later translation of the Chinese translation of the original French sentence, which itself has not been preserved. Regardless, it is the Chinese translation alone that Wang was able to hear and understand. This translation has two versions, or, to be more exact, can be translated in two different ways. All of the nuance resides in the choice of conjunction: either 'but' or 'only'.

First, 'China doesn't have philosophy, it *only* has thought.' This was the version published in the collection of Wang's writings.[1] It was also the interpretation of certain Chinese intellectuals. Consequently, the conversation between Derrida and Wang resuscitated amongst these intellectuals the old debate around the question of whether or not China has its own philosophy.

Second, 'China doesn't have philosophy, but it *does however* have thought.' We believe that this was what Derrida was trying to say. Between 'only' and 'however' there is a difference of stress. Nonetheless, this difference implies two completely opposing conceptions of Chinese thought.

As we know, for Derrida, 'philosophy' is centred on *logos* and is prisoner to it; presumably his aim in visiting China was thus not to identify the same structure in Chinese thought. Derrida did not understand Chinese, but we need only refer to his criticism of alphabetic writing, in *Of Grammatology* for example – a writing that is for him intrinsically linked to *logos* –– to understand what he may have hoped for from the Chinese language and Chinese thought. That China had no *logos*, and therefore no 'philosophy', presented an opportunity to Derrida's eyes, as it does to all Western philosophers who find in 'Chinese thought' a way of reviving or regenerating their 'philosophy'.

Unfortunately, those Chinese listeners who heard Derrida's sentence ignored this probable intention and interpreted his words as a negative value judgement, one that placed Chinese thought in an inferior position vis-à-vis Western philosophy. The reaction of his Chinese interlocutor was therefore to establish in 'Chinese thought' those aspects that had most in common with 'Western philosophy', particularly its logic and metaphysics. And yet Derrida went to China neither to find 'philosophy' nor to speak ill of 'Chinese thought'. In fact, to foresee the provocative effect of his comment, he would have needed to understand the history of the modernisation of China to see why the Chinese could not but be extremely sensitive to this kind of assessment. The idea that China has no philosophy, no natural science, has nothing related to Western modernity, was historically regarded as a fatal danger, insofar as China had almost perished at the hands of technologically superior Western powers.

---

* The writing of this article was supported by the research project 'The Relationship between Western Philosophy and Chinese Thought in Jesuits' Writings', funded by the China Postdoctoral Science Foundation Grant (No. 2018M633266) and the Fundamental Research Funds for the Central Universities (No 18wkpy67). It was first published in French in B. Cassin et F. Gorog (dir.), *Psychanalyser en langues, Intraduisibles et langue chinoise* (Paris: Demopolis, 2016), 47–76. We thank Demopolis for permission to translate it here.

Derrida was not the first to say that China does not have philosophy. For Wang, for whom the work of Hegel is more familiar than that of Derrida, the condescending simplification of Chinese thought is also found in Hegel's *Lectures on the Philosophy of History*, where we read:

> He [Confucius] is for the most part a moral educator. He was a moralist as such, not actually a philosopher; for in his case we do not find theory that occupies itself in thought as such. ... We have one of his books [the *Lün yü*] in a modern translation; according to the reviews, however, it does little to enhance his reputation. He is not to be compared to Plato, Aristotle, or Socrates.[2]

Despite their differences, Derrida's valorisation and Hegel's devaluation of Chinese thought have one thing in common. To put it in Foucauldian terms: 'For the West, the East is everything that it is not, yet it must search it to find its own primitive truth'.[3] From this perspective, saying that China does not have philosophy isn't really saying anything at all. By reducing China to that which the West is not, all we see in it *is* the West. In other words, we remain stuck in logocentrism.

Is there philosophy in China?

Undeniably China did not originally have 'philosophy' in the Greek or Western sense of the word, but today in China people speak of both 'Western philosophy' and 'Chinese philosophy'. This is an effect of translation. Philosophy has been given a name in Chinese; it has been ascribed a neologism, 哲学 (transcribed in pinyin as *zhe xue*), which means, literally, the study of wisdom.[4] *Logos* on the other hand has only been given a phonetic transcription that does not make literal sense. In other words, 'philosophy' has become a common noun – which is why we can talk about 'Western philosophy' and 'Chinese philosophy' – but the word '*logos*' has remained a proper noun. As such, there is no Chinese *logos*. The problem is not that the Chinese language lacks a word into which to translate the word '*logos*'. The fact that the word '*logos*' has not been sinicised when the majority of concepts from Western philosophy, even the most recent, already have a Chinese equivalent, means that the problem is not related to a gap in the Chinese language itself. After all, if Derrida had said that China did not have *logos*, his listeners would presumably not have been particularly shocked.

In the phrase '*logos* is a proper noun', which gives my essay its title, I want to make clear, then, two points. The first is that *logos*, like all foreign proper nouns, has no translation but only a transcription in Chinese. Secondly, *logos* is seen by Derrida, as by other Western philosophers and the Chinese, as something that belongs to the West. The question mark in my title indicates that we are posing the question here of both why the word *logos* is untranslatable, and why it belongs to the West.

In this respect, it seems useful to recall Heidegger's conversation 'between a Japanese and an Inquirer'. In the version recounted by the German philosopher (as translated into English), we discover an exchange that seems like an anticipation of the misunderstanding that would arise decades later between Derrida and Wang:

> **Inquirer (Heidegger):** The danger of our dialogues was hidden in language itself; not in *what* we discussed, nor in the *way in which* we tried to do so.
>
> **Japanese:** But Count [Shūzō] Kuki had uncommonly good command of German, and of French and English, did he not?
>
> **I:** Of course. *He* could say in European languages whatever was under discussion. ... it was *I* to whom the spirit of Japanese language remained closed – as it is to this day.
>
> **J:** The languages of the dialogue shifted everything into *European*.
>
> ...
>
> **J:** The language of the dialogue constantly destroyed the possibility of saying what the dialogue was about.
>
> **I:** Some time ago I called language, clumsily enough, the house of Being. If man by virtue of his language dwells within the claim and call of Being, then we Europeans presumably dwell in an entirely different house than East-asian man.
>
> **J:** Assuming that the languages of the two are not merely different but are other in nature, and radically so.
>
> **I:** And so, a dialogue from house to house remains entirely impossible.[5]

Heidegger, while praising German as 'more Greek than Greek' because it is the language of philosophy, remains imprisoned in his own 'house of Being' and could only hopelessly imagine the possibility of a dialogue with 'the man from the Far East'. Similarly, Derrida discovers that his wish to escape from logocentrism turns back upon itself. For both philosophers, given that they cannot think in the language of their interlocutor, and so continually draw non-European thought back into European logic, their dialogues are fated to remain monologues – ones in which they can only hear themselves.

The dilemma of the Heideggerian 'house of Being' is that it serves simultaneously to confirm man in his relation to Being and to enclose the Europeans in their own house, since they have no other language than that of Greek and European *logos*. I would like to propose, however, another reading of the dialogue between Heidegger and his Japanese interlocutor. From the thesis that languages are radically other in nature, we do not have to conclude that a conversation between houses remains entirely impossible. That the language of the dialogue constantly destroys the possibility of saying what the dialogue is about is only true if there is only one language of dialogue, in this case German or French, or, indeed, any European language. But what if there is more than one? What if Heidegger and Derrida spoke the language of their interlocutor, Japanese or Chinese, and could therefore understand its differences from their own tongue?

We can agree with Heidegger: there is a fundamental difference between languages. And with Derrida: China does not have philosophy in the sense given by logocentrism. Yet, this does not entail a belief in *logos* as the house of Being. Humanity does not dwell in its house in the same way that Being dwells in *logos*: Being can only exist in *logos*, in Greek and German, whilst humans can and must communicate with their neighbours, be welcomed into their homes and receive them in turn. This is linguistic and cultural pluralism, and it is the very condition of human existence, today more than ever. The possibility of communication between houses and cultures comes through translation, because translation is the very dialogue between languages. By translation, however, I do not mean the work of translators who appear to save speakers from linguistic barriers while in fact keeping them locked within them, but, rather, the recognition of linguistic differences by the speakers themselves.

The first encounter of China and *logos*

My aim here is not to answer, therefore, the question of whether China has philosophy, but, rather, to tease out the complexity of the question itself with the help of one of the foundational texts of philosophy and of *logos*; a text that was also one of the first Western philosophical texts to be translated into Chinese: Aristotle's *Organon*.

The text that served as the basis for the Chinese translation of the *Organon* is to be found in a book entitled *Commentarii Collegii Conimbricensis, e Societate Jesu, in Universam Dialecticam Aristotelis Stagiritae* ('Comments from the Coimbra College of the Society of Jesus on the whole dialectic of Aristotle of Stagire'), which was published in Cologne in 1611. The Chinese translation, *Ming li tan* (名理探), which dates from 1631, was, like most Jesuit translations of the period, the result of a collaboration between a foreign missionary and a Chinese scholar: in this case, Francisco Furtado, a Portuguese Jesuit, and Li Zhizao, a mandarin who had converted to Christianity. Unlike Derrida, Furtado had the advantage of speaking Chinese and of living in China. By comparison with contemporary Chinese scholars, Li also had a 'parental' link with traditional Chinese thought, a link that has in a sense been broken in the process of Chinese modernisation. Furtado was among the first Westerners to learn Chinese, while Li was among the first in China to encounter Aristotle's philosophy.

The Jesuits' reason for translating Western philosophy into Chinese was recorded anecdotally in a letter from Andrea Lubelli, S.J., to the General in Rome from 15 December 1683:

> When the Emperor of China heard Father Verbiest speaking of our [European] philosophy, he bestowed the task upon this Father to transmit this [philosophy] in Chinese characters; because in China there is no philosophy in whatever form, unless one takes into account some philosophical sayings, acutely published by *literati* and written unsystematically, without [philosophical] bases [*sine fundamento*], improvised [*ex improvise*] … and without [logical] order [*sine ordine*].[6]

This is probably the first version of the thesis that 'China does not have philosophy', given that the Jesuits were the first Westerners to establish an intellectual exchange between Europe and China. Indeed, Lubelli's words seem almost a paraphrase of Derrida's and Hegel's formulations cited above. Or rather, Derrida and Hegel only repeat what the Jesuits had already said centuries earlier.

From the perspective of the Christian mission, the Jesuits were not in China searching for the irreducible otherness of the West. Their strategy of 'assimilation'[7] had the opposite intention: searching the Chinese classics, especially Confucius, to find elements that could echo the Sacred Scriptures. A later group of Jesuits, known as the 'Figurists', went as far as interpreting the hexagrams of the *Classic of Changes* as messages from the bible. The Jesuits therefore had no interest in drawing out the difference between China and the West. Why shouldn't China have philosophy like that of the West? It would certainly make conversion easier.

Yet Lubelli's letter can also be read from the other side of a strategy of assimilation: as a way of attracting the attention and interest of Chinese academics to Western culture by presenting what it did best from all different branches of knowledge.[8] It was with this intention in mind that mathematics, astronomy and cartography were brought to China by the Jesuits, and this also explains why Lubelli speaks proudly of 'our philosophy'. In short, portraying China as bearing traces of Christianity, or as being devoid of philosophy, are two ways of thinking that serve to justify the same end.

Thus, those theses according to which China has no philosophy, or Chinese language has no grammar, were first pronounced by the Jesuits. Today the tendency in sinology is rather to say that the Chinese language does not lack grammar and that China, even if it does not have philosophy, does at least have sophists, logicians, mathematicians, etc. Have we got past the Jesuits then? The answer is no. Everything was already there in nucleus in the first encounters between the West and China. Perhaps the Jesuits' most important legacy is to have shown that it is always possible to claim China as either the same or different to the West, depending on what one wants to do. In fact, to say that China lacks a certain thing that exists in the West, or on the contrary that China does have something in common with the West, comes to the same thing: we never escape ethnocentrism, because this kind of comparison continues to draw on the Western system of reference; it is a reduction rather than a comparison, which thereby undermines the coherence of Chinese thought that is simply not built upon the same questions. For both comparativists and anti-comparativists, the difficulty of avoiding such a practice comes from the fact that there is no understanding of the other that is not conditioned by our prior self-understanding. In the case of Chinese culture, for both Westerners since the Jesuits and Chinese people who are today under the influence of the West, there is no prior understanding of Chinese culture other than that formed through a Western lens. For Japan, which became westernised in slightly different circumstances to China, the existence of 'Japanese philosophy' is still questioned in a very similar way.[9] It is therefore useless to want to refuse comparative philosophy – whether for an Eastern or Western researcher – as concerns the East, because the background is itself always Western.

Unable as we are to extract ourselves from Western pre-understanding, we can at least take critical distance from such comparative philosophy with the help of the *Ming li tan* because this text was written before the modernisation of China; that is to say, in a non-modernised, non-westernised China. In what follows, I want to place this text under the microscope in order to focus solely on one thing: the translation of the word 'logic' as *ming li* (名理), or 'name-principle'. It is this translation which already contains an answer to the question of whether China has philosophy.

The translation of Aristotle's *Organon* by Furtado and Li is the first attempt in Chinese history to seek, at the lexical level, a Chinese equivalent to the word 'logic'. Strictly speaking, their translation is a new creation in that before them there was no Chinese equivalent. It is not completely new however, as the translation was not made by means of a neologism; the words *ming* and *li* were already part of the Chinese language. The problem is that the mode of reasoning implied in *ming* and *li* is not at all the same as that of Aristotelian logic.

The word *Ming*

Ming means 'name'. To begin with Confucius:

> When names are not correct, what is said will not sound reasonable; when what is said does not sound reasonable, affairs will not culminate in success; when affairs do not culminate in success, rites and music will not flourish; when rites and music do not flourish, punishments will not be exactly right; when punishments are not exactly right, the common people will not know where to put hand and foot. Thus when the gentleman names something, the name is sure to be usable in speech, and when he says something this is sure to be practicable. The thing about the gentleman is that he is anything but casual where speech is concerned.[10]

This is the famous Confucian theory of the 'rectification of names', which is essentially a theory of the art of governing. Given the way in which Confucius approaches the question of names, Hegel's remark quoted earlier is unsurprising: 'He was a moralist as such, not actually a philosopher; for in his case we do not find theory that occupies itself in thought as such.' Yet, it should be noted that Confucius' names refer to individual titles in the family and society, such as sovereign and minister, father and son. The importance of names consists in each person behaving in accordance with his or her name; not their own name, but their title or social position.

In China as in Greece, the theory of names is above all a theory of the relation between *ming* (名), 'name', and *shi* (实), 'reality', the thing designated by the name. However, there are two principal differences. First, for Chinese thinkers, a name is not any noun, but relays an individual's 'reputation'; reality does not refer to any given worldly thing, but mainly to people's behaviour in society. Second, following Confucius' example, almost all Chinese thinkers concerned with language have accorded particular importance to the rectification of names. By contrast, Greek logic is concerned with predication: the combination of noun and verb, subject and predicate. For Aristotle the link between language and reality is apophatic; language designates an extralinguistic fact. The verb 'to be' is what brings out the structure of predication, as Aristotle demonstrates in the *Metaphysics*: 'The senses of essential being are those which are indicated by the figures of predication; for "being" has as many senses as there are ways of predication. ... There is no difference between "the man is recovering" and "the man recovers"; or between "the man is walking" or "cutting" and "the man walks" or "cuts".'[11]

The word *Li*

The notion of *li* is closely linked to the Study of *li* (理学/li xue), a current of thought that dates from the eleventh century and that provides the context for the philosophical and religious exchanges between the Jesuits and Chinese academics in the sixteenth century. *Li* is usually translated into English as 'principle' (or *principe* in French).[12]

Ming li tan begins by presenting the notion of philosophy: 'The love of wisdom, which Westerners call *fei-lu-suo-fei-ya* (斐录琐费亚), is the name for all the knowledge concerned with *principles*'.[13] The guiding maxim for the Study of *li* is *ge wu qiong li* (格物穷理), 'examining things and fathoming principles'. *Li* in the sense of principle can be seen as an alternative term for *dao*. But unlike the ancient thinkers of *dao* who saw it as a union of human and heaven and the principles of the human behaviour, the grand masters of the Study of *li* had a strong interest in the internal principles of ordinary things; for them the understanding of such principles was an indispensable step towards achieving the union of human and heaven. It is this importance of *li* that led to the analogy between the Study of *li* and philosophy, the supreme knowledge of the West. This is why, for those Chinese academics in contact with the Jesuits, Western philosophy corresponded to the Study of *li* in Chinese thought.

Nicolas Standaert sees in *li* the element that allowed the Jesuits to introduce Western knowledge into China, the common ground between the Study of *li* and Jesuit teaching being a shared interest in the real. *Li* is reached by examining real things, while, for the Jesuits, understanding of the real world leads to God.[14] The only common point is in the means, but these means serve two completely different ends: the experience of God in Christianity, and the self-cultivation in Confucianism, *i.e.* becoming a sage. Although *li* has a common element with positive knowledge, its pursuit is the realisation of Confucian morals.

The literal meaning of *li* is 'to carve in jade'. This means that it originates in a verb. Among the figurative meanings of the verb are: to manage, to handle, to put in order, etc. From the verb *li* there is also the noun *li*, referring to the veins in jade and other related ideas such as wood fibre, blood vessels, order, norm, reason. The *Grand dictionnaire Ricci de la langue chinoise* provides the following definitions of the word:

> 1. The lines that guide the constitution and determine the qualities of beings and things: the natural structures of the animation of a being; 2. the sensible qualities of beings and things; 3. the structuring principle that determines the form and fate of everything that exists (neo-Confucianism); 4. the principle of things, which makes possible and determines the substantial expression of vital energy 气 (qi); 5. to reason: to find the lines of force in beings and events.

Obviously the first definition is closely related to the veins in jade. Given the central role of jade in Chinese culture since ancient times, it is unsurprising that it is at the origin of an important philosophical concept. The date of birth of the word *li* is difficult to establish, but it appears in the oldest literature of pre-imperial China.

If *li* is usually translated into French as 'principle', it is in the sense, it seems to me, of principle as origin of the universe, as in the Greek *arkhê*. All the definitions from the *Grand Ricci Dictionary* could be united under the word 'principle' understood in its widest sense. For traditional Chinese thinkers, it is always the same principle that determines the natural world and human society. As the principle of human society, *li* also comes close to the other definition of 'principle' as law or rule. As the Chinese sage lives in the union between man and heaven, so the principle of the two worlds, natural and social, must be the same.

The term *Ming li*

Christoph Harbsmeier notes that the term *ming li*, which is at least as old as the Han dynasty (third century BC), came into regular usage during this period and served as a 'vague general word for logic' until the twentieth century.[15] He adds that the word can also be anachronistically translated as 'analytic philosophy'. Yet, arguably, translating it as 'logic' is no less anachronistic. Analytic philosophy is a more recent development than logic in the history of Western philosophy, but in both China and the West – or in Western sinology – the branch of knowledge known as 'Chinese logic' and the sorting of certain ancient doctrines under this heading only began at the start of the twentieth century. Moreover, the Chinese of the third century never used *ming li* as 'the vague general word for logic'. In fact, Furtado and Li were the first to translate *ming li* in this way.

Ming li is a common noun that can be found in dictionaries. The *Grand Ricci Dictionary* gives the following example:

> 名理 'Names and principles': distinguishing denominations and analysing constitutive principles, a discipline practiced by the neo-Taoists (dyn. 晋 Jin), which involves going back to principles through right and proper names.

Why, in the *Ming li tan*, does the term *ming li* become the translation for the word 'logic' in the sixteenth century? Does the definition of the *Grand Ricci*, which is only valid in the context of the Jin dynasty, give a precise reason? Or is it worth taking Harbsmeier's position on the term into account? The following discussion thus focuses on two further queries: First, what is the concrete subject of this discipline that distinguishes denominations and analyses principles? Second, what does the term *ming li* usually mean in its 'vague and general' sense?

The movement that characterises the period from the third to the sixth centuries of China's intellectual history is known as *qing tan* (清谈), 'pure conversations'. The link between *ming li* and *qing tan* resides in the fact that *ming li*, as names and principles, designates the object and content of *qing tan*. The expression *ming li* comes from *bian ming xi li* (辩名析理), 'to distinguish names and analyse principles'. It is this link that no doubt led Harbsmeier to translate *ming li* as 'analytic philosophy'. *Qing tan* covers names and principles, and takes the form of a kind of discussion that has much in common with dialectic in the Aristotelian sense of the word.

The names (*ming*) in *bian ming xi li* are initially the same as those in Confucius's 'rectification of names'. Their scope also include the qualities of a governor, humanity's general moral qualities and other related ideas, like heaven and *dao*, and it is this scope that explains the relation between names and principles. The criteria for distinguishing names are founded on human nature, itself justified by *li*, the ultimate principle and foundation of everything. To correctly differentiate between names, one should analyse principles.[16] We can thus say that in *qing tan*, which aims to distinguish names and analyse principles, names and principles relate to the same notions of *ming* and *li* that were treated separately above.

It is primarily the object of its research that distances *qing tan* from Aristotelian logic. While its original motivation was political, *bian ming xi li* eventually transformed into commentaries on Confucian and Taoist classics. The horizon for intellectual reflection in this period, as is generally the case in all periods of traditional China, was still centred on the moral ideal of the sage. The way in which this was considered and discussed was fairly subtle and speculative in this period compared to others, but the validity of arguments was not a primary concern, as it is in Aristotle. It would be a little too optimistic to believe in the possibility of genuine communication between a way of thinking born of the need for good governors, and a philosophy that was stimulated by the Greeks' awe at natural phenomena.

Let us now turn to the problem of the term *ming li* taken as a 'vague and general' word. The expression *kong tan ming li* (空谈名理), 'idle discussion of names and principles', became in the third century a common term by which to indicate a dismissive evaluation, often conveyed solely with the term *ming li* itself: to talk about names and principles means to do nothing useful. The *literati* of the Wei and Jin dynasties turned against Confucianism because of their disengagement from politics, and subsequently *ming li* has been retained as a way of describing a mind inclined towards questions that are theoretical, abstract, speculative; in short, contrary to the political ideal of Confucianism.

Ming li is therefore both part of ordinary Chinese today and a word that is 'vague and general'. It is not however the 'vague and general word for logic' that Harbsmeier claims it is, but a word that carries in itself the idea of a discourse that is vague and general. The *Ming li tan* discusses the names and principles of language and thought as opposed to the names and principles of things, and is thereby aligned more or less to the tradition of *qing tan*. *Ming li* can also be taken as 'the principles of names'.

Insofar as Chinese language philosophy is a philosophy of names, the principles of names are no other than the principles of language. In the expression *ming li*, 'name' and 'principle' are therefore not of the same order; the 'name' is ruled by the 'principle'. This makes sense from the perspective of the subordination of logic to philosophy in the case of the West, and of the *Ming li tan* to the Study of *li* for the Chinese.

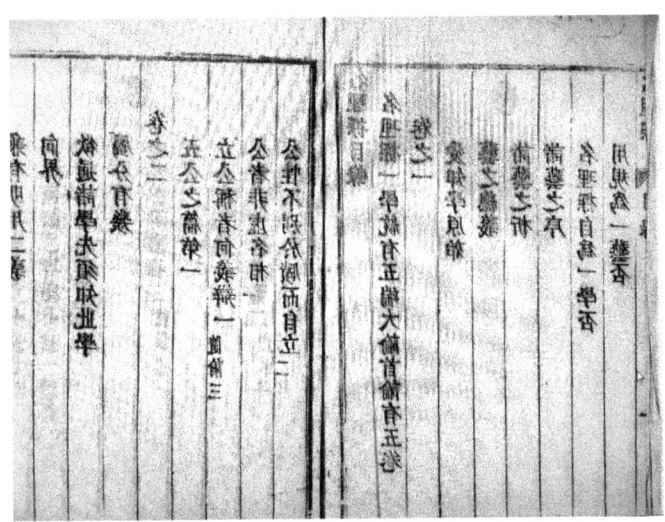

Translating the word 'logic' after the *Ming li tan*

Between the *Ming li tan* and the twentieth century, the number of nouns that the Chinese have invented to translate the word 'logic' is estimated to be more than fifty.[17] I will discuss two of them. Both were put forward by people who were pioneers of Chinese 'modernisation'; Yan Fu (1854-1921), translator and advocate of Western science, and Sun Yat-sen (1866-1925), revolutionary and founder of the Chinese Republic. The fact that these two men each offered their own translation of the word 'logic' based on their own understanding of logic as a Western science is proof enough of the importance accorded to this science in the process of modernisation – as well as in the survival of their country.

Yan translated J. S. Mill's *A System of Logic, Ratiocinative and Inductive* under the title *Mu le ming xue*, meaning 'Mill's science of names'. In his preface he justified this translation choice against Furtado and Li's:

> Titles like '(Ming li) tan' and 'Bian (xue qi meng)' capture neither the depth nor the scope of this science. In an effort to stay as close as possible to the original language,

29

we will render it provisionally as *Ming xue* [science of names]. In Chinese, only the word *ming* has an intention as subtle and rich as the word *logos*.[18]

It is interesting to note that, while defending his own translation of the word 'logic', Yan does not translate but only transcribes the word *logos* as 逻各斯 (*luo ge si*). His translation of 'logic' as *ming xue* – *ming* here is the same as in *Ming li tan*, and thus makes reference to the general theory of names from ancient China – has not been retained by posterity. His phonetic transcription of *logos* has however come into official usage. Ultimately, Yan reconsiders the word 'logic' with more prudence: 'This science [of logic] contains so much. What our country possessed in the pre-imperial era simply cannot accommodate the entirety of its content, but relate only to its very earliest preoccupations.'[19]

After the revolution that put an end to the imperial regime, Sun, as President of the Chinese Republic, published a series of articles under the title 建国方略 [*Jian guo fang lue*], or *Fundamentals of National Reconstruction*, to share his ideas about how Western science was necessary for both the conservation of traditional Chinese culture and the construction of a new modern country. He believed that writing was one of the reasons why China was lagging behind Western countries, and since grammar and logic were two things that had until then belonged to Western languages but were lacking in China, their absence was the cause of this delayed development.

However remarkable it was, Chinese literature had never developed an awareness of itself, because there was neither grammar nor logic in Ancient China. If today we can speak about 'Chinese grammar' and 'Chinese logic', this does not prove Sun wrong, but simply shows that these notions have since been constructed according to the framework of the Western versions of these sciences. Sun himself introduced these two sciences in the following way:

> I deliberately use the expression 'reasoning in writing' (文理) as a translation for the word 'logic' not because it is the best fit, but because in my view logic applied to writing implies a process of reasoning. Modern authors generally apply this science to the act of establishing correct conclusions. Others define logic as 'the science of argumentation' [论理学], while still others call it 'the science of names'. In reality these definitions are not exact. The science of correct deductions comprises only one aspect of logic; Yan's translation as the 'science of names' is proof of his lack of culture. These definitions are imprecise, and do not cover logic as a whole. ...
> What is logic therefore? What does the word mean? Those familiar with this science know that it is the basis for all others, the science of sciences, which controls both thought and action. Many think logically without ever having learnt it directly. In China, this science has no name. It could, in my view, be given that of *li ze*.[20]

Sun thus proposes two neologisms for the word 'logic': 文理 (*wen li*) and 理则 (*li ze*). The first could be rendered as 'writing a reasoning', but I prefer to translate it as 'principles of writing'. The expression *wen li* recalls 文法 (*wen fa*) in the same text. The latter is Sun's translation of the word 'grammar'. *Wen fa* is literally 'the law of writing'. In the case of both *wen li* and *wen fa*, the word *wen* is not the verb 'to write', even though it can have this meaning, but a noun that is able to modify the domain of the 'law' or of 'principles' given its relation to the law and principles of (written) language. Sun is talking first and foremost about written language. His second neologism, 理则 (*li ze*), could be translated as 'principles and rules'.[21] The word *li* in the expressions *wen li* and *li ze* is the same *li* that we saw earlier with the name 'principle'. It can mean the purpose of a thing, specifically of a well-argued text, but not that of human reasoning. Sun does not say what he means by *li ze*, but the translation 'principles and rules' makes sense in terms of what Sun says about the content of this science: 'the basis for all others, the science of sciences, which controls both thought and action'. From my point of view, however, the word *li ze* is inconvenient because, while rejecting Yan's 'science of names' and its failure to encompass all of logic, Sun's translation lacks the link between logic and language that is suggested by the word *ming*, 'name'.

So while Yan kept the word *ming* as his name for logic, Sun preferred the word *li*. They made the same choice as the translators of *Ming li tan*. Clearly in traditional Chinese thought, *ming* and *li* are two of the closest concepts to that of *logos*.

Starting with Furtado and Li, this long quest to find a semantic equivalent to the word 'logic' ended up in a purely phonetic translation, 逻辑 (*luo ji*). This is probably because with their advancing understanding of the Western science of logic, the Chinese become more aware of its specificity. Sinicising logic would risk masking some of the richness proper to this science. It can thus be argued that 'logic' has no Chinese equivalent, and since the word 'logic' is derived from 'logos', it is unsurprising that 'logos' too lacks a translation.

The problem of translating the word 'logic' into Chinese reveals the differences, then, between two ways of thinking. Logic, as established by Aristotle, consists in the determination of reasoning's formal conditions of truth at their most general and universal. But what the Chinese example could question is precisely this claim to universality. The universality of thought has been challenged for as long as thought has been linked to language, or, more precisely, to linguistic pluralism. Is *logos* universal if it does not even translate into Chinese? The debate around this question has resulted in diametrically opposed positions. For example, Benveniste has shown how Aristotelian logic is dependent upon the Greek language, in particular for the ten categories.[22] Does this dependence, in the words of Pierre Aubenque, 'lead us to relativise the metaphysics of being in line with the Greek language, or, instead, to exalt the Greek language in the name of metaphysics, which is, as Heidegger wrote, the most powerful of all languages and closest to the language of the mind?'[23]

The Heideggerian position also gives rise to variations that are opposed. For Derrida, given that *logos* is Greek, China cannot have philosophy. For Aubenque however, given that metaphysics is only ever Western, and that this metaphysics engendered the science and technology that have conquered the entire world, Greek *logos* cannot *not* be universal, and even China cannot escape it. As Aubenque writes, 'Aristotle's philosophy constitutes a decisive mutation in the essence of language … making it available to all the demands of scientific representability, mathematical calculability, and even the technical transformation of the world. … [W]hile it is possible to do without metaphysics, the fact remains that there is only Western metaphysics and that this metaphysics has generated the science and technology whose planetary domination shapes the relationship of all humanity to the world.' For Aubenque, 'we are provided with a verification of this fact by civilisations that did not undergo a revolution like that under Aristotle, no doubt because their language was less suited to it.'[24] Sun provides just such a verification in his 'attributing of the technical and political delay in China to the fact that the Chinese had no logic and their language had no grammar'.[25] One can agree that without logic there is no science or technology, because this is what historical reality shows. However, the question remains of whether the fact that Western technology has dominated all other civilisations, and that capitalism has spread worldwide, is in itself 'logical' proof that Western logic is universal.

In fact, I would argue, the history of the translation of the word 'logic' in Chinese is exemplary of Barbara Cassin's notion of *untranslatability*: 'I suggest to call "untranslatable", not that which we do not translate, but that which we never cease translating, and thus also that which we never cease not translating.'[26] As concerns the philosophical exchange between Europe and the East, untranslatability is not opposed to translation, but is the process of translation itself.

I would like to end with a further translation of the word *logos*, the only 'translation' of which I am aware, which appears in the Chinese version of the Bible. The Gospel of Saint John begins with the following sentence:

In Greek: Ἐν ἀρχῇ ἦν ὁ λόγος.
In English: In the beginning there was the Word.
In Chinese: 太初有道 (*Tai chu you dao*).[27]

To translate the Chinese: 'In the beginning there was the *dao*'. In this translation, the word 'logos' is both translated and not translated into Chinese. It is rendered as *dao*, which, like *logos*, is a polysemic word that serves as the central concept for a whole system of thought. As for its meaning, the translators got it right: *dao* can mean, among other things, the word. John's sentence also recalls Laozi's famous line: 道生一，一生二，二生三，三生万物 ['*Dao* gives birth to one, one to two, two to three, and three to ten thousand things']. *Logos* and *dao* are therefore both at the origin of everything. Since *dao* is not usually translated but transcribed in French, as is also the case for other Western languages, the word 'logos' is arguably still a proper noun in this sentence because *dao* is a proper noun too. In other words, the great untranslatable word of Western thought for the Chinese is translated as the great untranslatable word of Chinese thought for the West. It is both translatable and not, because from the beginning there has been, on the one side, *logos*, and, on the other, *dao*.

Translated by Sophie Eager

Yijing Zhang is a postdoctoral researcher in the Department of Philosophy at Sun Yat-Sen University, Guangzhou, China.

Notes

1. Yuanhua Wang, 王元化, *Qing yuan jin zuo ji* 清园近作集 [Recent Collected Works from Qingyuan] (Shanghai: Wenhui chubanshe, 2004), 23–34. The meeting is recorded in Chinese in the form of an interview by a third person. We therefore cannot know which exact words Derrida used. Given that Derrida didn't speak Chinese, and Wang didn't speak English, the dialogue, organised by the French General Consulate in Shanghai, required a translator as an intermediary, and fell prey to all the problems of translation and assumption.

2. G. W. F. Hegel, *Lectures on the Philosophy of World History*, vol. 1, trans. R. F. Brown and P. C. Hodgson (Oxford: Clarendon Press, 2011), 240–241.

3. '… l'Orient est pour lui tout ce qu'il n'est pas, encore qu'il doive y chercher ce qu'est sa vérité primitive.' Michel Foucault, 'Préface de *Folie et Déraison. Histoire de la folie à l'âge classique*', in *Dits et Écrits*, tome I (Paris : Gallimard, 1994), 161.

4. In the seventeenth century, the Jesuits created the first Chinese translation for the Latin word *philosophia* with *qiong li xue* (穷理学), 'study of the principle'. The meaning of the word 'li' (principle) is explained below. The neologism *zhe xue* (哲学) was created by Japanese translators of Western philosophy in the nineteenth century and then reintroduced into Chinese.

5. Martin Heidegger, 'A Dialogue on Language', in *On the Way to Language*, trans. Peter Hertz (New York: Harper & Row, 1971), 4–5.

6. Noël Golvers, 'Verbiest's introduction of *Aristoteles Latinus* (Coimbra) in China: New Western Evidence', in *The Christian Mission in China in the Verbiest Era: Some Aspects of the Missionary Approach*, ed. Noël Golvers (Leuven: Leuven University Press, 1999), 40–41.

7. Jacques Gernet, 'Ciel des Chinois, Dieu des Chrétiens', in *Chine et christianisme. La première confrontation* (Paris: Gallimard, 1991).

8. Hubert Verhaeren, 'Aristote en Chine', in *Bulletin Catholique de Pékin* 22 (1935), 417.

9. Cf. Sugimura Yasuhiko, 'Auto-éveil et témoignage – philosopher autrement: L'école de Kyoto en comparaison avec la philosophie française post-heideggérienne', in *Philosophie* 125 (2015), 44–62.

10. Confucius, *The Analects*, Book 13, trans. D.C. Lau (Hong Kong, The Chinese University Press, 1983), 121.

11. Aristotle, *Metaphysics*, trans. Hugh Treddenick (Cambridge, MA: Harvard University Press, 2014), 237.

12. We reserve judgement on the translation of *li* by the English 'theory' in Robert Wardy, *Aristotle in China, Language, Categories and Translation* (Cambridge: Cambridge University Press, 2000), and as 'pattern' by Joachim Kurtz, *The Discovery of Chinese Logic* (Leiden and Boston: Brill, 2011).

13. P. Francisco Furtado, *Ming li tan. Traité de logique*, accessed 4 April 2019, https://gallica.bnf.fr/ark:/12148/btv1b9006070t/f1.image.r=Ming%20li%20tan

14. Nicolas Standaert, 'The investigation of Things and the Fathoming of Principles (格物穷理/*Gewu Qiongli*) in the Seventeenth-Century Contact Between Jesuits and Chinese Scholars', in *Ferdinant Verbiest (1623-1688): Jesuit Missionary, Scientist, Engineer and Diplomat*, ed. John W. Witek (Nettetal: Steyler Verlag, 1994), 396–99.

15. Christoph Harbsmeier, *Joseph Needham, Science and Civilisation in China*, vol. 7, *Language and Logic* (Cambridge: Cambridge University Press, 1998), 353–54.

16. Tang Yijie 汤一介, *GUO Xiang yu weijin xuanxue* 郭象与魏晋玄学 [GUO Xiang and the *Xuanxue* of the Wei and Jin dynasties] (Beijing: Pekin UP, 2000), 19–38.

17. Zhou Zhenghe, et al. 周振鹤等, *Zhishu wuya* 智术无涯 [The Cross-Disciplinary Art of Thinking] (Tianjin: Baihua wenyi chubanshe, 2002), 161–162.

18. '曰探、曰辨，皆不足与本学之深广相副。必求其近，姑以名学译之。盖中文惟``名''字所涵，其奥衍精博与逻各斯字差相若…'. Cf. Yan Fu 严复, *Mule Mingxue* 穆勒名学 [Mill's Logic] (Beijing: Shangwu yinshuguan, 1981 [1905]), 2.

19. '此科所包至广，吾国先秦所有，虽不足以抵其全，然实此科之首事…'. Cf. Sun Yingxiang and PI Houfeng, eds., 孙应详 皮后峰, *Yan Fu Ji Bubian* 严复集补编 [Further Selected Writings of Yan Fu] (Fujian: Fujian renmin chubanshe, 2004), 100.

20. Cf. Sun Zhongshan 孙中山, *Jianguo fanglue* 建国方略 [Fundamentals of National Reconstruction], accessed 18 November 2018, https://zh.wikisource.org/wiki/心理建設/第三章 ; Sun Yat-sen, *Souvenirs d'un révolutionnaire chinois*, trans. E. Dalter, (Paris: Les éditions d'aujourd'hui, 1933), 59–61.

21. The French translator of Sun's text paradoxically transcribes this as 'litchich', as though Sun were rendering the word 'logic' as a proper noun.

22. Emile Benveniste, 'Catégories de pensée et catégories de langue', in *Problèmes de linguistique générale* (Paris: Gallimard, 1976), 63–74.

23. Pierre Aubenque, 'Aristote et le langage', in *Problèmes aristotéliciens* (Paris: Vrin, 2009), 26.

24. Aubenque, 'Aristote et le langage', 29.

25. Aubenque, 'Aristote et le langage', 29.

26. Barbara Cassin, *Parménide, sur la nature ou sur l'étant. La langue de l'être?* (Paris: Seuil 'Points bilingues', 1998), 9.

27. There are several Chinese translations of the Bible made by different groups of missionaries at different points in history. This phrase, which is familiar to Christian and non-Christian alike thanks to its formulation in Chinese terms both linguistically and conceptually, comes from the 'Chinese Union Version' (1906), the official edition of the Chinese Protestant church. The 'Studium Biblicum Version' (1968), used by the Chinese Catholic Church and only recognised by the Roman Curia, translates the same phrase as: 在起初已有圣言. The word 'logos' is translated as 'sheng yan' (sacred word).

Dossier: Social reproduction theory

On the value of social reproduction
Informal labour, the majority world and the need for inclusive theories and politics

Alessandra Mezzadri

Radical feminist analyses have always placed considerable emphasis on the crucial role played by social reproduction for the development of capitalism. Early social reproduction analyses – primarily premised on housework but also more broadly concerned with wagelessness – developed a robust critique of Marxian views that identified processes of value-generation only with the productive sphere, and *de facto* deployed 'productive' and 'paid' labour as synonyms.[1] Some more recent approaches, by contrast, propose social reproduction as a 'theory' (SRT), and deploy the concept in order to focus on how labour is regenerated daily and inter-generationally through private and public institutions in contemporary contexts.[2] This second set of studies seem concerned with analysing the circuits of care that reproduce the worker as *connected yet distinct* to those of capital and value-generation. At the same time, however, they are committed to avoiding what they consider 'dual theories', conceptualising patriarchy and capitalism as separate systems.[3]

Starting from a review of the social reproduction debate, old and new, and focusing on the rise and spread of informal and informalised labour, the following analysis argues that only interpretations of social reproduction activities and realms *as value-producing* can advance our understandings of labour relations of contemporary capitalism. In fact, reproductive activities and realms play a key role in shaping such relations and in the processes of surplus extraction they are embedded in, particularly, (albeit not only), developing regions; that is, in the 'majority world'. Specifically, this analysis argues that reproductive realms and activities contribute to processes of value-generation through three channels: first, by directly reinforcing patterns of labour control, expanding rates of exploitation; second, by absorbing the systematic externalisation of reproductive costs by capital, working as a *de-facto* subsidy to capital; and, third, through processes of formal subsumption of labour that remain endemic across the majority world. I conclude that the exclusion of informal and informalised labour from debates on the relation between social reproduction and value creation will inevitably lead to problematic – in fact, dualist – understandings of capitalist development. I discuss by way of conclusion the political relevance of stressing the value-producing nature of wagelessness for a politics (and theory) of inclusion, able to capture the leading features of the contemporary world of labour, and aimed at building solidarities between productive and reproductive struggles.

Social reproduction debates, new and old

The recent publication of Tithi Bhattacharya's edited collection *Social Reproduction Theory* (2017) has revamped debates on social reproduction, and its role and (re)configuration under capitalism. The collection aims at making a number of contributions. First, it proposes to engage in a Marxian theorisation of class where social oppression is not treated in merely epiphenomenal terms, but rather is seen as co-constitutive of processes of class formation.[4] Second, it aims at illustrating the process of reconfiguration and commodification of social reproduction during the neoliberal phase of capitalism. The essay by Nancy Fraser stands out in in this regard by virtue of its ability to re-sketch the whole history of capitalism in terms of different regimes of social reproduction, and in its analysis of the current neoliberal phase;[5] while Susan Ferguson's essay on childhood also significantly contributes to our understanding of neoliberal 'socialisation'. Third, the collection aspires to 'reconcile' Marxian and feminist analyses of capitalism, in the context of a 'unitary theory' of capitalism.[6] While the agenda of this project is certainly worthy, and the book succeeds in confirming the key role that social reproduction plays in contemporary capitalism, some of the contributions are, arguably, overly adversarial towards other theorisations moved by compatible intellectual and political concerns – for instance, David McNally's rather selective critique of intersectionality theory – or towards older analyses of social reproduction.[7] The latter is the main object of discussion here. Specifically, some social reproduction theory (SRT) studies do not sufficiently acknowledge the huge contributions made by early social reproduction analyses in explaining the role played by reproductive realms and activities in structuring capitalism and generating value by producing the 'unique' commodity, labour power.[8] In fact, one could argue that the very packaging of social reproduction as a 'theory' might be seen – rightly or wrongly – as an attempt to reincorporate earlier analyses into a somewhat broader (Marxist) remit.

On the other hand, undoubtedly one of the most contentious areas of difference between the 'old' and 'new' social reproduction debates is the role that social reproduction does or does not play in processes of value-generation. This is by no means a minor issue within Marxist debates. In fact, if, for some, the greatness of early radical feminist analyses of social reproduction lay, among other things, in their subversive approach to what constitutes value, for others it is this that constitutes their limitation. The analysis that follows aims to underline the strong theoretical foundations of the early social reproduction debate and its take on value. It also aims at illustrating why, focusing on the contemporary world of informal and informalised labour, and so shifting attention from 'The West' to 'The Rest'[9] – namely, the *majority* world, where the lion's share of the people on this planet labour – we cannot easily dismiss these earlier analyses and claims. In fact, once we move away from western-centric analyses and study the features of actually existing labour relations for the majority of people globally, we come to appreciate the role that social reproduction plays in processes of labour surplus extraction and value-generation. In short, from the perspective of the livelihood of the majority world, social reproduction is indeed value-generating, and in a Marxian sense.

The (great) value of social reproduction: the early debate

There is little doubt that, in relation to issues of value and wagelessness, the social reproduction debate first originated with the publication in 1972 of *The Power of Women and the Subversion of the Community* by Selma James and Maria Rosa Dalla Costa. This largely political pamphlet, which focused on housework but was more broadly concerned with wagelessness, was the first to highlight how capitalism was first and foremost dependent on processes of generation and regeneration – biological as well as social – of the worker and of commodity labour power, which mostly took place outside what were considered the classic domains of production and value-generation. While the pamphlet hardly engaged in an in-depth theoretical analysis of how social reproduction generated value, following its publication several radical feminist scholars sought to provide the argument with the theoretical depth it deserved.

Looking at housework but also at sex work, Leopoldina Fortunati explored the ways in which reproductive work is *de facto* socially constructed as the realm of 'non-value' within productivist schemas, and hence was excluded from orthodox Marxian understandings of value-generation. She argued that its non-valorisation should therefore be considered as a sort of self-fulfilling prophecy.[10] Silvia Federici's feminist analysis of primitive accumulation as a brutally gendered process entailing the dispossession, devaluation and domestication of women, and the barbaric destruction of their bodies through witchcraft accusations and trials, is also constructed around a similar theoretical project. In *Caliban and the Witch*, whose earlier version in Italian was in fact co-written with Leopoldina Fortunati (*Il Grande Calibano*), Federici shows how capitalism was first and foremost built on imperial and colonial dispossession, and on the expropriation and exclusion of some cohorts of people from realms of generation (or appropriation) of value. Her feminist theorisation of primitive accumulation illustrates how all these events predated the far better known processes of land enclosure usually considered to characterise the initial phases of capitalism.[11] Equally, Federici's project aimed to subvert more traditional analyses of value, by showing the complex (and bloody) politics and history delineating its social perimeters and boundaries, which stretch far beyond transformations in the sphere of production. The entire work of the German feminist sociologist Maria Mies, which started off with her magisterial 1982 analysis of the *Lacemakers of Narsapur* in Andra Pradesh, India, also aims at debunking the mythology of value as merely generated within productive realms. Indeed, Mies' analysis of home-based work challenges theorisations that propose a neat separation between the realms of production and reproduction, and suggests how processes of *housewifisation* of women's labour have systematically blurred sources of value, both by hiding women's productive contributions to the market, and by devaluing those contributions as non-value-producing. Mies expanded these insights into housewifisation further in *Patriarchy and Accumulation on a World Scale*,[12] where, like Federici, she also analyses at length the interconnections between patriarchy and capitalism in relation to imperialism.[13] Here, Mies analyses the variation of housewifisation across the world economy. In fact, the work of Rhoda Reddock illustrates how this played out very differently for female slaves and indentured labourers.[14] For these women, housewifisation primarily worked to contain the rising costs of death or sexually transmitted diseases for slaves and plantation labourers. This is a point also made by Angela Y. Davis in *Women, Race and Class*, with specific reference to black women slaves in the United States.[15]

A far less well-known author, internationally, is the Marxian feminist economist Antonella Picchio, who arrives at similar conclusions about the exclusion of socially reproductive activities from sources of value. In fact, by proposing a compelling exploration of the ways in which the cost of labour has been treated in classical political economy, not only by Marx but also by Adam Smith and David Ricardo, Picchio highlights how the exclusion of reproductive activities from value calculations is not only a political issue, but one derived from the ways in which the whole *corpus* of classical political economy dealt with the *value* of labour; namely, as an exogenous parameter given by the general reproductive conditions of a given society at a given point in time. This treatment of the value of labour as an exogenous factor, then, facilitated its inaccurate conflation with its cost, namely the wage, instead of regarding it as endogenous to the capitalist system. On the other hand, who is waged and who is unwaged has always been a largely political – in fact, legal – issue, as Picchio goes on to demonstrate with reference to the British Poor Laws, and their legal, gendered distinction between abled (that is, male) and unable bodies.[16]

Undoubtedly, it is the reification and fetishisation of the wage as the value rather than the cost of labour that provides the premises for productivist understandings of value generation.[17] Obviously, productivist Marxist understandings do not theorise the wage as the 'true' value of labour, as they must account for the rate of exploitation. However, they do aim to resolve the issue of the value of the commodity labour-power within the same schema that deploys it as the measure of the value of all other commodities.[18] In fact, this is the main problem with productivist analyses. They want to stretch the labour theory of value far beyond its proposed remit; namely the realm of commodity production. Specifically, they try to deploy the theory in order to assess the value of the commodity that is set as the very measure of value itself; that is, labour-power. This results in a paradox. The 'special' commodity 'labour-power', whilst recognised and celebrated as unique by the SRT approach, seems to receive the same rather poor treatment as any other 'vulgar' one, when it comes to its value.

The centrality of the labour theory of value to Marxian analyses of capitalism is, of course, a much-debated issue. Recently, David Harvey, for instance, has questioned the extent to which one can find a coherent 'theory' of value in Marx, or if, instead, the original Marxian analysis aimed primarily at showing the limitation of Ricardian understandings of value.[19] Indeed, the biggest lesson from Marx should be that all value is generated by labour in production, and is not the result of capitalist efforts to combine production 'inputs'. In this sense, as brilliantly put by another feminist economist, Diane Elson, more than a labour-theory of value in Marx one finds a value-theory of labour.[20] However, I do not feel one has to go as far as posing more complex ontological questions about the labour theory of value in order to build the case for the value-producing nature of social reproduction. One has simply to remark how the question lies entirely outside the remit of the labour theory of value. On the other hand, as SRT acknowledges – in line with the earlier social reproduction feminist scholars analysed above – Marx is mostly silent about the circuits producing the most extraordinary commodity of all under capitalism; namely, the worker.

Marx's silence can be taken in different ways. One way of addressing this theoretical gap is to stretch the labour theory of value to also include how the worker is produced under capitalism. This seems to be the choice of many within SRT, who stress the relevance of the distinction between use value and exchange value when it comes to differentiating 'labour' (seen as a use value) and 'labour power' (an exchange value, once productively consumed). This view, which falls within a more orthodox Marxian interpretation, would tend to club together all activities apt at reproducing 'labour' as linked to use value and hence as non-value-producing, and all those linked to labour-power as value-producing. This is the path undertaken by the Marxist scholar Paul Smith, who some of these analyses rely on.[21] Smith dismissed the issue of housework producing value precisely on the basis of the use value / exchange value distinction, deriving from this dualism the impossibility for reproductive work to ever become social labour. However, this view seems merely tautological. It does not demonstrate that social reproduction is not value-producing; it assumes it.

Another way of addressing the theoretical gap related to the production and reproduction of capitalist 'life' – namely, human beings as well as the capitalist relations of production of which they are part [22] – is simply to accept the far more limited remit of the labour theory of value, whose reach, for Marxian analysis, was only ever to be understood as working within the realm of capitalist commodity production. In short, rather than obsessing about how to theorise social reproduction and the 'making' of the worker, one could simply note that this question never was the subject of the original Marxian analysis of value in the first place. It was not simply an omission;[23] it was not its key concern. So, while the theoretical observations of early social reproduction analysts on value are sadly often dismissed on the basis of their supposed overly 'emotive' or 'emotional' drive – in fact, a stereotypical criticism widely deployed to attack women writers – I would argue that accounts that remain rigidly caged within the labour theory of value, whilst exploring processes residing outside its focus, are far more irrational, theoretically shaky and emotionally driven.[24] Moreover, empirical evidence concerning *actually existing labour and labour relations* for the majority on this planet suggests the need to account for the value-producing nature of reproductive realms and activities. It is to this issue that I now turn.

From the West to the 'Rest'

Geography always matters for the ways in which we explore the world and interpret its logics. So it is highly significant that early feminist theorists of social reproduction, eager to insist on the value-producing nature of social reproduction, were either based in or studying countries where wagelessness – and not only narrowly related to housework – was endemic. For example, Dalla Costa, Fortunati and Picchio are Italian scholars whose enquiry is not only likely to have been affected by the considerable presence of women's unpaid housework in Italy (and elsewhere), but also by the broader conditions of wagelessness and informality that characterised – and still characterise – Italian development as a whole.[25] Silvia Federici's thought was clearly influenced by observations about the conditions of work of women and men in former colonies during the Fordist and Post-Fordist phases.[26] Maria Mies studied India throughout her life, and her observation of home-based work and *housewifisation* in Narsapur was clearly crucial to the development of her entire body of work.

By contrast, scholars within the SRT group generally focus on Europe and North America. Indeed, their focus on the institutions and capitalist architecture of care and their transformations during neoliberalism makes a lot of sense in relation to the trajectories of these regions. However, these regions are not representative of the world economy as a whole. Moreover, social reproduction and care are not synonyms, an inaccuracy that already characterises some of the work of liberal feminist economics analyses. The very term social reproduction, as also acknowledged by SRT, is meant to be far broader than notions of care, and encapsulates both the reproduction of life and of capitalist relations *at once*;[27] that is, of both labourers and labour power. However, not many within the SRT camp – and virtually none of the contributors to the SRT edited volume – focus on labour relations and practices or the labour process. In fact, SRT seems primarily concerned with what Lasslett and Johanna Brenner have already defined as 'societal reproduction', hence moving the gaze of the analysis towards more classic Marxist notions of reproduction concerned with the transmission of inequality under capitalism.[28] While this is indeed a worthy area of enquiry, it risks narrowing down the social reproduction debate. Moreover, focusing primarily on institutions, it is hard to address concerns over the nature and boundaries of value, insofar as its source, in Marxian analysis, is *labour*. Arguably, once we shift attention from the institutions of care (or social reproduction more narrowly defined) to the labour relations dominant under contemporary capitalism, and we shift our geographical focus from 'the West' to 'the Rest'[29] – that is, we look at the majority world and how it toils – we cannot so easily dismiss the subversive, radical claims of early feminist theorists of social reproduction.

The majority of people on this planet labour in the informal economy, or are subject to labour relations that are greatly informalised. According to the International Labour Oganisation, 85.8% of total employment in Africa, 71.4% in Asia and the Pacific, 68.6% in the Arab States and 53.8% in the Americas is either informal – located in the informal economy – or informalised – in formal production realms but still *de facto* based on informal relations.[30] The total estimate of informal employment for the whole emerging and developing economies bloc is set at 69.6%. Given the considerable weight of this bloc vis-à-vis the world's total workforce, even at a world level (i.e. including developed regions) 61.2% of total employment is classified as either informal or informalised. This huge world of informal and informalised employment includes casual labourers and the self-employed, who can either be highly vulnerable petty commodity producers[31] or various disguised forms of wage labour, also known as 'classes of labour'.[32] Once upon a time wrongly considered one of the key features of 'backwardness', and of the domestic 'traditional' socio-economic fabric of developing regions, informality has not only reproduced itself exponentially during the neoliberal global era, but it has also found new channels of transmission.[33] These channels are systematically continuing to reproduce labour as a highly precarious relation in developing contexts, and are now also doing so in developed regions, with the rise of the gig economy, crowd-work and what has been called, rightly or wrongly, the 'precariat'.[34]

The rise of global commodity chains and production networks, in particular, has produced endless circuits of propagation, redefinition and expansion for informal labour relations. In surplus labour economies like India or China, global commodity chains can rely on labour being informalised in myriad different ways. Informalisation can be based on rural-urban mobility and mediated by legal status, as in the case of China and its reliance on the *hukou* system,[35] which mediates the movement of around three hundred million migrants from villages to cities every year. Alternatively, it can rely on 'traditional' forms of social stratification interweaving social oppression with class, as in the case of India, where informalised labour is structured along gender, caste and mobility lines, shaping forms of 'conjugated oppression'[36] and where surplus value extraction interacts with subordination to regimes of social stigma.[37]

Crucially for the arguments developed here, within this complex scenario of endemic and ever-expanding informal and informalised labour relations, it would be hard and completely misleading to try to distinguish between value-producing and non-value-producing activities and realms, strictly based on tasks and/or payments. In fact, an analysis of how exploitation unfolds in these contexts suggests that social reproduction realms and activities are directly crucial to the structuring of processes of labour surplus extraction; expand rates of exploitation; and hence build (exchange) value. In particular, there are at least three ways in which reproductive realms and activities become directly value-producing.

The first is through their ability to deepen labour control far beyond work-time. Evidence from China,[38] Vietnam,[39] the Czech Republic,[40] and also, more selectively, India,[41] suggests that the rise of dormitories and industrial hostels is expanding the ability of employers to control labour well beyond the actual labour process. The tightening of labour control, on the basis of what Pun Ngai and Chris Smith have defined as the 'dormitory labour regime', has direct effects on the expansion of exploitation rates. In these contexts, any distinction between work and reproductive time becomes blurred, as social reproduction becomes fully individualised and subsumed into the value-generating process. Moreover, as noted by Hannah Schling with reference to the Czech Republic, in dormitories 'non-waged time' becomes fundamental to the production of compliant labouring subjects.[42]

The second way in which social reproduction realms and activities directly contribute to value-generation across today's 'global factory'[43] is through their absorption of the systematic externalisation of costs of social reproduction.[44] Across the greatly informal and informalised majority world, social reproductive realms – the household, the village, the community – and activities – housework as well as other forms of unpaid work generally (albeit not only) performed by women[45] – are deployed as a systematic subsidy to capital. In fact, in contexts where neither employers nor the state bear any of the costs for socially reproducing labour, everything is dumped onto the shoulders of workers and their kin, family and community ties. While in the West the externalisation of costs of social reproduction has been explained in terms of a crisis of care or crisis of social reproduction more broadly,[46] in contexts that neither experienced the welfare state nor its disciplining role on capital, this externalisation can be better understood as directly serving the purpose of shaping the capitalist relation in ways that impose unpaid, wageless work and life as a direct subsidy to production. Again, the effect is one in which exploitation rates can be expanded, through a cut in wages and social contributions, with losses naturalised and internalised by the labouring poor and their social and economic networks.

Finally, as I have discussed at length elsewhere with reference to the Sweatshop Regime,[47] a third way in which social reproduction realms and activities directly constitute value is through the expansion of processes of formal subsumption of labour, made possible by the fragmentation and decomposition of labour processes worldwide. The proliferation of tasks and activities decentralised to armies of home-based workers shows the crucial role that formal subsumption of labour still plays vis-à-vis processes of value-generation. Hardly a remnant of the past, as it is often portrayed, this process makes any distinction between production and social reproduction – or work and life – irrelevant, as their times are conflated, and all is subject to the laws of value. Since Maria Mies wrote *The Lacemakers of Narsapur*, thousands more villages have been swallowed by the logics of contemporary neoliberal capitalism, where 'unfree' labour relations represent a stable 'form of exploitation'.[48] These informal and wageless workers live, at once, within and beyond the Marxian labour theory of value, subverting and blurring our theoretical categories, and challenging our politics.

Theories of inclusion for a politics of inclusion

One may rightly ask, at the end of this analysis: why should we care at all about theoretical distinctions and divisions, if these can be overcome in politics? In short: can we still support a theory where value-generation remains anchored to the realm of commodity production, if our politics can then transcend its boundaries? I argue that this would be difficult for two reasons. First, theoretical distinctions are always political. The theoretical exclusion of social reproduction realms and activities from the arena of value-generation posits, implicitly or explicitly, a hierarchy of exploitation, while also constructing the category of 'labour' on highly unequal terms, premised around the wage form. As the wage is the cost of labour, but not necessarily its value, this choice embraces a capital-centric conceptualisation of toil, productivity (too often conflated with exploitation) and reward.[49] In political terms, arguing that labour struggles can articulate with the struggles of the wageless is not quite the same thing as enlarging the social parameters of what is defined as a labour struggle to accommodate all those whose work is subjected and subordinated to the capitalist relation in more hidden ways. The former approach still presupposes a distinction, in the struggle, between the waged and the unwaged; it indirectly embraces the 'primacy' of wage-labour over work, and, as such, cannot but fracture solidarities. The latter approach, by contrast, is far more likely to provide a broader basis for organising and include all struggles (of the waged or unwaged) as labour (and, ultimately, reproductive) struggles.

Second, if we are serious about the need to develop a 'unitary theory' of capitalism, and avoid dualist understandings of the mode of production, we cannot conflate the (current) western experience of labour and work with that 'normalised' across the world economy. In fact, the western experience is hardly representative of how the majority toils on this planet. In contexts dominated by the informal economy and informalised labour – in which almost two-thirds of the people of the world make their livelihood – approaches to value proposing a neat separation between what produces and what does not produce surplus are based on an inaccurate and highly dualistic understanding of how capitalism works.[50] While undoubtedly we need to avoid dualist theories conceptualising capital and patriarchy as autonomous social relations,[51] at the same time we cannot develop any unitary theory of capitalism based on understandings of value generating other highly problematic dichotomies.

In mapping the vast world of India's unorganised labour, Barbara Harriss-White and Nandini Gooptu highlight the ways in which large segments of informal and informalised labour – in India and elsewhere – are not so much engaged in class struggle, as they are still trapped in 'struggles over class'.[52] They are still fighting to be recognised as a labouring class and develop their own consciousness. We can help the wageless in their struggle for recognition, and support them through a politics of inclusion, only by developing inclusive theories and categories of analysis in the first place.

Alessandra Mezzadri is Senior Lecturer in Development Studies at SOAS, University of London, and author of The Sweatshop Regime *(2017).*

Notes

1. Maria Rosa Dalla Costa and Selma James, *The Power of Women and the Subversion of the Community* (Bristol: Falling Wall Press, 1972); Leopoldina Fortunati, *The Arcane of Reproduction: Housework, Prostitution, Labour and Capital* (Autonomedia, 1981; originally published in Italian as *L'Arcano della Reproduzione: Casalinghe, Prostitute, Operai e Capitale*, Venezia: Marsilio Ed-

itori, 1981); Leopoldina Fortunati and Silvia Federici, *Il Grande Calibano: Storia del Corpo Sociale Ribelle nella Prima Fase del Capitale* (Milano: Franco Angeli, 1984); Maria Mies, *The Lace Makers of Narsapur: Indian Housewives Produce for the World Market* (London: Zed, 1982); Maria Mies, *Patriarchy and Accumulation on a World Scale: Women in the International Division of Labour* (London: Zed, 1986); Antonella Picchio, *Social Reproduction: The Political Economy of The Labour Market* (Cambridge: Cambridge University Press, 1992); Silvia Federici, *Caliban and the Witch: Women, the Body and Primitive Accumulation* (Brooklyn: Autonomedia, 2004).

2. Tithi Bhattacharya, ed. *Social Reproduction Theory: Remapping Class, Re-Centering Oppression* (London: Pluto, 2017).

3. Bhattacharya, 'How Not to Skip Class', in *Social Reproduction Theory*, 68–93; see also Cinzia Arruzza, 'Functionalist, Deterministic, Reductionist: Social Reproduction Feminism and its Critics', *Science and Society* 80:1 (2016), 9–30.

4. See also Lisa Vogel, *Marxism and the Oppression of Women: Toward a Unitary Theory* (London: Pluto, 1983).

5. Nancy Fraser, 'Crisis of Care? On the Social Reproductive Contradictions of Contemporary Capitalism', in Bhattacharya, ed. *Social Reproduction Theory*, 21–36; see also Nancy Fraser 'Behind Marx's Hidden Abode: For an Expanded Conception of Capitalism', *New Left Review* 86 (2014): 55–72.

6. Arruzza, 'Functionalist, Deterministic, Reductionist'.

7. David McNally 'Intersections and Dialectics: Critical Reconstructions in Social Reproduction Theory', in *Social Reproduction Theory* pp. 94–111. On the basis of a broader review of scholarship on Intersectionality, and in the context of what I see as a worthy intellectual and political project, Ashley Bohrer has recently highlighted productive ways in which Marxism and Intersectionality approaches may articulate and complement each another. See Ashley Bohrer 'Intersectionality and Marxism: A Critical Historiography', *Historical Materialism* 26:2 (2018).

8. Dalla Costa and James, *The Power of Women*; Fortunati, *The Arcane of Reproduction*.

9. Jan Breman and Marcel Van der Linden, 'Informalising the Economy: The Return of the Social Question at a Global Level', *Development and Change* 45 (2014): 920–40.

10. Fortunati, *The Arcane of Reproduction*.

11. Federici, *Caliban and the Witch*; Fortunati and Federici, *Il Grande Calibano*.

12. Mies, *The Lacemakers*; Mies, *Patriarchy and Accumulation*.

13. In fact, already in her study of lacemaking Mies understands housewifisation as a capitalist patriarchal arrangement and an imperial import, at once. Indian women were underpaid to produce in peripheral homes what British women performed unpaid in imperial homes.

14. Earlier these women were denied any right to a family as an economic unit as envisaged under capitalism for the 'free' industrial working classes. They were only 'granted' these rights so that capital could externalise social and biological reproduction costs and health replenishment to 'the home'. See Rhoda Reddock, *Women, Labour and Struggle in 20th century Trinidad and Tobago, 1898-1960* (The Hague: Institute of Social Studies, 1984). For a gendered account of indenture, illustrating the violent ways in which women were coerced into reproductive servitude, including sexual servitude, see Gaiutra Bahadur's masterful *Coolie Woman: The Odyssey of Indenture* (London: Hurst and Co, 2013).

15. Angela Y. Davis, *Women, Race and Class* (New York: Random House,, 1983).

16. Picchio, *Social Reproduction*.

17. Sebastien Rioux, 'Embodied Contradictions: Capitalism, social reproduction and body formation', *Women's Studies International Forum* 48 (2015), 194–202.

18. Karl Marx, *Capital, Volume I* (London: Penguin Classics, 1990; reprint of Pelican Books edition, 1976).

19. David Harvey, 'Marx's Refusal of the Labour Theory of Value', accessed 1 March 2018, http://davidharvey.org/2018/03/marxs-refusal-of-the-labour-theory-of-value-by-david-harvey/

20. Diane Elson, 'The Value Theory of Labour', in *Value: the Representation of Labour in Capitalism*, ed. Diane Elson (London: CSE Books, 1979).

21. Paul Smith, 'Domestic Labour and Marx's Theory of Value', in *Feminism and Materialism (RLE Feminist Theory): Women and Modes of Production*, eds. A. Kuhn and A.M. Wolpe (London and New York: Routledge, 1978), 198–220).

22. Cindi Katz, 'Vagabond Capitalism and the Necessity of Social Reproduction', *Antipode* 33 (2001), 709–728; Catherine Mitchell, Sally Marston and Cindi Katz, 'Introduction: Life's Work: An Introduction, Review, and Critique', *Antipode* 35:3 (2003), 415–42; Isabella Bakker, 'Social Reproduction and the Constitution of a Gendered Political Economy', *New Political Economy* 12 (2007), 541–556.

23. Rioux, 'Embodied Contradictions'; see also Timothée Haug, 'The Capitalist Metabolism: An Unachieved Subsumption of Life under the Value-form', *Journal for Cultural Research* 22:2 (2018), 191–203; and Rohini Hensman 'Revisiting the Domestic Labour Debate: An Indian Perspective', *Historical Materialism* 19:3 (2011), 3–28.

24. In many instances, the dismissal of arguments connecting social reproduction to value is based on their mischaracterisation as claims merely stressing the 'deserving', 'worthy' or 'useful' nature of reproductive work or realms. It is on the basis of this mischaracterisation that such arguments are depicted as emotional. However, feminist analyses stressing the value-producing nature of social reproduction do engage with Marxian notions of value, as linked to processes of labour surplus extraction. It should also be noted that one of the most irrational comparison deployed by orthodox Marxism to dismiss reproductive work as non-value producing is the impossibility of increases in its productivity. However, first, as argued here, this schema should not be imposed beyond the remit of the labour theory of value. Second, even if we were to engage with the argument on its own ground, we should at least acknowledge that productivity and exploitation are not the same thing. In *Capital*, Marx presents them as an identity to *deconstruct* productivity as a bourgeois concept, and show how surplus value is instead generated by labour. Moreover, we know from Marx that relative surplus value extraction (linked to productivity) is only one way to appropriate surplus. The other is through absolute surplus value extraction, which expands the working day to its very limits and totalises the workers' subsumption into the pro-

duction cycle. Arguably, the total involvement required by some reproductive activities, and the bodily depletion they entail, can be easily equated with processes of absolute surplus extraction. In a similar vein, Silvia Federici sketches the link between reproductive activities and processes of formal subsumption of labour. Silvia Federici, 'Marx and Feminism', in *TripleC* 16:2 (2018), 468–75.

25. See also more recent studies on homework in Italy, for example Tania Toffanin, *Fabbriche Invisibili: Stories di Donne, Lavoranti a Domicilio* (Ombre Corte: Invisible Factories: Stories of Women, Homeworkers, 2016).

26. Silvia Federici, *Revolution at Point Zero: Housework, Reproduction, and Feminist Struggle* (Brooklyn: PM Press, 2012).

27. For example, Katz, 'Vagabond Capitalism'; Bakker, 'Social Reproduction'.

28. Barbara Laslett and Johanna Brenner, 'Gender and Social Reproduction: Historical Perspectives', *Annual Review of Sociology* 15 (1989), 381–404.

29. Breman and Van der Linden, 'Informalising the Economy'.

30. ILO, *Women and men in the informal economy: A Statistical Picture*, third edition (Geneva: ILO, 2018), available at: http://www.ilo.org/wcmsp5/groups/public/---dgreports/---dcomm/documents/publication/wcms_626831.pdf

31. Barbara Harriss-White, 'Labour and Petty Production', *Development and Change* 45 (2014), 981–1000.

32. Henry Bernstein, 'Capital and Labour from Centre to Margins', Keynote Address at 'Living on the Margins, Vulnerability, Exclusion and the State in the Informal Economy', Cape Town, 26-28 March 2007; Henry Bernstein, *Class Dynamics of Agrarian Change* (Halifax and Winnipeg: Fernwood, 2010).

33. Alessandra Mezzadri, *The Sweatshop Regime: Labouring Bodies, Exploitation, and Garments Made in India* (Cambridge: Cambridge University Press, 2017).

34. See Guy Standing, 'Understanding the Precariat Through Labour and Work', *Development and Change* 45:5 (2014), 963–80; for a critique see Jan Breman, 'A Bogus Concept', *New Left Review* 84 (November-December 2013).

35. Anita Chan, 'Globalisation, China's free (read bonded) labour market, and the Chinese trade unions', *Asia Pacific Business Review* 6:3-4 (2000), 260–281; Sarosh Kuruvilla Ching Kwan Lee and Mary Gallagher, *From Iron Rice Bowl to Informalisation: Markets, Workers, and the State in a Changing China* (Ithaca: ILR Press, 2011); Pun Ngai, *Made in China: Women Workers in a Global Workplace* (Durham, NC: Duke University Press, 2005); Alessandra Mezzadri and Lulu Fan, 'Classes of Labou' at the Margins of Global Commodity Chains in India and China', *Development and Change* (2018).

36. Alpa Shah, Richard Axelby, Dalaal Benbabaali, Brendan Donegan, Jayaseelan Raj, and Vikram Thakur, *Ground Down by Growth: Tribe, Caste, Class and Inequality in the 21st Century* (London: Pluto, 2017). A superb account showing the co-constitutive and intersecting nature of gender and caste in shaping processes of class formation can be found in Leela Fernandez, *Producing Workers: The Politics of Gender, Class and Culture in the Calcutta Jute Mills* (Philadelphia: University of Pennsylvania Press, 1997).

37. Mary John, 'The Problem of Women's Labour: Some Autobiographical Perspectives', *Indian Journal of Gender Studies* 20:2 (2013), 177-–212; Mary John, 'The Woman Question: Reflections on Feminism and Marxism', *Economic and Political Weekly*, LII-50(2017): 71–79.

38. Pun Ngai and Chris Smith, 'Putting Transnational Labour Process in its Place: The Dormitory Labour Regime in Post-Socialist China', *Work, Employment and Society* 21:1 (2007): 27–45.

39. Michela Cerimele, *Informalising the Formal: Work Regimes and Dual Labour Dormitory Systems in Thang Long Industrial Park* (Hanoi, Vietnam), Working Paper, copy given by the author (2016); Pietro Masina and Michela Cerimele, 'Patterns of Industrialisation and the State of Industrial Labour in Post-WTO-Accession Vietnam', *European Journal of East Asian Studies* 17 (2018), 289–323.

40. Rutvika Andrijasevic and Devi Sacchetto, 'Made in the EU: Foxconn in the Czech Republic', *Working USA: The Journal of Labour and Society* 17:3 (2014), 391–415.

41. Mezzadri, *The Sweatshop Regime*.

42. Hannah Schling, (Re)production: Everyday Life in the Workers' Dormitory', *Society and Space* (2017), Forum on Social Reproduction, available at: http://societyandspace.org/2017/11/07/reproduction-everyday-life-in-the-workers-dormitory/

43. Massimo De Angelis, 'Trade, The Global Factory and the Struggles for New Commons', paper presented at the CSE conference 'Global Capital and Global Struggles: Strategies, Alliances and Alternatives', London, 1-2 July 2000, available at: https://libcom.org/files/NewComm.pdf ; Daeoup Chang, 'Informalising Labour in Asia's Global Factory', *Journal of Contemporary Asia* 39:2 (2009), 161–79.

44. Mezzadri, *The Sweatshop Regime*; see also Bridget O'Laughlin, 'Land, Labour and the Production of Affliction in Rural Southern Africa', *Journal of Agrarian Change* 13 (2013), 175–96.

45. Hensman, 'Revisiting the Domestic Labour Debate'.

46. Fraser, 'Crisis of Care?'; Fraser, 'Behind Marx's Hidden Abode'.

47. Alessandra Mezzadri 'The Informalisation of Capital and Interlocking in Labour Contracting Networks', *Progress in Development Studies* 16:2 (2016), 124–169; Alessandra Mezzadri, 'Class, Gender and the Sweatshop: on the nexus between labour commodification and exploitation', *Third World Quarterly* 37:10 (2016), 1877-1900.

48. Jairus Banaji, *Theory as History: Essays on Modes of Production and Exploitation* (Leiden and Boston: Brill, 2010).

49. Michael Denning, 'Wageless life', *New Left Review* 66 (2010), 79–97.

50. Jan Breman, *At Work in the Informal Economy of India: A Perspective from the Bottom-Up* (New Delhi: Oxford University Press, 2013).

51. Arruzza, 'Functionalist, Deterministic, Reductionist'; Bhattacharya, *Social Reproduction*.

52. Barbara Harriss-White and Nandini Gooptu, 'Mapping India's World of Unorganised Labour', *Socialist Register* 37 (2001), 89–118.

After the housewife
Surrogacy, labour and human reproduction
Kalindi Vora

Human reproduction in the form of pregnancy, childbirth, breastfeeding and nurturing of infants and children has been at the core of Marxist feminist understandings of reproductive labour. When this labour is overtly commercialised, as in the case of surrogacy, it brings together biological processes of gestational and social processes of nurture and parenting into market relationships. Just as feminist scholars have had to work to theorise how domestic labour, sex work and service are economically and socially productive activities, researchers are now extending and building upon those theories to encompass practices like commercial surrogacy as hired human reproduction, and in general the biological processes of bodies (i.e. clinical trial subjects) and tissues (novel cells in the lab that come from an individually important body) as sites that generate economic value.

Commercial gestational surrogacy is a practice in which someone enters a paid contract to gestate an embryo and deliver an infant for one or more commissioning (also called 'intended') parents. Embryos are created by in vitro fertilisation, a lab-based process in which ova from an intended mother or donor are fertilised with sperm from an intended father or donor. The resulting embryo (or embryos) is then transferred to the uterus of the gestational carrier, which has been prepared by hormones to allow the embryo to attach, and thereby start pregnancy and gestation.

The first documented gestational surrogacy in India was in 2004. A small industry quickly grew from this success, with as many as 3,000 operating clinics in late 2015 when transnational surrogacy arrangements were banned by the Indian government.[1] At the Manushi clinic in northwestern India, where I conducted ethnographic research on transnational surrogacy arrangements between 2008 and 2015, surrogates were strongly encouraged to move into residence hostels after the first trimester of pregnancy. Here, they would eat a regulated diet, receive regular preventative medical exams in line with the Euro-American standards of prenatal care, and participate in sanctioned activities which the clinic described as preserving them from manual and other paid work, as well as household work for their own families. These conditions were described by current surrogates as very different from pregnancies with their own children, which were almost exclusively overseen by local midwives outside the clinic and the practice of allopathic medicine.

The surrogate is a complicated subject of labour. First, there is the social location of surrogacy as *mothering* labour and the cultural economic weight of the household/family economic unit which comes with that location. Second, gestation and childbirth are imbricated with the body and subject of the surrogate in a way that makes it difficult to distinguish between what is labour and what is not. Finally, because women becoming surrogates in India are at a disadvantage in terms of financial resources, political influence, mobility and access to knowledge, the idea that surrogacy contracts are freely entered into with informed consent is also complicated.[2] Moreover, the women I spoke to who were pregnant as surrogates offered their own theories of what surrogacy was: for instance, many described the value and meaning of surrogacy as different from a job, as apart from categories of kinship new or old, and as apart from clinic and market discourses. There was instead an emphasis on a feeling that carrying a child for a couple that could not otherwise have a child was something so extraordinary that it was almost a divine act; this aspect of the arrangement was more important than money as a motivation. As I have written elsewhere: 'Discourse about the divine aspects of surrogacy points to simultaneous and competing logics for the social meaning and value of gestational surrogacy. These meanings cannot be easily organised or communicated through the genetic definition of a biological parent, though it is a condition of possibility for commercial surrogacy, or even through the economic logic of the value of the labour of surrogacy as underpaid and technologically mediated 'women's work' in the global economy.'[3]

My argument, then, is that commercial surrogacy involves both biological and affective labour (for example self-care and surveillance in addition to gestation), but also produces value through more than just labour.[4] Like most forms of gendered labour, these biological and affective processes are difficult to separate from the body and person of the woman acting as a surrogate. This makes the work of surrogacy a form of labour that engages histories of race and colonialism and, at the same time, in the reproduction of the human that supports social reproduction, is pertinent to the arguments of materialist feminists for the need to classify and compensate reproductive labour.

Transnational surrogacy contracts in India

The context in which women enter surrogacy contracts as their best employment option, which includes privatisation of land and other resources, resulting in the loss of family farms, and a subsequent shift to urban employment, is one where entering surrogacy is like entering the industrialised workforce. Yet, because these conditions engage the history of colonialism, which instrumentalised consent, freedom and choice, alienation, and sexual and reproductive relations that do not register as 'labour', it is easy to overlook them.[5] The history of India's rule as a colony to be exploited for labour and resources left behind infrastructure that continues to affect the hyper-availability of racialised and gendered bodies.[6] The emergence of women in working and lower middle-class India as gestational surrogates fits into a pattern where advances in biotechnology make the bodies and body parts of workers more sellable and mobile than their labour, what Lawrence Cohen calls 'bioavailability'.[7] The structural adjustment policies to liberalise India's economy in the early 1990s contributed to the conditions under which women cannot find sufficient work other than by finding some way to make their value travel to meet capital when labour migration is not financially possible; here through transnational surrogacy. In fact, Kamala Kempadoo argues that neoliberal reforms imposed by the World Bank and IMF upon these formerly colonised nations have effectively been a process of re-colonisation of female, reproductive work.[8] While all biological life represents a site of speculation and potential biological production and accumulation, the legacies of imperialism continue to affect the hyper-availability of racialised and gendered bodies. In the case of transnational gestational surrogacy contracts in India, which were in place between 2004 and 2016 when the practice was officially banned, the colonial prehistory of contemporary globalisation and outsourcing of labour and labouring populations influences how we can understand the very nature of the work being performed.[9]

The biological and affective nature of women's participation as surrogates under paid contract challenges the analytical frameworks most often used to quantify or even identify an activity as labour. As scholars studying the bioeconomy have argued, this challenge to the labour categories of political theory characterises a number of emerging biological markets.[10] However, contrary to the newness of the technologies that make gestational surrogacy contracts possible, the difficulty in accounting for embodied and therefore gendered labours of care, affect and the body is not new. In fact, both materialist feminist analysis of housework and black feminist analysis of women's reproduction and bodies under chattel slavery have raised problems with the labour theory of value and the privileging of the subject of labour. For example, Leopoldina Fortunati has argued that reproductive labour has a dual function in capitalism: work occurring in the domestic or otherwise non-public realm that produces service, whether bodily, physical or emotional, represents itself and the person performing it as nonvalue, yet it simultaneously channels the value it actually does produce into the capitalist system through the visibly productive workers who consume it.[11]

Maria Mies argues that the modern marriage contract sets up a model of unpaid labour in the private sphere, the home, that is then extended through globalisation to encompass the formerly colonised world's labour economies.[12] We can add casualised labour, including many forms of crowdsourced digital labour and sweatshop work, as extending from this model of unpaid and under-paid labour in the gendered private sphere. The former colonial metropole, in the position of patriarch, commands the gendered labour of globalised service economies in the position of 'wife' – sweatshop garment work, customer service call centre work, long-distance tutoring and distance education, or crowdsourced microtask work like that managed by platforms such as Amazon Mechanical Turk. These forms of labour have little in common except that they are deemed to be uncreative or reproductive, and therefore while they are performed by people of any gender, the work itself is feminised, a process that Mies called 'housewifisation'.

After the housewife

Contracted surrogacy involves a spectrum of intimate and bodily actions that are still being theorised and catalogued as labour. As the paid work of pregnancy, gestation and childbirth, surrogacy falls into a category of bodily work in the private sphere that is not only devalued in Fortunati's terms, but becomes difficult to regulate, and given the limits on other choices and informed consent, walks a line between free and coerced participation. In the context of transnational commercial surrogacy contracts, the intended parent then becomes the commissioning parent, a type of profit-based patient. Doctors, formerly agents of pastoral care, become paid service providers who manage the technical, medical and social supervision of the process being commissioned. The clinic provides a portal for the transition of surrogates into the global service economy and, ironically, their transition into an industrialised labour force.

Women of colour feminists have critiqued the racialised nature of domesticity and free labour, whether or not it is performed in the home, pointing out that capitalism has grown not just because of so-called productive and reproductive labour, but also through the exhaustion of life past the possibility of its reproduction.[13] For example, the reproductive labour and bodies of women under slavery weren't comparable to unpaid housewives, as enslaved women were legally considered property, rather than a subject who could exchange labour for a wage. Children born to women under slavery remained slaves, and therefore the property of slave owners. The domination of women under slavery meant that the first issue of concern wasn't the lack of the wage for their work; it was the fact that they were property, rather than subjects who could sell their labour.

Other women of colour feminists in the US, including Evelyn Nakano Glenn and Grace Chang, among others, have pointed out that immigrant and low-resourced women have always done their own household labour, plus additional under-paid wage labour in the households of wealthier, often white, families.[14] Angela Y. Davis also argues that, historically, the reproductive work of the household in Black families has not been socially valued in the US. For example, in 1971, Davis described the domestic or reproductive work of women under slavery in the U.S., which was performed not in the family household, but for men and children who were not necessarily a family group under conditions of complete domination. She goes on to theorise this domestic space as the main space of resistance, because this reproductive labour was the only work not fully claimed by the slave owner, and while reproducing the lives of the enslaved, also created the conditions for resistance.[15] In the early 1980s, Davis critiqued the 'Wages for Housework' campaign by arguing that Black women and other women of colour had been performing paid housework for decades, in other words making housework a public responsibility, and that this had not improved the valuing of that labour, which was still low-waged work. Supplementing Fortunati's argument about middle-class white women's labour in the household, Jennifer Morgan argues that Black women's bodies were as essential to the success of chattel slavery as their labour in the antebellum U.S. south.[16]

Like domestic workers in the home who create the opportunity for middle-class women to work outside the home, outsourced service work is supposed to supply lower-valued, often feminised tasks so that other workers can be freed to do more highly valued, masculine tasks. First performed by women, then by hired women of colour and female immigrant workers, and finally sent to overseas workers, these tasks do not lose the association of being feminised and therefore unskilled, resulting in low compensation and social valuing. New technologies, like the biotechnologies discussed earlier, have historically marked what kinds of labour are considered replaceable and reproducible, and those that are productive and therefore highly valued. Long-distance telecommunications allowed for the outsourcing of voice-based customer service, and the Internet extended this to text and visual based labour.

Surrogates, like the figure of the housewife in the Wages for Housework campaign, but also other workers isolated to labour in the private sphere, (including domestic workers and intellectual pieceworkers doing crowdsourced work, among increasing numbers of others), have inherited the feminisation, and therefore devaluation, of the home as a workplace. They are also positioned in a global division of labour that has mapped itself onto the decolonising world to feminise developing labour markets. At the same time that commercial surrogacy upholds Davis's point that the 'housewife' is limited as a bourgeois figure that represents only the tip of the iceberg of women's labour and experience, surrogacy illustrates the enclosure and expropriation of women's bodies discussed by Silvia Federici.[17] More than the class-specific, race-delimited and advanced capitalist location of the housewife, Federici's observation of the enclosure of women's bodies to harness and control reproductive capacity explains why commercial surrogacy is continuous with the logic of capitalist accumulation via women's bodies and reproductivity.

Surrogacy as a site of resistance?

Bringing together materialist feminist, women of colour critique, and contemporary work on reproduction presents an urgent need to decolonise reproduction and to imagine domestic labour as a site of resistance. In the case of surrogacy, this should include empowering the models for sharing of resources advocated for by surrogates who see their work as above and beyond what can be represented by a labour contract, which imposes a regime of property and privacy where many surrogates expect ongoing social relation and reciprocity.[18] In my ethnographic study of surrogacy, women who were currently engaged in surrogacy contracts talked about the value and meaning of surrogacy in two ways. On the one hand, there was the feeling that such bodily work, so closely associated with adultery in carrying the child of a man not your husband, was dangerously stigmatising.[19] On the other hand, there was an emphasis on a feeling that carrying someone else's child was extraordinary, almost divine. While the need for income was the impetus to become a surrogate, this extraordinary aspect of surrogacy was much more heavily weighted, and in fact, inspired a common-sense expectation for ongoing social relations and social support of their own families by the commissioning parents. In this sense, women refused the alienation of the commercialisation of their surrogacy through the contract, insisting on its meaningfulness as social reproductive activity even though it is outside the area of the household proper. These women undertaking surrogacy thus describe their understanding of the risks and future potential of their work in terms that acknowledge, but also exceed, the clinic's discourse of surrogacy as simply the paid service of gestation and rented use of an otherwise unused uterus. Their 'unreasonable' expectation of a sense of indebtedness on the part of commissioning parents could be seen as an attempt to 'potentialise' relationships formed through the clinic and to stabilise one of the competing meanings of surrogacy as exceeding what is represented by the contract.

Kalindi Vora is an Associate Professor at the University of California, Davis and author of Life Support: Biocapital and the New History of Outsourced Labour *(2015).*

Notes

1. It is difficult to get comprehensive statistics for the nature and outcome of births associated with ART clinics in India right now because there is no required reporting (Sama Resource Group for Women and Health 2010).
2. See Kalindi Vora, 'Limits of Labour: Accounting for Affect and the Biological in Transnational Surrogacy and Service Work', *The South Atlantic Quarterly* 111:4 (2012), 681–700; Kalindi Vora, *Life Support: Biocapital and the New History of Outsourced Labour* (Minneapolis: University of Minnesota Press, 2015).
3. Kalindi Vora, 'Potential, Risk and Return in Transnational Indian Gestational Surrogacy', *Current Anthropology* 54: Supplement 7 (2013), S97–S106.
4. See Kalindi Vora, 'Re-Imagining Reproduction: Unsettling Metaphors in the History of Imperial Science and Commercial Surrogacy in India', *Somatechnics* 5:1 (2015), 88-103; Kalindi Vora, 'Experimental Sociality and Gestational Surrogacy in the Indian ART Clinic', *Ethnos: Journal of Anthropology* 79:1 (2014), 1–18; Kalindi Vora, 'Limits of Labour'.
5. See Vora, 'Limits of Labour'; *Life Support*; 'Re-Imagining Reproduction'.
6. Vora, 'Re-Imagining Reproduction'.
7. Lawrence Cohen, 'Operability: Surgery at the Margins of the State', in *Anthropology in the Margins of the State*, ed. Veena Das and Deborah Poole (Santa Fe: School of American Research Press, 2004), 79–106.
8. Kamala Kempadoo, 'Continuities and Change: Five Centuries of Prostitution in the Caribbean', in *Sun, Sex and Gold: Tourism and Sex Work in the Caribbean*, ed. Kamala Kempadoo (New York

and Oxford: Rowman & Littlefield, 1999).

9. Vora, *Life Support*.

10. See Catherine Waldby and Melinda Cooper, 'The Biopolitics of Reproduction', *Australian Feminist Studies* 23:55 (2008), 57–73; Catherine Waldby and Melinda Cooper, 'From Reproductive Work to Regenerative Labour: The Female Body and the Stem Cell Industries', *Feminist Theory* 11:1 (2010), 3–22; Melinda Cooper and Catherine Waldby. *Clinical Labour: Tissue Donors and Research Subjects in the Global Bioeconomy* (Durham, NC: Duke University Press, 2014); Kaushik Sunder Rajan, *Biocapital: The Constitution of Postgenomic Life* (Durham, NC: Duke University Press, 2006).

11. Leopoldina Fortunati, *The Arcane of Reproduction: Housework, Prostitution, Labour and Capital*, ed. Jim Fleming, trans. Hilary Creek (New York: Autonomedia, 1989).

12. Maria Mies, *Patriarchy and Accumulation on a World Scale* (London: Third World Books, 1986).

13. Angela Y. Davis, 'Reflections on the Black Woman's Role in the Community of Slaves', in *The Angela Y. Davis Reader*, ed. Joy James (London: Blackwell, 1998), 111–129; Grace Hong, 'Existential Surplus: Women of Colour, Feminism and the New Crisis of Capitalism', *glq: A Journal of Lesbian and Gay Studies* 18 (2012), 87–106; Jennifer Morgan, *Labouring Women: Reproduction and Gender in New World Slavery* (Philadelphia: University of Pennsylvania Press, 2004).

14. Evelyn Nakano Glenn, 'From Servitude to Service: Historical Continuities in the Racial Division of Paid Reproductive Labour', *SIGNS: Journal of Women and Culture in Society* 18 (1992), 1–43; Grace Chang, *Disposable Domestics: Immigrant Women Workers in the Global Economy* (Cambridge, MA: South End Press, 2004).

15. Davis, 'Reflections on the Black Woman's Role'.

16. In *Labouring Women*, Morgan writes, 'The obscene logic of racial slavery defined reproduction as work, and the work of the colonies – creating wealth out of the wilderness – relied on the appropriation of enslaved women's children by colonial slave owners ... The effort of reproducing the labour force occurred alongside that of cultivating crops' (145).

17. Silvia Federici, *Caliban and the Witch: Women, the Body and Primitive Accumulation* (Oakland, CA: Autonomedia, 2004).

18. See Vora, 'Experimental Sociality'; *Life Support*; 'Re-Imagining Reproduction'.

19. See also Amrita Pande, 'Not an Angel, Not a Whore: Surrogates as Dirty Workers in India', *Indian Journal of Gender Studies* (2019), https://doi.org/10.1177/097152150901600201

Social reproduction and empire in an Egyptian century

Mai Taha and Sara Salem

In one of the newspaper dailies, I read an article by an author who criticised the recent women's renaissance for focusing on the right to vote and be elected without addressing the problems facing women as wives and mothers. And this, he argues, signals a complete collapse of the roads leading to the true path of the nation.[1]

Writing in 1949, Doriya Shafik, one of the most prominent Egyptian feminists and founder of the journal *Bint al-Nil* [Daughter of the Nile], engages with the various meanings of a 'housewife'.[2] Shafik, who studied philosophy at the Sorbonne, saw that elite women of the palace and the upper classes needed to use their moral and material resources to transform the dreadful conditions of the poorer Egyptian population. In fact, they had 'a special mission' to bridge the gap between women from the upper classes and those from poorer ones.[3] Responding to the author of the article cited above, who voiced a common sentiment at the time, she argued:

> [T]he primary role of women is in making the life of the people [*al-sha'b*]. And any demand for rights is nothing but a vehicle to achieve the higher social goals for the Egyptian woman: building new generations of perfect wives and mothers.[4]

Shafik's position was consistent with a new family ideology that had reached widespread acceptance by the 1920s among the upper classes of Egyptian society.[5] This ideology propagated the conjugal family as the elemental unit of society, the welfare of which was necessary for the development of the nation. The new ideology entailed the education of women who would then become better companions for their husbands, and more suitable for their role of child-rearing and household labour, more broadly. While this new ideology was not concerned with women's rights, it became a precursor for the feminism of that period,[6] of which Doriya Shafik was a proponent. She claimed that women's education and political rights were 'all for the happiness of the Egyptian home with its "housewife" whose presence and dedication was always expected.'[7] This labour, exerted in the production of life almost exclusively done by women, is, in the words of Maria Mies, the 'perennial precondition of all other forms of productive labour.'[8] This insight was not present in elite feminist circles at the time, and yet by the time of the founding of Egypt's postcolonial state, we see debates around social reproduction, or 'making the life of the people', become increasingly prominent. What explains this shift, and how can we trace the presence of social reproduction in feminist debates from the 1950s onwards?

The following contribution looks at social reproduction in the context of Egypt, beginning with the period during which Doriya Shafik was active – the founding of Egypt's postcolonial state – and then moving to the beginning of Egypt's neoliberal project in the 1970s. Social reproduction, initially conceptualised as a Marxist feminist framework for understanding the unpaid work that goes into reproducing both the household and the labour force, asked the famous question: 'If labour produces the commodity, who produces labour?'[9] Challenging the tendency of orthodox Marxist scholarship to ignore the importance of unpaid labour – often done by women – to the evolution of capitalism, social reproduction as a theory made a crucial intervention into Marxist analysis. Nevertheless, its emphasis on gender as the primary means of understanding social reproduction meant that it became a narrow approach to the question of unpaid labour and capitalist exploitation. We aim here to critically analyse the intersecting social structures that come together around social reproduction, building on the Black feminist tradition and the Italian autonomous feminist tradition: in particular Claudia Jones's concept of 'triple oppression',[10] to read how colonialism, class and gender come together at different points in Egyptian history; and Silvia Federici's analytical approach that takes imperialism as central to the workings of social reproduction.

Focusing on the context of Egypt, we look at different historical moments during which debates on care work and motherhood cropped up and ask what these debates tell us about broader questions of capitalist reproduction.[11] Increased empirical attention to the everyday workings of social reproduction in postcolonial contexts can shed light on the ways social reproduction theory is imagined, and what it would mean to resist unpaid labour. We have chosen to structure this article around two examples – spanning the twentieth century – to highlight how social reproduction was embedded within debates around colonialism, capitalism and gender. Echoing Frantz Fanon, we emphatically believe that by situating our analysis in the colony/postcolony, Marxist analyses of capitalism must be re-conceptualised to account for colonial difference.

'As if the child has sprouted from the land – that is, her mother': Social reproduction in the post-colonial moment

During the British colonial period, social reproduction came to be defined by the parameters of colonial capital and changes in property relations, as well as a domestication of some colonial myths about the nature of 'Eastern women'. This period saw changes in the land tenure system, accompanied by urbanisation, industrialisation and investments in key sectors of the economy. This was in addition to social reforms that targeted the nuclear family as the foundation of national progress through new policies on population and reproduction. These new policies entailed legislation on women's labour, specifically limiting their night work, as well as a new interest in the subject of birth control.

Contestation over the meaning of Egyptian womanhood during this period was part of the debates surrounding domesticity, culture and modernity that developed in the late nineteenth century with British colonialism.[12] Through the figure of the 'ignorant and oppressed Muslim woman' in Egyptian families, British colonial officials questioned the moral and political authority of Egyptians for self-governance.[13] Remarkably, various colonial tropes of 'modern motherhood' were adopted later by nationalist elites constructing a new vision for a modern and independent Middle East.[14] In fact, modern motherhood became essential for the collective dream of independence, where the household would serve as a microscosm for the nation. The modern mother would nurture the children of the nation through her reproductive labour. This also came with a new family ideology that changed the precolonial idea of the 'maintenance-obedience relationship', where women received financial support from their husbands in return for their obedience and docility, albeit without an explicit legal obligation to do housework or care for the children.[15] While women still did all the housework, it was viewed as something beyond what was expected of them. This was partly because the obedient wife, almost like a prisoner, restricted herself to the home. Accordingly, husbands were expected to treat their wives with respect and to tolerate their 'overbearance', especially with the prevalence of patriarchal notions surrounding their 'deficiency in intellect and faith'.[16] With the new colonial family ideology, women's obedience came to be understood as an obligation to do housework.[17] This new ideology cultivated 'modern motherhood' as a remedy for backwardness and inability of self-rule.[18] Modern motherhood, it was argued, was to be cultivated through the science of home economics and sound principles of child rearing. At the turn of the century, courses on washing, ironing, sewing and cooking were being offered to women across all social classes.[19]

After independence, all of this changed, largely because of the emergence of 'state feminism', which was one of the principles that defined the new nation-state. Egypt, like other post-independence states in Africa and Asia, embarked upon a comprehensive legal, economic and cultural programme that consolidated the power and political legitimacy of the post-colonial regime.[20] Women were granted the right to vote in 1956, and new labour laws iterated the principle of non-discrimination on the basis of gender.[21] Women were entitled to fifty days of paid maternity leave, and employers were forced to provide day care if they employed more than one hundred women.[22] Accordingly, as Mervat Hatem argues, the state 'made reproduction a public concern'.[23]

Women's liberation was seen as necessary for building a new, modern, republican and anti-colonial nation-state.²⁴ Even in the political union with Syria, solidarity between Syrian and Egyptian women was viewed as instrumental to the cohesion of the United Arab Republic (1958-1961). In its April 1958 issue, *al-Hilal*, one of the oldest and most influential cultural magazines of the Arab world, ran an article celebrating the role of women in the union with Syria written by author and professor of literature, Aisha Abel-Rahman. Writing with her pen name *Bint al-Shati*, she argues that Egyptian and Syrian women are conscious of the role of virtuous motherhood in the collective national struggle, and mindful of their responsibility in uniting the forces of the nation that were divided by the pretences of colonialism. 'From the heart of Asia to the African Maghreb', women are struggling to unite the Arab nation.²⁵ 'The daughter of Algeria is standing in her war for independence immortalising in history the most heroic and beautiful scene of women's anti-colonial struggle.'²⁶ In another 1958 article published in *al-Hilal*, and written by the inspector of art at the Ministry of Education, the author celebrates mothers' day through depictions of motherhood in ancient and modern art. An ancient Egyptian sculpture depicts the child as part and parcel of the mother's body 'as if the child has sprouted from the land – that is, her mother.'²⁷ The depiction of the *fertile* land and the nation as a mother in works of art is a common imagery used by nationalists.²⁸ Beth Baron and other feminist writers have shown how Egypt was centred in the national imagination as a woman and a mother.²⁹

However, while the imagery of the mother served the national consciousness, it effaced her labour at home, subsuming it under the allusive category of 'love' and national duty. State feminism adopted this metaphor to consolidate the role of women as both active participants in the public sphere, and as dutiful mothers serving the nation through social reproduction. Domestic labour was as central to the formation of a new, modern state, and yet it was erased in the celebration of women as equal citizens working in the new public sphere of the postcolonial nation. The expansion of women's visible and, accordingly, also invisible labour, meant that dramatic shifts were happening in gender relations, even if told only through changes to the former. However, this cannot be understood outside of the particularities of anti-colonialism, which centred on modernising the nation, with all the gendered effects this entailed.

One way in which we can see these dramatic changes expressed in the everyday is through novels and other forms of writing published during this period. For instance, even the celebrated feminist novel, *The Open Door*, written by Latifa al-Zayat in 1960 (and its later rendition into a film directed by Henri Barakat in 1963), links domestic work with immorality and promiscuity.³⁰ The novel was written at the height of Nasser's popularity, a few years after the nationalisation of the Suez Canal, but was set during the anti-colonial struggles of the 1940s and 1950s. The novel links the patriarchy of middle-class sensibilities to complicity with the colonial authority. While the novel successfully makes the connection between the liberation of women with the liberation of the nation, it fails to address the complexitites of domestic work. In fact, it participates in a familiar discourse that devalues and denigrates this form of labour.

Laila, the main protagonist, is in love with her cousin Essam who has a kind heart and loves her back. Essam gradually disappoints her with his possessiveness and his cowardice when he doesn't volunteer in the peoples' resistance against the British in Port Said. Laila loses faith in love when she sees him being seduced by Sayeda, the sexualised and 'immoral' maid. Promiscuous Sayeda is pitted against Laila whose freedom from the confines of the family becomes tied to the freedom of the nation. As Laila is breaking from old norms of middle-class respectability through her anti-colonial political activism, domestic work remains devalued and tied to notions of immorality and female promiscuity. When she finds love again in the figure of Hussein, it is tied to her duty to the nation. In a rare depiction of women rejecting hypocritical middle-class moralities as a happy ending, the last scene shows Laila leaving her family with its conservative beliefs. She runs after a train heading to Port-Said full of volunteers, including Hussein, to participate in the resistance movement against the tripartite aggression after the nationalisation of the Suez Canal in 1956.

The novel, considered a feminist literary manifesto, linked women's individual freedom to the collective national liberation, capturing the spirit of a new vision of post-colonial modernity where women became active participants in the political life of the nation. While the new state broke older taboos on women's role in the public sphere, reflecting a radical and progressive shift, it also accommodated a conservative stand on the role of women in the household and family by maintaining the idea that propriety and respectability for women lay at home, where domestic labour continued to be denigrated and devalued. Regarded as 'unstable emotional beings,' women could not be trusted with the right to divorce except in cases of impotence or incurable illness.[31] In fact, all efforts to reform the personal status law failed, and it remained in its pre-revolution formulation. While women were celebrated as the drivers of modernity and progress in the public sphere, they were denied their autonomy should they decide to abandon the household or the 'social factory' as Federici puts it.[32] A woman's labour outside of the home, as well as her active participation in political life, was considered complementary to her duties in the household. Showcasing the successes of import substitution and industrialisation policy, the state introduced household management devices to help the working mother.[33] Through the washing machine, the gas stove and the vacuum cleaner, women would be able to balance between their work outside and inside of the home.[34] The nuclear family came to be governed by the new family planning programme that propagated contraception as the way forward for the modern working-class Egyptian family. Through contraception and industrialisation, the post-colonial state configured its identity, and in the process maintained the double burden placed on women in society. In what follows, we discuss the complete disintegration of this regime, which, albeit imperfect, provided basic social services for women that would soon disintegrate with the *infitah*.

'I'm 23 but I feel like I'm 50': Egypt's neoliberal project and a deepening domestic burden

The 1970s saw the emergence of a new global project, premised on freeing the market from state intervention in order to create economic growth. This project can be read as a counter-revolution against both anticolonial movements and socialist movements that had dominated much of the world since the 1950s. The 1970s, therefore, marked the defeat of anticolonialism, and, in the particular context of Egypt, Nasserism. Anwar el Sadat became president of Egypt in 1971, heralding the start of a neoliberal transformation. One of the most significant shifts was the 'opening up' of Egypt's economy to foreign investment and imports, known as *infitah*. This coincided with the IMF and World Bank intervention into much of the Global South through structural adjustment programmes which had massive effects on public social services that had been established under Nasser. In particular, structural adjustment targeted health and education as sectors within which states were 'over-spending' – the same sectors within which cuts would have major ramifications for social reproduction.[35]

The IMF-led structural adjustment – which can be understood as a form of neo-imperialism – is therefore central to tracking changes in social reproduction in postcolonial contexts, highlighting the intersections of empire, nation and gender, and the importance of taking an intersectional approach to social reproduction. What the IMF saw as Egypt's extremely slow liberalisation process led them to increasingly pressure Egypt into signing a structural adjustment deal, which it did in 1977. The major aspect of this deal was Sadat's promise to cut subsidies and reduce government spending for public services. Alongside this, there was a concerted effort to construct the private sector as the engine of economic growth, which included opening up to foreign capital and turning towards the goal of profitability rather than national development. This was to have very particular gendered effects. On the one hand, Nasserism's state-centric approach to gender equality, which was very much built on the public sector and women's labour within it, was abandoned. On the other hand, the shift to the private sector opened up opportunities for a very small minority of women. Moreover, even for those middle-class women for whom opportunities were now available, these often came at the price of an increased work load given the continuing presence of social reproductive work. As Mervat Hatem writes:

> With the retreat of the state as a social and economic agent of change, many official commitments to gender inequality were either ignored or abandoned within and without the state sector. It is the young lower-middle-class and working-class women who bore the brunt of these painful economic and social adjustments.[36]

Additionally, the benefits offered by the private sector did not match the ones the public sector had been able to provide, notably job security, long maternity leaves, and fixed working hours. Perhaps most importantly, how-

ever, *infitah* had the effect of feminising a certain part of the labour force: 'The inflation and migration that were products of the open-door system served to push urban and rural working-class women into the labour force. While most male workers were interested in the better paying jobs of the private sector and/or of the Gulf economies, in order to deal with spiralling prices, women workers preferred employment in the public sector because it offered such benefits as subsidised transportation, child care, and maternity leave.'[37] It is thus clear that the gendered effects of *infitah* in the public sphere were multiple. What we are interested in here is what happened to the gaps that opened up after cuts to subsidies and reduced government spending. Because these gaps were most notably felt in the public sector provision of social welfare, they had very clear gendered effects.

To trace some of these gaps, we turn here to Sonallah Ibrahim's *Dhat*, beginning with the 1952 revolution and ending in the late 1980s, which explores Egyptian politics through the life of the central character, Dhat, as well as her family and friends, as she navigates new challenges in the face of an ever-changing political economy. Sonallah Ibrahim is one of Egypt's most prominent novelists and a self-defined communist intellectual. Born on the day of the 1952 revolution, Dhat herself is very much symbolic of Egypt as a nation, and all of the changes it has undergone. As Samia Mehrez writes, 'This is not a novel that critiques a regime of the past. Rather, it is one that hits hard at the present, in all its manifestations – social, economic, cultural, ideological, religious, political.'[38] The word *Dhat* itself is also symbolic: Mehrez points out that when used alone, the word Dhat means 'self' in Arabic, a tactic Ibrahim used to displace the focus from an individual onto the collective. In other words, the linguistic suggestion is that 'Dhat' means the self; the viewer is in a sense encouraged to relate to the character. This is not a story about an individual Egyptian woman named Dhat, but a story – or a series of stories – about Egypt and Egyptians. The text offers an incisive commentary on how political and economic changes seep into the ordinary-ness of the everyday,[39] indeed, social reproductive work can often only be traced through a focus on the everyday. It is precisely in the changing rhythms and tempos of everyday life that we can see the deepening of the domestic burden following *infitah*.

Here we focus specifically on the theme of work and exhaustion that permeates much of the novel during the era of *infitah*, and how this is represented through the everyday travails of Dhat. Indeed as we move from the 1960s into the 1970s, it increasingly seems to be the case that Dhat is always working. Whether at home or at her job at a national news agency, she barely has time to recover, let alone relax. She is in a constant state of movement, which in turn means she is in a constant state of tiredness. In contrast, her husband Abdel-Meguid is portrayed very differently: although he goes to work, once he comes home he spends his time relaxing.

For Dhat, work outside and inside merge into one endless day. Many of the scenes in this section become a repetitive representation of this endless cycle, where Dhat wakes up, goes to work, comes home, only to begin what appears to be a second shift. This invokes feminist understandings of the 'second' or 'third' shift, where coming home after work – supposedly in order to relax – often means nothing more than starting a new shift, or what can even seem like an entirely new work day. In addition to this – and in addition to her full-time job in the public sector – we also begin to see Dhat getting involved in numerous small business schemes, from selling electric cooking pots to sewing lingerie. This very much captures the spirit of *infitah*, where entrepreneurship was encouraged and the economic burden individualised. Prices of everything begin to steadily increase, and the flood of luxury imports creates pressure on middle-class or socially mobile families to purchase items seen as representative of class privilege. Brought together, this created immense pressure on families to add other sources of income, despite the idea that this was an era during which Egyptians could supposedly *all* prosper. We see Dhat do the laundry, cook, clean, and take care of the children, all while seemingly exhausted. Indeed the images that stay with you from many of these scenes focus on the increasing tiredness Dhat embodies, and the ways in which her pace slows down over time. This eventually culminates in her saying, 'I'm 23, but I feel 50.' Such reference to social reproductive work and its effects on the body and mind is telling; it is precisely in the body that women often feel the effects of simply doing too much.

One coping mechanism we see Dhat make use of is that of retreating into the bathroom. Several times, Dhat slowly walks to the bathroom, locks herself inside, sits down on the closed toilet seat, and proceeds to cry. What is interesting about the bathroom is the steady decay that overtakes it. The bathroom is not only an escape from financial and marital difficulties, but also a physical manifestation of those difficulties. In one scene in the television show based on the novel, the bathroom is run down, broken, and leaking water into their neighbour's apartment, leading to a crisis in the family. After a visit to a couple who had been her university friends and who are now evidently wealthy, Dhat comes away feeling even worse about her own apartment, and specifically her bathroom. It is only after Dhat uses her own money – which she saved through exhausting sewing work late at night – that the bathroom is fixed and rendered respectable.

The bathroom is interesting from a metaphorical perspective, particularly in its representation of Egypt's decaying infrastructure during this period. Indeed we see decay – both in terms of infrastructure and in terms of public services – become the central theme in the novel from the late 1960s onwards. The refusal by the government to attend to infrastructural weaknesses results in a rapid increase in accidents and collapses, and we also see the collapse of the education and healthcare sectors following the withdrawal of the state. This is consistently represented against the lack of decay during the Nasser years, when Dhat and her husband attended well-funded public schools. Their children, on the other hand, must attend private schools, which their parents have to work extra hard in order to afford. This burden affects both Dhat and her husband, but as we see throughout the novel, has especially high ramifications for Dhat who already has an extremely heavy social reproductive workload.

Sonallah Ibrahim's masterpiece thus provides a fascinating lens for looking into the gendered changes brought about by varying national projects in Egypt, highlighting the connections between gender, empire and capital in relation to increasing workloads. We see how *infitah* has had very particular ramifications for women, especially because of the withdrawal of social services and the individualisation of the economic burden. The novel not only shows the multiple 'shifts' Dhat has to complete each day to support her family, but also the embodied nature of this extra work, and the toll it takes on her. Where during her youth under Nasser, she appears healthy, happy and light, this image drastically transforms after her marriage and the increasing pressures created under Sadat.

Conclusion

Social reproduction was always-already part of the story of modern Egypt. From colonial notions of 'modern motherhood', to anti-colonial nationalist approaches to gender equality, to free market utopias, we have highlighted why a social reproductive approach that takes empire and colonialism seriously is productive. Rather than conceptualise this as a theoretical argument, we see it as the beginnings of a research agenda in a context such as Egypt, considering what it would mean to think about social reproduction in the postcolony through multiple structural inequalities.

We have focused here on the 1950s–80s, but it is worth mentioning that changing economic patterns throughout the 1990s and 2000s were also intimately linked to changes in social reproduction. The turn towards hiring foreign domestic labour, the increased ostentatiousness of Egypt's upper-middle and upper class, and the increased presence of 'cultural traits' as part of the domestic labour market are all symptomatic of a deepening economic crisis in Egypt at the hands of deepening neoliberalisation. The individualisation of economic traits and the increased tendency to represent and sell labour based on characteristics it possesses – in this case, cultural characteristics – represents a particular phase of late capitalism. Following on from scholarly work that has highlighted the ways in which 'culture' comes to stand in for 'race', it is pertinent to pay closer attention to the mobilisation of culture in the creation of hierarchies in the labour market. In Egypt, this has manifested in the creation of a 'marketplace' of domestic labour in which there exists a hierarchy that positions women according to their country of origin.

Ideas about which countries produce the 'best' domestic workers or the most 'hardworking' nannies can be seen as producing very material effects in terms of hiring practices and the production of a racialised marketplace. This builds on an increasingly large field within critical feminist development studies, that looks at race, migration, the international division of labour and social reproduction. Through tracing realities such as the 'global care chain', feminist development scholars have shown that race and location are embedded within social reproduction at a global scale.[40] Material and ideational movement is part and parcel of these chains, as who is seen as 'valuable' on the domestic worker market often determines migration patterns. This is so to the extent that countries such as the Philippines soon began to represent themselves as providing the 'best quality' domestic workers, in order to become competitive internationally. Notions of race, work and gender therefore come together explicitly and implicitly when we think of migration and domestic work in our contemporary moment. Contemporary Egypt and the widespread tendency among a certain social class to displace its reproductive burden on to foreign domestic workers remains an understudied development that can also shed light on the coming together of social reproduction, gender, empire, race and capital.

Returning to the question 'If labour produces the commodity, who produces labour?', we suggest that the answer is never simply 'women'. Processes of race, empire and class constantly complicate the multiple power relations embedded within social reproduction. Colonisation and the IMF / World Bank structural adjustment programmes both increased the social reproductive burden of women, but of which women? Moreover, these processes also often increase the social reproductive labour of men, a point sometimes missed in the process of gendering social reproductive work.[41] As Claudia Jones has shown us, capitalist exploitation is already racialised *and* gendered;[42] women of colour face a different set of economic, political and social problems because of this. Addressing the imbalances of social reproduction, then, means thinking through the intersections of multiple structures, from patriarchy and capitalism to imperialism and racism.

Mai Taha is Assistant Professor in the Department of Law at the American University in Cairo. Sara Salem is Assistant Professor in Sociology at the London School of Economics.

Notes

1. 'Doria Shafik, 'Sayyedat al-Bayt' [The Housewife], Bint al-Nil Journal 1 (1949); translation is our own. The idea behind Bint al-Nil was developed in 1945 by Shafik who saw that there needed to be a magazine devoted completely to women, especially Egyptian and Arab women. She was particularly concerned with conservative interpretations of the Quran that rendered women as obedient and docile. See Cynthia Nelson, *Doria Shafik, Egyptian Feminist: A Woman Apart* (Cairo: American University in Cairo Press, 1996), 126.
2. Ibid.
3. Cynthia Nelson, *Doria Shafik, Egyptian Feminist*, 114.
4. Shafik, 'Sayyedat al-Bayt' [Housewife].
5. Kenneth Cuno, *Modernising Marriage: Family, Ideology, and Law in Nineteenth and Early Twentieth Century Egypt* (Syracuse, NY: Syracuse University Press, 2015), 77.
6. Cuno, *Modernising Marriage*, 77.
7. Shafik, 'Sayyedat al-Bayt' [The Housewife].
8. Maria Mies, 'The Social Origins of the Sexual Division of Labour', *Institute of Social Studies* 85 (1981).
9. Silvia Federici put forward the most complex articulation of social reproduction, which did not centre gender but rather took seriously race, class and nation in articulating social reproduction. This paper very much builds on her work, and suggests that more recent understandings of social reproduction depart from this complex and intersectional moment signalled by Federici's work.
10. Claudia Jones, *An End to the Neglect of the Problems of the Negro Woman!* (New York: Jefferson School of Social Science, 1949).
11. Himani Bannerji, *Thinking Through: Essays on Feminism, Marxism, and Anti-Racism* (Toronto: Women's Press, 1995), 30.
12. Laura Bier, *Revolutionary Womanhood: Feminisms, Modernity, and the State in Nasser's Egypt* (Stanford: Stanford University Press, 2011), 27.
13. Ibid., 27.
14. Ibid., 27.
15. Cuno, *Modernising Marriage*, 80.
16. Ibid., 88, 89.
17. Ibid., 80. For a longer analysis on the relationship between imperialism and motherhood, see Ana Davin, 'Imperialism and Motherhood' in *Tensions of Empire: Colonial Cultures in a Bourgeois World*, ed. Frederick Cooper and Ann Stoler (Berkeley: University of California Press, 1997).
18. Lisa Pollard, *Nurturing the Nation: The Family Politics of Modernising, Colonising, and Liberating Egypt (1805-1923)* (Berkeley: University of California Press, 2005), 123.
19. Pollard, *Nurturing the Nation*, 123.
20. Mervat Hatem, 'Economic and Political Liberation in Egypt and the Demise of State Feminism', *International Journal of Middle East Studies* 24 (1992), 231.
21. The right to vote came after years of struggle for suffrage by feminists like Doriya Shafik who was put under house arrest during the Nasser period. See Hatem, 'Economic and Political Liberation in Egypt', 232.
22. Ibid., 232.
23. Ibid., 232.
24. Bier, *Revolutionary Womanhood*, 7.
25. Bint al-Shati, 'Al-Masriyyat wa al-Suriyyat fi Ma'raket al-Wihda' [Egyptian and Syrian Women in the Struggle for Union] (April 1958), *al-Hilal*, 60, 61; translation is our own.
26. Ibid.
27. Abi Saleh al-Alfly, 'Gamal al-'Umuma fi Badae' al-Fann al-Qadim wa al-Hadith' [The Beauty of Motherhood in Ancient and Modern Art] (April 1958), *al-Hilal*, 53, 57; translation is our own.
28. Beth Baron, *Egypt as a Woman: Nationalism, Gender and Politics* (Berkeley: University of California Press, 2005), 7.
29. Ibid., 1.
30. Latifa El-Zayyat, *al-Bab al-Maftouh* [The Open Door] (1960).
31. Hatem, 'Economic and Political Liberation in Egypt', 232.
32. Silvia Federici, *Revolution at Point Zero: Housework, Reproduction and Feminist Struggle* (Oakland: PM Press, 2012), 7.
33. Bier, *Revolutionary Womanhood*, 81, 82.
34. Ibid., 81, 82.
35. Nazih Ayubi, *Overstating the Arab State* (Oxford: Oxford University Press, 1994).
36. Hatem, 'Economic and Political Liberalisation in Egypt', 233.
37. Ibid., 238.
38. Samia Mehrez, *Egyptian Writers Between History and Fiction* (Cairo: American University in Cairo Press, 1994), 129.
39. Sonallah Ibrahim, *Dhat* (Cairo: Dar Al Adab, 2013).
40. See John Connell, *The Global Health Care Chain: From the Pacific to the World* (London: Routledge, 2008).
41. Majella Kilkey, 'Men and Domestic Labour: A Missing Link in the Global Care Chain', *Men and Masculinities* 13.1 (2010), 126--149.
42. Jones, *An End*.

Social reproduction theory
History, issues and present challenges
Silvia Federici

As the articles contained in this issue of *Radical Philosophy* indicate, 'social reproduction' is today more than ever at the centre of feminist debates. Yet the same articles also express a legitimate concern that recent theorisations obfuscate the political significance of this concept and its ability to describe the changes that have taken place in the production of labour-power in the present phase of capitalist development.

In the notes that follow, I summarise the key issues emerging from this dossier, and then sketch a tentative program of analysis and action that I think is made necessary by the crisis of reproduction that women are experiencing worldwide. First, however, I would like to briefly comment on the history of the concept, to dispose of the assumption that to speak of 'social reproduction' is by itself to take a radical stance. This may seem a minor point in the context of the present debates, but I think it is worth emphasising that the idea of social reproduction originated in the context of bourgeois economics to indicate the processes by which a social system reproduces itself. This is how 'social reproduction' was first conceptualised by the François Quesnay (1694–1774) and other Enlightenment-era Physiocrats who, according to Marx, were the first economists of capitalist society, and also the first theorists to identify the nature of productive labour with agricultural work.

Contrary to an assumption that runs through recent works on social reproduction, to look at social reality from this viewpoint *is not itself to take a Marxist or a radical stand generally speaking*. Social reproduction theorists have included a wide range of promoters of capitalist development. Thus, as an analytic category 'social reproduction' cannot be adopted as a form of a political identification, as it is done by feminists describing themselves as 'social reproduction theorists'.

What made the discussion of social reproduction by wages for housework theorists and activists in the 1970s 'revolutionary' (in my view) was not the field that they examined, but what they discovered, which is the existence of a large area of exploitation until then unrecognised by all revolutionary theorists, Marxist and anarchist alike. It was discovering that unpaid labour is not extracted by the capitalist class only from the waged workday, but that it is also extracted from the workday of millions of unwaged house-workers as well as many other unpaid and un-free labourers. It was redefining the capitalist function of the wage as a creator of labour hierarchies, and an instrument serving to naturalise exploitative social relations and to delegate to wage-workers power over the unwaged. It was unmasking the socio-economic function of the creation of a fictional private sphere, and thereby re-politicising family life, sexuality, procreation.

This is what made the work of Mariarosa Dalla Costa, Selma James, Leopolda Fortunati and many others a turning point in feminist political thinking, not the fact that they looked at the world from the viewpoint of social reproduction. Scores of bourgeois thinkers – not just Marx – had done that before us.

Placing the spotlight on the work that produces the work-force has made possible a new understanding of the mechanisms by which capitalist society has been reproduced. It explains why the process that Maria Mies has defined as housewifisation has been exported throughout the former colonial world and – as the article here by Mai Taha and Sara Salem indicates – it persisted even in the state planning of the postcolonial period. This was plausibly because the goal of social development was still defined by the postcolonial state in terms of capital accumulation. Yet, the fact that Nasser's government 'made reproduction a public concern' clearly indicates, as the authors again underline, a decisive political shift, redirecting social investment this time to the support of the national workforce, although this new commitment never translated into a remuneration of the women in charge of this work.

Clearly, important changes have occurred in the organisation of social reproduction, with the restructuring of the global economy and the international division of reproductive work, that need to be theorised. As Mai Taha and Sara Salem point out, Egypt's adoption under Anwar Sadat of a neoliberal agenda has reversed the effects of Nasserism's social reproduction policy that strongly supported investment in the public sector. My own work has repeatedly focused on the consequences – worldwide – of the marketisation of reproductive activities that the neoliberal turn has produced, as well as the struggle of women in Africa and Latin America to create more cooperative forms of reproduction in response to this marketisation. Dalla Costa as well has written extensively on the effects of land privatisation, structural adjustment programs and the growing commercialisation of agriculture on subsistence economies and people's lives in the communities affected. In a co-authored work, entitled *Our Mother Ocean*[1] she has also extended her analysis of the neoliberal reorganisation of social reproduction to a description of the destruction of the greatest commons on earth – the seas, the oceans – caused by the industrialisation of fishing as well as by many forms of poisoning and contamination.

There is an immense work in which we, as feminists, have to engage, to denounce the profound crisis of social reproduction that entire populations across the world are experiencing because of the impoverishment capitalist development is producing, due to the defunding of social programs, the politics of extractivism and the now permanent state of warfare. We also need to write about the war that is being conducted against proletarian children and public schools, about the misery in which many elderly people are living, about the new forms of slavery constructed through the mass incarceration of black youth, and above all, about the struggle that can be made against these injustices.

What we do not need are new exercises in Marxology, which seek to demonstrate that reproductive work is not 'productive'. I will not reiterate the arguments against such efforts and resulting theories; Alessandra Mezzadri has already provided an exhaustive, excellent critique of them here, in her analysis of its articulation in some of the articles contained in the recent collection *Social Reproduction Theory*.[2] I will only question why it continues to be so important for feminists to deny something so evident as the fact that those who produce the producers of value must be themselves productive of that value. I would also add that value production is not a linear process, but one that occurs through constant displacements, as value is most often realised not where it is produced. But the question is why should it matter so much to feminists to deny a proposition that reflects a position of power for women in our negotiation and confrontation with capital and the state.

We can well imagine, for instance, what a difference it would have made if, in the 1970s and 1980s, in the face of the most racist attacks on women on welfare in the United States, feminists had gone to the streets to support their struggle and, together with them, demonstrate that every mother is a working woman and a producer of social wealth. In this context, I particularly appreciate Mezzadri's acknowledgement that given 'the expanding informal and informalised labour relations, it would be hard and completely misleading to distinguish between value-producing and non-value producing activities and realms, strictly based on tasks and/or payments', also considering that to deny the productivity of unpaid work activities is to assume that much of the world population is irrelevant to capital accumulation, which means that it cannot make the claim that the wealth that capitalism produces is also the fruit of its labour. Such denial evokes the orthodox Marxist view that only the (predominantly white) waged industrial workers qualify as makers of the communist revolution. But most important it leaves open the question of what power do we have to force the state to return to us the resources we need for our reproduction.

Many feminists in the 1970s and today as well have rejected the thrust of our campaign for wages for housework. However, nothing has so far been put forward as an alternative, except for timid calls for state-provided childcare and the sharing of housework with men. Meanwhile, women, in the United States among other places, are now so in need of money of their own that they have children whom they will never know or care for, and whom they essentially sell to others for a stipulated price. According to Kalindi Vora's 'Surrogacy, Labor and Human Reproduction', in India, surrogate mothers engage in this practice with the expectation that it will open the way to 'ongoing social relations and social support of their own families by the commissioning parents.' It is inconceivable, in fact, for many women that such an important act as giving a child to another family should not create affective ties and other obligations among all the people involved. This expectation, however, is destined to be cruelly frustrated, as it is one of the key requirements of surrogacy contracts that the children thus produced be immediately delivered to their new parents, a legal clause that has traumatic consequences, especially for the new-born infant who is separated from a body in which they have grown for nine months, the body whose voice and smell they recognise, and from which they expect their nourishment. Thus, as Vora, among others, has underlined, surrogacy can be taken as exemplary of the ways in which the extension of capitalist relations deepens the social hierarchies and the colonial structuring of the world economy, with the further racialisation of the activities considered to be of least value, beginning with the very process of procreation itself.

It is to be regretted that the feminist movement of the 1970s did not change the social status of such a vital activity as reproductive work, and it did not struggle to guarantee that women should not be denied the possibility of being mothers; an omission that means the predicament of African American women in slavery who were forced to produce children that would be taken away from them, finds echoes in the present context of commercial surrogacy. How to achieve such goals, how to construct a feminist agenda and a feminist struggle that in the words of a contemporary feminist slogan 'places life at the centre', valorising the process of its reproduction remains an open question for feminist movements internationally. It is the task of feminist theories of social reproduction to see how these questions can be answered.

Silvia Federici's books include Wages Against Housework *(1975) and* Caliban and the Witch: Women, the Body and Primitive Accumulation *(2004).*

Notes

1. Mariarosa Dalla Costa and Monica Chilese, *Our Mother Ocean: Enclosure, Commons, and the Global Fishermen's Movement* (Chico, CA: Common Notions Press, 2015).
2. Tithi Bhattacharya, ed., *Social Reproduction Theory: Remapping Class, Recentering Oppression* (London: Pluto Press, 2017).

OUT NOW £19.99

COUNTERFACTUALS

By Christopher Prendergast

'If kangaroos didn't have tails, they'd fall over.'

From the absurd to the densely philosophical, counterfactuals appear throughout literature, history, cosmology and more. Richly and sometimes treacherously present in the everyday, their influence over the ways our lives are imagined and lived is not to be underestimated.

In this original and lively work, Christopher Prendergast takes us on a dizzying journey through the landscapes created and inhabited by counterfactuals, and the consequences of their use.

www.bloomsbury.com/counterfactuals

BLOOMSBURY

CRMEP BOOKS

edited by
PETER OSBORNE
ÉRIC ALLIEZ
ERIC-JOHN RUSSELL

Éric Alliez
Étienne Balibar
Tithi Bhattacharya
Boris Buden
Sara R. Farris
John Kraniauskas
Elena Louisa Lange
Maurizio Lazzarato
Antonio Negri
Peter Osborne
Eric-John Russell
Gayatri Chakravorty Spivak
Keston Sutherland

Capitalism: concept, idea, image
Aspects of Marx's *Capital* today

AMAZON UK£12/US$18   FREE DOWNLOAD   www.kingston.ac.uk/crmep-cap

Centre for Research in Modern European Philosophy

1ST ANNUAL GILLIAN ROSE MEMORIAL LECTURE

'Deadlines (literally)'
REBECCA COMAY   University of Toronto

THURSDAY 23 MAY 2019
5.00–6.30 pm

Clattern Lecture Theatre,
Penrhyn Road campus,
Kingston upon Thames, KT1 2EE

Kingston University London

The event is free but registration is required:
www.kingston.ac.uk/crmep
The lecture will be followed by a reception.

Generously supported by
the Tom Vaswani Family Trust

Late style and contrapuntal histories
The violence of representation in Jean-Luc Godard's *Le Livre d'image*
Alex Fletcher

If the category 'late' has generally served to designate an ever-extending period of Jean-Luc Godard's filmmaking career – typically dated from his return to cinema at the end of the 1970s when Godard was approaching fifty – with the release of his latest feature, *Le Livre d'image: Image et parole* [*The Image Book: Image and Word*] (2018), we are now well into the period of *late* late Godard. Beyond a mere periodising label, however, the category 'late', as James S. Williams has noted, more critically conveys the kinds of artistic and communicational forms and strategies that Godard has developed over these years, and which can be productively understood by turning to Edward Said's reflections on the idiom of 'late style'.[1]

Said takes the phrase from Adorno's essay fragment 'Spätstil Beethoven' [Late Style Beethoven] (1937), where the German philosopher employs the term to capture how Beethoven's late compositions, rather than attain a sense of 'harmony and resolution', are instead marked by 'intransigence, difficulty and unresolved contradiction', as well as 'a peculiar amalgam of subjectivity and convention'.[2] Following Adorno, the 'remorselessly alienated and obscure' character of Beethoven's late style becomes for Said a 'prototypical modern aesthetic form' by virtue of its insistence on an increasing and unyielding sense of 'apartness' and 'exile' from bourgeois society, which late style 'expresses and, more importantly, uses to formally sustain itself'. Where one would expect to find expressions of maturity, transcendence or unity, in late style artists such as Beethoven – as well as late style thinkers such as Adorno – one is instead confronted with bristling challenge, resolute negativity and unsynthesised fragmentariness.[3] 'In the history of art', as Adorno writes, 'late works are the catastrophes.'[4]

Since the early 1980s Godard has repeatedly presented himself, to borrow Said's characterisation of both Beethoven and Adorno, as 'a figure of lateness' itself: an 'untimely' commentator on the present whose alienation from society is expressed not only through the obstinate difficulty and fragmentary character of his work, but in his geographic apartness from the metropolitan 'centres' of contemporary art and filmmaking, producing much of his work close to home in the small Swiss village of Rolle.[5] While the countless films, videos, exhibitions, CDs and books Godard has produced over this period diverge in terms of their content, medium and formal techniques, a central theme that pervades almost all of this work is what Godard views as the coming to pass of cinema, or, more specifically, a certain idea and history of cinema – a subject most notably explored in his eight-part video project *Histoire(s) du cinéma* [*(Hi)stories of Cinema*] (1988-1998). As Godard states in his long interview about *Histoire(s)* with Yousseff Ishaghour for *Trafic* in 1998:

> We can say broadly that a certain idea of cinema … which I myself feel quite close to – that idea of cinema has passed, as the Fontainebleau School passed, as Italian painting passed … As Hegel said, an epoch has ended. Afterwards things are different. One feels sad because childhood has been lost. But it's normal too. Now there's a new cinema, and a different art, whose history will be made in fifty or a hundred years.[6]

Godard's innumerable pronouncements on the twilight of a particular cinematic history are, however, rarely articulated wholly in terms of mourning or melancholia, but, as Christopher Pavsek observes, are generally shot through with 'utopian energy'.⁷ Indeed, the reason that the utopian possibility of cinema lives on for Godard, as Pavsek contends, is precisely because, as Adorno famously said of philosophy, 'the moment to realise it was missed'.⁸ As Godard expresses it in his 1983 video-letter to Freddy Buache (a film critic and director of the Swiss Film Archive): 'You and I are too old, and cinema will die soon, very young, without giving everything it could.'⁹ It is, accordingly, this 'sentiment of dusk' for an obsolete (or soon-to-be obsolete) cinematic project that gives Godard the 'desire' to continue working in it until he dies, construing his death as somehow coterminous with the death of the medium. As he relates in an interview from the same year: 'I say to myself that the cinema and myself may die at the same time.'¹⁰ Godard's conviction that his life is directly imbricated with the life and death of his artistic medium is emblematic of late style artists, who, as Said writes, 'care enough about their métier to believe that it too ages and must face death with failing senses and memory.' Rather than 'admit the definitive cadences of death' into his work, however, as Adorno said about Beethoven, Godard's reflections on lateness – of being '*in*, but oddly *apart* from the present' – are predominantly refracted through an allegorical or ironic mode.¹¹ Exemplary here is Godard's tendency since the early 1980s to perform his condition of lateness or anachronism in his films and video works by assuming the role of an outdated geriatric, a holy fool or idiot prince, quixotically pursuing the unfulfilled utopian potentials of cinema's past.¹²

This combination of romantic irony and utopian promise in relation to the imminent demise of both Godard and the cinema resurfaces at multiple moments in *The Image Book*. 'The world's masters should be ... wary of Bécassine', a clipped epigraph to the film reads, 'she is silent'. The name of an iconic Breton comic book heroine (usually portrayed without a mouth), the word 'Bécassine' has also come to mean 'fool' in French. An image of the provincial peasant, with whom Godard appears to be identifying, crops up later in the film, her raised arm pointing upwards. It serves as an ironic counterpoint to another more mysterious image of a hand that appears at the opening and near the end of *The Image Book*, *détourned* from what is widely thought to be Leonard da Vinci's final painting, *St. John the Baptist* (1513-1516).

The painting depicts the titular figure against a shadowy background, smiling enigmatically, index finger pointing toward the heavens, a gesture intended to denote salvation through baptism. Drained of colour, as if photocopied several times, Godard severs the hand from its original context, enabling it to float free in a void of empty black space, detached from any definitive meaning. Does the pointing digit symbolise Godard's approaching departure, or humanity's impending doom or salvation? Is it about to teach us a lesson or warn us of where the planet appears to be heading (the Old English word for forefinger, *tæcan*, can mean to teach, direct or warn)? Is it an accusatory gesture – an angry *J'accuse...!* – directed at the 'world's masters'? Or perhaps it indicates Godard's long-held belief in the ostensive power of the cinema to *index* (deriving from the Latin *indicō*: 'to point out'), and possibly redeem, the visible world? 'Even scratched to death', as he proclaims in *Histoire(s)*, 'a simple thirty-five millimetre rectangle saves the honour of reality'.

This romantic-ironic conjunction of gallows humour and utopian promise, bodily finitude and possible redemption, appears again towards the end of *The Image Book's* post-credits coda, where, over a black screen, Godard reads a passage from the French translation of the third volume of Peter Weiss's historical novel, *The Aesthetics of Resistance* (1975-1981).¹³ As Godard intones in a faint and gravelly voice, 'even if nothing would be as we hoped it would change nothing of our hopes, they would remain a necessary utopia'. Continuing to speak about 'immutable expectations' and 'resistance' his voice gives way to a cigar-deepened cough. Throughout *The Image Book*, and especially at this moment, we are made to hear what Roland Barthes termed the 'grain' of Godard's voice – the 'materiality' of his fragile and ageing 'body speaking' – which, due to the film's multi-channel sound design, was dispersed around the space of the movie theatre, making it seem as if Godard was in the space delivering the text live (an experience that is lost when viewing the film on a laptop).[14] The sudden cacophony that was created by the layering of multiple voice-tracks in the moments leading up to Godard's fit of coughing, moreover, gave the impression that the cinema itself was about to croak.[15] Godard nonetheless coughs his way through, with odd phrases, such as 'ardent hope', still audible. The film then cuts to fin-de-siècle Paris, to a ballroom scene taken from Max Ophüls's *Le Plaisir* (1952), in which an old man, disguised as someone younger, dances frenetically in circles until he collapses – another veritable allegory for Godard's condition of lateness. Over this black-and-white image – which, like all the archive footage in *The Image Book*, is significantly faded, as if sourced from a degraded VHS copy – Godard superimposes the opening and elegiac piano chords of Hans Otte's *Das Buch der Klänge* [*The Book of Sounds*] (1984). Phrases from Otte's minimalist score, which oscillates between melodic repeating patterns and dissonant horror-movie-esque chords, recur throughout *The Image Book*, where its cyclical swings between irenic harmony and agitated discord serve to dramatise Godard's tragic-romantic portrayal of history as an endless spiral of dread, barbarism, despair and transient hope.[16] The clip from *Le Plaisir* similarly has multiple historical and personal resonances. Made following the German-born Jewish director's exile in the United States, it was described by Godard in 1965 as the best French film 'since the Liberation', and represents the rebirth of national cinemas in Europe following World War II, which would subsequently give rise to Godard's career (first as a critic and then a filmmaker) in the French New Wave: a movement typically viewed by Godard as one of the final flickers of resistance to the occupation of cinema by a uniform (and Americanised) film industry.[17] The image of *Belle Époque* Paris further invokes a period of regional peace and artistic flourishing ominously foreshadowed by the catastrophic wars of the twentieth century, as well as the years when the cinema (or cinematograph) first came into existence.

If Godard's post-1979 works are less overtly political than those of the late 1960s and early 1970s – particularly the agit-prop style of his films produced under the moniker Groupe Dziga Vertov (1969-1970) – they nonetheless remain politically charged in their insistence on the idea of cinema, and art more generally, as a form of *resistance* to the aesthetic, cultural and economic imperialism of a tendentially global capitalist system.[18] Emblematic here is Godard's televisual-short, *Changer d'image* [*To Change the Image*] (1982), which reflects on the (im)possibility of making what he refers to as 'an image of change' when cinema and television are 'occupied' by capital and the state; a situation that is literally acted out through a scene in which Godard, tied to a chair, is beaten by a male interrogator. During this scene we hear a third-person male voice-over recount Godard's failed project, undertaken in the late 1970s, to work with the socialist government of the newly independent Mozambique in their establishment of the country's first television station – a symbol of the failure of Third Worldism and of socialist projects across the globe more generally (including that of Mitterrand's presidency in France), as well as the idea that television might serve as a communicational tool in such struggles.[19] The video ends with Godard relating a comic anecdote from his childhood about his grandfather who, when driving Godard and his siblings around, would never leave first gear. The children would cry from the backseat, 'change, grandfather, change'. Whether Godard has become the grandfather unable to change or is still the child in the back crying out for change is left open to interpretation.

Contrapuntal histories

Godard's venture in *The Image Book* to irradiate and excavate densely layered histories through the constellation and superimposition of fragmentary audio-visual citations extends the historical montage method he developed in *Histoire(s)*; a work which, as Michael Witt details, presents less a history of cinema than a story of what became of the experimental potentials of early silent cinema in the age of the talkies and television.[20] As Godard rehearses this in his series of screenings and lectures given in Montreal in 1978 – his first significant exploration of cinema history – the early experiments of silent film brought about 'a different way of seeing' that 'gradually came to be called montage', an operation 'that filmed not things, but the connection between things'.[21] The essential 'mystery' of the cinema, as Godard advances it in *Histoire(s)*, lies in its capacity to present what he terms 'a form that thinks' [*une forme qui pense*]: to construct enigmatic relations between images and

61

sounds that induce, rather than forestall, reflection and interpretation.[22] Akin to the micrological and constructivist method of literary montage in Walter Benjamin's *Arcades Project*, in *Histoire(s)* Godard carries the cinematic principle of montage 'into history', fashioning an interstitial and 'stereoscopic' mode of historical perception wherein far-off times and remembered events interpenetrate with the present.[23] The double irony of *Histoire(s)*, and late period Godard more generally, then, is that while repeatedly declaring cinema's death, his work nonetheless breathes new life into the medium's corpse by revitalising the cinematic potential of montage to generate new audio-visual figures and forms of thought and perception. This work of resurrection, moreover, is undertaken with one of the technologies said to have destroyed the cinema's aura: video. As Godard relates on a number of different occasions, his grand scheme to tell the history of cinema with the medium of cinema – that is, made with and projected on 35mm film – was 'unrealisable'.[24] Instead, *Histoire(s)* presents only a (videographic) 'souvenir' or 'trace' of this utopian project.[25]

As with other video works made during and following the completion of *Histoire(s)*, *The Image Book* effectively functions as an additional episode or footnote to Godard's potentially infinite video series, the impossible task of which, as he declared at the outset of Chapter 1A, was to tell and show 'all' the histories of cinema that 'have been', 'might have been' and 'will be'.[26] *The Image Book* is comprised of five chapters or movements, corresponding to the five fingers of the hand. The first, 'REMAKES' – which is later transformed into 'RIM(AK)ES' (containing the word *rimes* [*rhymes*]) – charts an endless cycle of war, conquest and genocidal violence in a manner reminiscent of the opening montage sequence of Godard's 2004 film *Notre musique* [*Our Music*] (2004), with images (both documentary and fictional) amassed from the history of cinema (including Godard's own oeuvre), television and the Internet. In one arresting sequence Godard cuts a scene from the end of Roberto Rossellini's neorealist war drama, *Paisan* (1946), showing Italian partisans being summarily executed by drowning, together with an online video of an Islamic State militia executing their victims by blood-stained water. 'Please, please', a voice repeatedly pleads over another clip from *Paisan* that follows this gruesome (yet disturbingly placid) footage, which is in turn followed by a clip from Hitchcock's *Vertigo* (1958), depicting Scottie (James Stewart) diving into the San Francisco Bay to save Madeleine (Kim Novak) from drowning. If read simply as a formalist operation of iconographic association, Godard's rhyming montage of three widely distant representations of historical and fictional scenes of execution and drowning comes across as strikingly crass. Yet the jarring pictorial resemblance between these images also draws our attention to how, as Joram ten Brink and Joshua Oppenheimer argue, the cinema 'has long shaped not only how political violence, from torture to warfare to genocide, is perceived, but also how it is performed'.[27] The cinema, as Chad Elias contends, 'does not just represent or thematise violence but also provides an imaginative resource for the (re)production of violence in the world' – an idea that Godard also seems to be suggesting with the cinematic phrase 'remakes'.[28] From 'powerful missiles and bombs that aim to shock and awe' to 'medieval-style decapitations brought straight to home computers', the last two decades, as Susie Linfield observes, have seen 'East and West' embraced 'in a diabolical pas de deux of violent of images and actions.' These documents of atrocity are 'neither mere images nor mere actions, but are *designed* to be both: they are propaganda of the spectacle and of the deed.'[29]

The ISIS video, however, can additionally be read as an extreme instance of what the French film critic Serge Daney characterised as 'a world "without cinema"'; that is, a world and media environment where the ethical and political dilemmas of how to show, or not show, the reality of violence and suffering no longer guides how images are produced and consumed; where, as Daney puts it, 'there are no longer good or bad ways to manipulate images.'[30] Like Daney's late film and media criticism, Godard's late works present a reflection on the production and consumption of images acquired from a deep and impassioned engagement with the history of cinema in which problems of form were seen as critical. Indeed, both saw themselves as belonging to a culture of cinephilia for whom, as Daney (paraphrasing Godard) asserts, even 'a tracking shot was a "moral affair".'[31] The decision to place the ISIS video alongside works by Rossellini and Hitchcock, then, should not be taken lightly.[32] If the formalist rhyming of Godard's montage can be seen to aestheticise and render equivalent the significant differences (in form and content) between such imagery,

this structural indifference and violent levelling is accordingly to be understood as evidencing a global media environment flooded with representations of war and violence, which makes for a condition of perceptual and cognitive anomie toward such images. This line of argument is of course not new, and already finds an early articulation in what Benjamin Buchloh characterised as the pronounced 'media pessimism' of Siegfried Kracauer's famous 1927 essay on photography, in which Kracauer portrayed the 'flood' or 'blizzard' of photographic imagery in Weimer Germany as carrying out an 'assault' on memory and understanding.[33] 'ARCHIVES AND MORAL', reads an intertitle near the opening of *The Image Book* that follows an image from Buñuel and Dali's *Un Chien Andalou* (1929) of an emotionless woman about to have her eyeball sliced open with a razor, indicating how the spectacle of ever-increasing generic representations of violence and death has served to empty images of their representative weight and ethical burden.[34]

The following three chapters of *The Image Book* continue to catalogue an 'anomic archive' (Buchloh's phrase) of representations of brutality, war, sex and scatology, featuring clips from films such as Pasolini's *Salò* (1975) and Gus Van Sant's *Elephant* (2003). Chapter 2, 'LES SOIREES DE ST. PETERSBOURG' [The evenings of St. Petersburg], begins with another faded ballroom scene, this time nineteenth-century Russia, and is framed around Joseph de Maistre's *St Petersburg Dialogues* (1821), whose deliberations on humanity's tendency toward violent destruction and extermination are considered to have presciently foretold the catastrophes of the twentieth century. The dialogues can be related back to Godard's argument, outlined in *Histoire(s)*, about the prophesising capacity of art, and the way in which a number of films from the 1920s and 1930s – such as Jean Renoir's *Le régle de jeu* (1939) – can retrospectively be seen to have foreseen 'the disintegration of Europe into war'.[35] The point here, as with the ballroom scene from *Le Plaisir*, appears to be less one of inevitable and unavertable fatalism, than an attempt to recover and return to a past moment when history could have veered in a very different direction. Rather than simply exhibit symptoms of melancholic attachment or mourning about a lost past, the aim of Godard's constellation of nonlinear relays of anticipated futures and reconstructed pasts is to break out of history's temporal loop of violence and trauma, as well as to open up the self-identity of the historical present and its claims on futurity. As with Benjamin's disjunctive citational method in the *Arcades Project*, Godard wrenches historical fragments from their immediate spatio-temporal contexts to create new grammatical constellations between past and present, so that each may be contemplated through a 'prism of historical time that is not its own'.³⁶

Chapter 3, 'CES FLEURS ENTRE LES RAILS, DANS LE VENT CONFUS DES VOYAGES' [Those flowers between the rails, in the confused wind of travels] (a line from Rilke's *The Book of Hours* [1905]), surveys cinema's long connection and fascination with the train, compiling clips from the Lumière's *L'arrivée d'un train en gare de La Ciotat* (1896), Buster Keaton's *The General* (1926), von Sternberg's *Shanghai Express* (1932), and Straub/Huillet's *Sicilia* (1999). Both the train and the cinema embody the radical transformations in travel and communication wrought by modern technology in the nineteenth century, with the train and the railway track coming to symbolise a vision of history as linear, progressive and propelled by irresistible technological advancement. Any sense of teleological progressivism is, however, swiftly undercut by a number of archival images that remind us of the railway system's implication in histories of colonial expansion and deportation, along with the cataclysmic horrors made possible by technological warfare. Godard's Benjaminian endeavour to trace the barbarism that underlies every document of civilisation, and to hold together the both liberating and destructive possibilities of modern technology, can be understood as performing an audio-visual version of what Said called a 'contrapuntal' reading of history and the archive.³⁷ Indeed, Godard gives an unprompted definition of musical counterpoint in chapter 5, which can be linked not only to the film's weaving together of independent movements, motifs, historical events and audio-visual elements to create a complex polyphony, but also Godard's general historiographical method.³⁸

To read 'contrapuntally', as Said outlines in *Culture and Imperialism* (1993), means to interpret history not as a univocal and symphonic harmony, but as an atonal ensemble of contrapuntally connected historical processes and experiences.³⁹ A contrapuntal approach to history, for instance, must take account of how a certain lifestyle in nineteenth-century Europe was made possible by overseas colonial exploitation, as well as the way in which dominant narratives work to forcibly exclude and repress particular histories and experiences, such as the history of French colonialism in Algeria. *The Image Book* notably includes clips from Godard's *Le Petit Soldat*, a film made in 1960 during the Algerian War of Independence, but censored by the French government until 1963 because of its portrayal of political violence and torture.⁴⁰

In chapter 4, 'L'ESPIRIT DES LOIS' [The Spirit of the Laws], this theme of historical counterpoint is connected to the question of law. The chapter – which features several scenes from John Ford's *Young Mr. Lincoln* (1939) of Abraham Lincoln (Henry Fonda) studying legal text books – takes its name from Montesquieu's 1748 political treatise on law, which argued for the need of constitutional systems of government to reflect the social and geographical aspects of a particular community or nation. The deployment of Montesquieu here appears to be bound up with the film's broader contestation of the violence of externally imposed forms of representation (whether legal, historiographic or artistic) that work to stamp out alterity and difference. These ideas are brought to bear on the final and longest chapter of *The Image Book*, 'LA REGION CENTRALE' [The Central Region] (a reference to Michael Snow's experimental 1971 film of the same name), which explores representations of 'the Arab world' in art and film history. The chapter features a number of audio-visual references to Godard and Anne-Marie Miéville's *Ici et ailleurs* [Here and Elsewhere] (1974), and can be seen to return to the latter's auto-critical inquiry into the problems encountered by Godard and Jean-Pierre Gorin when filming and editing the material for their unfinished film project, *Jusqu'à la victoire* [To Victory] (1970); in particular, the way in which the two filmmakers had superimposed their own Western (and patriarchal) political discourse over images of the Palestinian resistance movement in Jordan, consequently failing to grasp the reality of the situation they sought to depict, and unintentionally drowning out the voices of those they purported to represent.⁴¹ 'Can the Arabs speak?', asks one intertitle in *The Image Book*, recalling the title of Gayatri Spivak's famous 1985 essay 'Can the Subaltern Speak?'. 'SOUS LES YEUX DE L'OCCIDENT' [Under Western Eyes], flashes another.⁴²

While 'Islam' at present holds 'the West's' attention 'politically', as Godard at one point comments, the great diversity of peoples, languages and cultures that make up 'the Arab world', as the chapter goes on to expose (in a critique echoing Said's work on the subject of Orientalism), are all too often swept aside in favour of falsely unifying rubrics and reductive Orientalist stereotypes.⁴³ The chapter references various Western literary and cine-

matic cultural representations of the Orient – from Alexandre Dumas's nineteenth-century fictional travelogue, *L'Arabie heureuse* [Happy Arabia], to Pasolini's *Arabian Nights* (1974) – which are counterposed with a number of images from the history of Arab cinema, including Youssef Chahine's *Cairo Station* (1958) and *Jamila, the Algerian* (1958), Nacer Khemir's *Wanderers of the Desert* (1984), and Abderrahmane Sissako's *Timbuktu* (2014). The latter function not only as an important rejoinder to the former, but also provide a critical addendum to the predominantly Eurocentric focus of *Histoire(s)*, highlighting the inevitably incomplete character of Godard's (self-consciously personal) cinema history project, and the need for further supplementation.[44] The chapter additionally incorporates passages from the 1984 novel, *Une Ambition dans le desert* [*An Ambition in the Desert*], by the Egyptian-born French writer Albert Cossery, which tells the story of Dofa, a fictional Gulf state whose absence of oil leads its ruler to stage fake terroristic acts in the hope of drawing international attention to his poor nation. 'Archaeology and Pirates', one intertitle announces, alluding to how the West is interested in the Arab world not only when it is turned upside down by acts of terror and conflict, but when it can be plundered for cultural artefacts or natural resources. As a counterpoint to these mythical and lurid historical and media representations, *The Image Book* is punctuated by high-definition and colour saturated images of everyday scenes and stunning landscapes shot in the north-eastern Tunisian coastal town of La Marsa.[45]

The violence of representation

A central problem raised in *The Image Book*, as the final chapter makes clear, is not simply the representation of violence, but the constitutive violence of representation itself. This problem is formulated most explicitly in chapter 5, where Godard quotes from a 1985 interview with Edward Said (although, as is typical of Godard's intertextual practice, Said is not directly cited).[46] '[R]epresentation', as the quotation reads,

> or more particularly the *act* of representing (and hence reducing) others, almost always involves violence of some sort to the *subject* of the representation, as well as a contrast between the violence of the act of representing something and the calm exterior of the representation itself.[47]

Whether considering 'a spectacular image, or an exotic image, or a scholarly representation', as Said continues in the interview, 'there is always this paradoxical contrast between the surface, which seems to be in control, and the process which produces it, which inevitably involves some degree of violence, decontextualisation, miniaturisation, etc.'[48] If acts of representation tend towards surface, or what Daney termed the 'sphere of the visible' (the image as unmediated objectivity), Godard in *The Image Book* works in the opposite direction, disrupting and splintering the calm exterior of representation through various forms of audio-visual manipulation. From abrupt changes of aspect ratio and colourisation, to slow, accelerated and saccadic motion, Godard continually foregrounds the process of manipulation and mediation behind the immediacy of the projected moving-image, calling attention to the violence of cinematic devices such as framing and cutting, as well as the fiction of cinematic forms of narrative continuity in smoothing over contradiction and otherness.[49] As if to highlight this absence of harmony and continuity in image resolution and ratio, the film begins with a rapid series of projection calibration charts, traditionally used by projectionists to test the focus, aperture and framing of the film projection. In contrast to the high-quality glossiness of contemporary cinema, however, the effulgent shots of La Marsa sit alongside bleached film clips, pixelated mobile phone footage and glitchy digital images.

As with the murky video quality of *Histoire(s)*, these 'poor images', as Hito Steyerl dubs them, testify to the accelerated circulation, dislocation and degradation of images in today's digital economy; an increasingly globalised image-space where the continuous displacement and reformatting of images has become the norm.[50] Yet whereas debates around digital technology have promoted notions of frictionless immaterial flows and the image as a de-realised entity, the stuttering image-track and discontinuous syntax of *The Image Book* instead attempts to re-inscribe its visual archive with an emphatic materiality and sensibility. Central here is the film's endeavour to put the human body back in the frame, which can be seen not only in the way that its sound design makes audible the grain of Godard's voice, but also its recurring focus on the human hand as an organ of expressive execution – manipulation, as Erika Balsom points out, is etymologically derived from the Latin 'manipulus', or 'handful'.[51] 'Man's true condition', as Godard comments in the opening moments of *The Image Book*, is 'to think with one's hands'. A citation from Denis de Rougemont's 1936 book *Penser avec les mains* [*To Think With One's Hands*], Rougemont's plea for an engaged and creative form of theoretical reflection, is linked by Godard (as it is in previous works) to the connection between hand, eye and mind in the practice of film editing – the quote follows from an image, taken from Godard's 1987 film *King Lear*, depicting hands at an editing table attempting to bind together two pieces of celluloid with a safety pin.[52]

As Godard remarked at the Cannes press conference for *The Image Book* – which was conducted via Face Time with Godard's collaborator, Fabrice Argano, holding up an iphone with Godard's face on it to the audience – 'editing, even digital editing, is done with the hands'.[53] While, with the introduction of video and digital technology, the craft of film editing has undoubtedly undergone a form of deskilling (replacing the physical cutting and gluing of film with the pressing of buttons), Godard's painterly manipulation of images works to underscore both the material and embodied nature of vision and filmmaking, as well as the continued power of the hand to reanimate and open to change what has become reified or neutralised by history and the archive.

The videographic montage and manipulation of pre-existing archival materials is accordingly seen by Godard, as Richard I. Suchenski notes, to 'deepen' rather than 'threaten' the integrity of a document (whether a film, a painting or a text) and its 'connection with history'.[54] Godard's (present-oriented) archaeological enterprise can here be compared with the archival film practice of Angela Ricci Lucchi and Yervant Gianikian, to whom a number of references are made in *The Image Book*.[55] In a similar way to Godard (albeit in a more rigorous fashion), Lucchi and Gianikian employ various (analogue) forms of visual manipulation – such as hand-tinting, speed alteration and re-framing – as a means to analytically and affectively scrutinise the naturalised violence of the colonial archive that their work investigates. As with Lucchi and Gianikian's analogue processing techniques, moreover, Godard's videographic manipulation of archival film clips works to foreground the surface texture and the essential alterity of images, performing what Peter Osborne, drawing on Paul Ricoeur, terms an 'acculturation' to the otherness or 'externality' of the historical past (typically figured as a relation to the otherness of others) as it is represented in the externality of the image.[56]

History is thus presented in Godard's archival video essays not as a settled archive of past monuments, but as 'an agonistic process still being made' (Said); a process which, as in musical counterpoint, 'will always remain open to changing combinations of sense and signification.'[57] The de- and re-contextualisation of audiovisual fragments in Godard's late works is accordingly not merely a formal or aesthetic exercise, but is inherently tied to his conception of history as an endless process of fragmentation and displacement, of destruction and reconstruction. As such, Godard's archival videographic practice brings to light that other critical moment of Kracauer's essay on photography (a moment that is downplayed in Buchloh's reading), which turns to the potentiality afforded by the 'warehousing' of history in the photographic archive when combined with the experimental techniques of cinematic montage. For Kracauer, the 'scrambling' of archival fragments through montage had the possibility to counter what he saw as photography's reification of social reality and history into 'a nature alienated from meaning', affording 'consciousness' not only with the capacity to reflect on a reality that, under conditions of industrial capitalism, 'has slipped away from it', but, in introducing an image of time and change into the world, to 'establish the *provisional status* of all given configurations'.[58]

If the ever-changing geo-political configuration that is 'Europe' and 'European' history becomes such a privileged subject in Godard's late work, it is, as Williams contends, as the site of an 'ongoing crisis of fragmentation and decontextualisation'. This crisis is perceived by Godard to undergo intensification following the fall of the Berlin Wall, and the subsequent generalisation of capitalist social relations across Europe, where 'the different processes of history and memory, as well as art and culture, risk being flattened if not cancelled out'. Godard's 'stubborn belief' in a 'pan-European imaginary' made up of diverse national cultures and histories, as Williams suggests, is to be understood as presenting a form of opposition to the increasingly commodified and administered project and vision of post-wall Europe, in which the violent conflicts and political struggles of Europe's past are forgotten or re-written as a superficial narrative of inevitable progress and final reconciliation.[59]

A work that directly engages this transformative moment of economic and political integration is Godard's 1991 film *Allemagne 90 neuf zéro* [*Germany Year 90 Nine Zero*], which was filmed in the post-industrial environs of former East Germany, and which contains the iconic of image of a Mercedes unceremoniously driving over a street sign, left in the gutter, bearing the name 'Karl-Marx Straße'. Films such as *Allemagne*, as Williams notes, 'revel in a polyglot, pan-European artistic and historical past imaginary' – in the film's opening moments we witness a scene in which two characters translate passages from different German and French editions of Hegel's *Lectures on the Philosophy of History*.[60] Themes of translation and non-translation become central in Godard's late works as another artistic means to resist the increasing standardisation of European culture, as well the pervasive invasion of (American) English as the new global lingua franca.[61] At least seven languages can be heard in *The Image Book* – French, Arabic, English, Italian, German, Greek and Russian. Yet, as with previous works, only a fraction of the voice and text is subtitled into English (and is often mistranslated), calling attention to the violence performed by translations that attempt to smooth over the differential specificity of particular languages.

Connected to this resistance against monological and monolingual uniformity, and the attempt to reduce complex and conflicted historical experiences to fixed and falsely unifying narratives, is Godard's tendency in his late works to present only fragments of paintings, photographs, film clips and textual excerpts, which are themselves constantly interrupted by various audio-visual elements, and which always gesture 'towards a narrative unity and whole located forever off-screen and thus forever deferred.'[62] Godard's montage of sound and image in all these instances is essentially allegorical – in the sense given to the term by Benjamin in his writings on the baroque *Trauerspiel* and Baudelaire – engendering a discontinuity between, as David Cunningham puts it, 'image and meaning, which disrupts the false appearance of "unity" located in the symbol'.[63] Indeed, rather than enact a 'montage of attractions' à la Eisenstein, the detached hovering of sound and image fragments in films such as *The Image Book* seem to evoke a feeling akin to what Benjamin described as the 'desolate, sorrowful dispersal' of allegorical emblems in baroque *Trauerspiel*.[64] Benjamin's analysis of Baudelaire's poetry as embodying a modern form of 'late allegory', in which the *correspondences* 'souvenir[s]' [*Andenken*] serve to express the recollection of experiences that have 'died out', provides a further model for understanding the melancholic sensibility of Godard's late works, as well as his characterisation of *Histoire(s)* as presenting only a (video) souvenir of his utopian cinematic project.[65] As in Baudelaire's poetry, furthermore, Godard's films and videos aim to represent the social world as a complex of signs and relics pointing beyond their present to things now disappeared – the final episode of *Histoire(s)* is notably titled '*Les signes parmi nous*' [The Signs Amongst Us], a phrase which reappears in *The Image Book*.

'Only a fragment carries the mark of authenticity', Godard comments in *The Image Book*, attributing the quotation to Brecht. The authenticity of the fragment as a form, for Godard, as it is for Early German Romanticism (a key influence on Godard from his youth), is premised on the essential incompletion it enacts, offering an image of both art and history as an open-ended project of association, translation, remembrance and renewal; a project whose 'real essence', as Friedrich Schlegel puts it in *Athenaeum* fragment 116, 'should forever be becoming and never perfected'.[66] This enactment of fragmentary incompletion is particularly manifest in the repetition of identical images, literary quotations and musical phrases throughout Godard's late corpus, which establish an intertextual axis of associations that cuts across the compositions of each individual work. The metaleptic repetition of audio, visual and textual fragments, which acquire new layers of meaning as they pass through different contexts, creates not only the impression of a sustained dialogue between the individual films and videos, but serves to underscore their provisional or essayistic character, whereby a problem or idea can always be revised or reconsidered at a later conjuncture. In *The Image Book*, this impossibility of narrative unity or closure is embodied in the film's recurring references to the finite and enclosed form of the book, forever dominated by the figures of bounded totality and the completion of meaning. As the tension between the film's absolutising title and its proliferating representations of and citations from various works of literature, as well as religious and legal texts, suggests, we may still be in an epoch of the book, but we no longer believe in any singular or absolute Book.[67] Modernity is for Godard, following Maurice Blanchot (another recurring reference in Godard's late works), the infinite movement between the desire for a total or absolute Book or Work and the 'worklessness' or 'unworking' [*désoeuvrement*] that leaves this desire for finality and higher synthesis in fragments.[68]

This is, finally, how we should approach the recurring theological motif of redemption or salvation in Godard's late works, which, as in Benjamin and Adorno, comes to stand for the impossible moment of totalising transcendence from which history and the present can be thought. As Adorno writes in the final aphorism of *Minima Moralia*:

> The only philosophy which can be responsibly practised in the face of despair is the attempt to contemplate all things as they would present themselves from the standpoint of redemption ... Perspectives must be fashioned that displace and estrange the world, reveal it to be, with its rifts and crevices, as indigent and distorted as it will appear one day in messianic light.[69]

Such a standpoint, however, as Adorno insists, remains practically unrealisable, as it would not come until the end of time: Judgment Day. It is correspondingly the unrealisability of this standpoint that Godard intimates with his recurrent deployment, in *Histoire(s)* and elsewhere, of the 'quasi-Pauline' phrase, 'the image will come at the time of the resurrection' – in *The Image Book* only a fragment of the phrase appears, cutting off the final part of the sentence.[70] While the *image* – which, for Godard, is always defined as the tensely articulated relation or association that is created through the rapprochement of disparate elements – carries with it the *idea* of reconciliation or redemption (an idea often represented in Godard's late works through the iconographic motif of hands reaching towards each other), it is the impossibility of receiving the image in its fullness that is instead suggested by this messianic phrase.[71]

This impossible fullness is figured in the increasingly dissociative and disjunctive form of Godard's late style, which works to deny any immediate sense of reconciliation or comprehension, resisting what Pavsek, following Adorno, terms 'the imperialism of the concept' – the violence of abstract conceptuality and universality exercised over individuality and particularity.[72] What is envisioned in Godard's 'paratactic revolt against synthesis', however, to borrow Adorno's remarks on the paratactic poetic syntax of Hölderlin's late poetry, is not the destruction of synthesis or meaning as such, but an attempt to evade and subvert hierarchical structures and subordinating grammars of logic and narrative in order to construct forms of unification and identity without the coercive anesthesis of difference and contradiction.[73] Godard's late works are accordingly not simply *about* remembering particular historical instances of artistic and political resistance, but aspire to performatively engage the spectator, at the level of form, in a process of 'internal self-resistance'.[74] By denying the spectator any positive forms of conceptual reconciliation or syntactical resolution, his films and videos can be seen to formally *figure* the immanent possibility, however minimal and uncertain, of resistance and historical change. It is, perhaps, to this horizon of historical possibility, rather than to any guarantee of future salvation, that St. John the Baptist's severed hand is now pointing.

Images from *Le Livre d'image* (2018). Copyright Jean-Luc Godard, Casa Azul Films and Ecran Noir Productions.

Alex Fletcher recently completed his PhD at the Centre for Research in Modern European Philosophy, Kingston University.

Notes

1. James S. Williams, *Encounters with Godard: Ethics, Aesthetics, Politics* (Albany: SUNY Press, 2016), 4.
2. Edward Said, *On Late Style: Music and Literature Against the Grain* (New York: Pantheon Books, 2006), 7, 12. 'Spätstil Beethovens' was included in the 1964 collection of musical essays, *Moments musicaux*. For an English translation, see Theodor W. Adorno, *Essays On Music*, trans. Susan H. Gillespie (Berkeley: University of California Press, 2002), 564–568.
3. Said, *On Late Style*, 17, 12.
4. Adorno, *Essays On Music*, 567.
5. Said, *On Late Style*, 14. Godard notably won the Adorno prize in 1995.
6. Jean-Luc Godard and Youssef Ishaghpour, *Cinema: The Archaeology of Film and the Memory of the Century*, trans. John Howe (Oxford: Berg, 2005), 112.
7. Christopher Pavsek, *The Utopia of Film: Cinema and its Futures in Godard, Kluge, and Tahimik* (New York: Columbia University Press, 2013), 25.
8. Theodor W. Adorno, *Negative Dialectics*, trans. E. B. Ashton (New York and London: Continuum, 2007), 3. As Adorno correspondingly puts it in *Aesthetic Theory*: 'If the utopia of art were fulfilled, it would be art's temporal end.' Theodor W. Adorno, *Aesthetic Theory*, trans. Robert Hullot-Kentor (London and New York: Continuum, 2002), 41.
9. The full title of the video is *Lettre à Freddy Buache: À propos d'un court-métrage sur la ville de Lausanne* [*Letter to Freddy Buache: About a Short Film on the Town of Lausanne*] (1981).
10. Jean-Luc Godard and Gideon Bachmann, 'The Carrots Are Cooked: A Conversation with Jean-Luc Godard', in *Jean-Luc Godard: Interviews*, ed. David Sterritt (Jackson: University Press Mississippi, 1998), 138.
11. Said, *On Late Style*, 24; Adorno, *Essays On Music*, 567.
12. See especially the films and videos: *Changer d'image* (1982), *Prénom Carmen* (1983), *Soigne ta droite* (1987), *King Lear* (1987) and *Les enfants jouent à la Russie* (1993).
13. Only the first volume of Weiss's novel has been translated into English. However, an English translation of the passage quoted by Godard can be read in Fredric Jameson's foreword to the book. See Fredric Jameson, 'Foreword: A Monument to Radical Instants', in Peter Weiss, *The Aesthetics of Resistance: A Novel, Volume 1*, trans. Joachim Neugroschel (Durham, NC: Duke University Press, 2005), xlviii. Thanks to Hannah Proctor for pointing this out to me.
14. Farbrice Argano – Godard's producer, co-editor and co-cinematographer – has noted how *The Image Book* was conceived as the cinematic equivalent of a chamber piece (as opposed to an orchestral/cinematic symphony), as well as Godard's plan to put on small screenings of the film in non-cinematic spaces so that the speakers could be arranged to their liking. See Daniel Kassman and Kurt Walker, 'The Chamber Piece: An Interview with Fabrice Aragno', accessed 14 February 2019, https://mubi.com/notebook/posts/the-chamber-piece-an-interview-with-fabrice-aragno.
15. Roland Barthes, 'The Grain of the Voice', in *Image-Music-Text*, trans. and ed. Stephen Heath (London: Fontana Press, 1977), 182.
16. Phrases from Otte's *The Book of Sounds* appeared in earlier works, such as Godard and Anne-Marie Miéville's video short, *De l'origine du XXIe siècle* (2000), which also features the ballroom scene from *Le Plaisir*. For a reading of the appearance of the clip in relation to the latter, see Daniel Morgan, *Late Style Godard and the Possibilities of Cinema* (Berkeley: University of California Press, 2013), 256–258.
17. See Morgan, *Late Style Godard*, 257.
18. This idea of art as a form of resistance can also be found in earlier works, such his 16mm short *Camera Eye*, made as a contribution to the collective film *Loin du Vietnam* (1967). It is an idea shared by both Adorno and Weiss. As Adorno writes in *Aesthetic Theory*: 'Art keeps itself alive through its social force of resistance', without which 'it becomes a commodity'. Adorno, *Aesthetic Theory*, 226. As Weiss correspondingly states in an interview from 1981 about *The Aesthetics of Resistance*: 'I tried to show how literature and art – so long as they're alive – al-

ways struggle against something … Artists – whether they are painters or writers – stand in opposition to their time and offer a kind of resistance; the aesthetic that they realise is an aesthetic of resistance.' Peter Weiss, Burkhardt Lindner and Christian Rogowski, 'Between Pergamon and Plötzensee: Another Way of Depicting the Course of Events', *New German Critique* 30 (Autumn 1983), 110.

19. *To Change the Image* was commissioned for television on the occasion of the one-year anniversary of Francois Mitterrand's election in 1981, who came to office on the promise of radical socialist change. Mitterrand's presidency, however, was characterised by a sharp move to the Right and the implementation of neoliberal economic policies. On Godard's work in Mozambique, see Daniel Fairfax, 'Birth (of the Image) of a Nation: Jean-Luc Godard in Mozambique', *Film and Media Studies* 3 (2010), 55–67.

20. Michael Witt, *Jean-Luc Godard, Cinema Historian* (Bloomington: Indiana University Press, 2013), 112.

21. Jean-Luc Godard, *Introduction to a True History of Cinema and Television*, trans. and ed. Timothy Barnard (Montreal: Caboose Books, 2014), 217–218.

22. See Williams, *Encounters with Godard*, 71.

23. Walter Benjamin, *The Arcades Project*, trans. Howard Eiland and Kevin McLaughlin, ed. Rolf Tiedemann (Cambridge, MA: Harvard University Press, 1999), 461, 458. For a discussion of *The Arcades Project* and Benjamin's theory of historical interpretation in relation to *Histoire(s)*, see Monica Dall'Asta, 'The (Im)possible History', in *For Ever Godard*, ed. Michael Temple, James S. Williams and Michael Witt (London: Black Dog, 2004), 350–363.

24. See Serge Daney, 'Godard Makes (Hi)stories', in *Jean-Luc Godard: Son + Image, 1974-1991*, 159.

25. As Godard says to Daney, it is only as a 'souvenir' that it was feasible to tell the 'projectable history' of cinema. In the Montreal lectures, Godard makes a similar comment: 'In the end, the history of cinema you make will be a trace, like a regret that it isn't even possible to make the history of cinema. But you'll see traces of that history.' Godard, *Introduction to a True History of Cinema*, 135.

26. As Godard noted to Ishaghpour, he did not consider the series in any way complete, explaining that it could have 'hundreds' of other chapters and 'even more appendices'. Godard and Ishaghpour, *Cinema*, 5. This desire to tell the history of cinema in its totality, as Witt points out, evokes not only the grand-sweep of André Malraux's iconographic art historical studies, but the Annales school historian Fernand Braudel, who approached history writing in terms of an interdisciplinary 'total history' [*histoire totale*]. See Witt, *Jean-Luc Godard*, 83.

27. Joram ten Brink and Joshua Oppenheimer, 'Introduction', in *Killer Images: Documentary Film, Memory and the Performance of Violence* (London: Wallflower Press, 2012), 1.

28. Chad Elias, 'Emergency Cinema and the Dignified Image: Cell Phone Activism and Filmmaking in Syria', *Film Quarterly*, 71:1 (Fall 2017), 25.

29. Susie Linfield, *The Cruel Radiance: Photography and Political Violence* (Chicago: University of Chicago Press, 2010), 152. What is 'new' here, as Linfield notes, 'is not just the ease with which such images are transmitted but the intimate relationship between the acts of violence and their documentation; it is hard to distinguish the two. Some terrorist groups now regularly send cameramen, just as the Nazis did, to film their missions, including attacks in Iraq and Israel; suicide bombings, especially in Iraq, are photographed as they happen and immediately broadcast.' Linfield, *The Cruel Radiance*, 163.

30. Serge Daney, 'The Tracking Shot in *Kapo*', in *Postcards from the Cinema*, trans. Paul Douglas Grant (Oxford and New York: Berg, 2007), 34.

31. Daney, 'The Tracking Shot in *Kapo*', 18.

32. This is despite Godard's apparently indifferent response, when asked about the connection between the scene from *Paisan* and the ISIS video, that they are simply two images of people being thrown into the sea: 'I don't see anything else'. See Jean-Luc Godard, Dmitry Golotyuk and Antonina Derzhitskaya, 'Words Like Ants', trans. Ted Fendt, accessed 14 February 2019, https://mubi.com/notebook/posts/jean-luc-godard-2018-words-like-ants.

33. See Benjamin Buchloh, 'Gerhard Richter's *Atlas*: The Anomic Archive', *October* 88 (Spring 1999), 131; Siegfried Kracauer, 'Photography', in *The Mass Ornament: Weimer Essays*, trans. and ed. Thomas Y. Levin (Cambridge, MA: Harvard University Press, 1995), 58. Linfield similarly returns to Kracauer's essay to characterise the way that media representations of violence work to preclude 'the development of analytic abilities' and 'historic understanding'. See Linfield, *The Cruel Radiance*, 170.

34. Chapter 3 notably begins with amateur pixelated footage of a father filming his daughter's expression in response to an approaching train, which is cut together with the Lumière's *L'arrivée d'un train en gare de La Ciotat* (1896), the first screenings of which represents one of the founding myths of early cinema; namely, that of a naïve audience made to flee the cinema because of their belief in the realism of the projected image.

35. See Witt, *Jean-Luc Godard*, 124. As Witt points out, Godard's argument here resonates with Siegfried Kracauer's identification in *From Caligari to Hitler* (1947) of the premonitions of fascism in the German cinema of the 1920s.

36. Gerhard Richter, *Thought-Images: Frankfurt School Writers' Reflections from Damaged Life* (Stanford: Stanford University Press, 2007), 64

37. See thesis seven of Benjamin's 'On the Concept of History' (1940), in *Selected Writings, Vol. 4, 1938-1940*, ed. Michael W. Jennings (Cambridge, MA: Harvard University Press, 2003), 389–400. Passages from 'On the Concept of History', particularly Benjamin's famous image of the angel of history, appear in a number of Godard's late works. See Witt, *Jean-Luc Godard*, 79–80.

38. As Godard states: 'Counterpoint is a discipline of superimposition. Melodies don't need to be identical. In harmony, the arrangements produce melodies. In counterpoint, it's the melodies which, to the contrary, become arrangements.' The latter definition recalls Godard's citation in *Histoire(s)* of Beethoven's axiom: 'The perfect union of several voices prevents, all in all, the progress of one towards another.' Quoted in Williams, *Encounters with Godard*, 74. Musical counterpoint is of course also central to the presentational form of Adorno's philosophical writings (particularly *Aesthetic Theory*), the paratactical arrange-

ments of which are partly modelled on musical serialism.
39. See Edward W. Said, *Culture and Imperialism* (New York: Vintage Books, 1994), 51.
40. Ibid., 66-67.
41. See Michael Witt, 'On and Under Communication', in *A Companion to Jean-Luc Godard*, ed. Tom Conley and T. Jefferson Kline (Chichester and Malden, MA: John Wiley, 2014), 319–322.
42. Since *Ici et ailleurs*, Godard has returned to the subject of Palestine in a number of films, most notably *Notre musique*, which features a cameo from the Palestinian poet Mahmoud Darwish, and a number of quotations from Darwish's poetry. As Rebecca Dyer and François Mulot note, instrumental to getting Darwish to agree to play the part in *Notre musique* was Godard's friendship with the translator Elias Sanbar, who translated Darwish's poetry from Arabic into French, and was originally asked by Godard and Miéville, while they were in the process of making *Ici et ailleurs*, to review and translate the voices in the footage of the Palestinian resistance that Godard and Gorin had filmed in Jordan. See Rebecca Dyer and François Mulot, 'Mahmoud Darwish in Film: Politics, Representation, and Translation in Jean-Luc Godard's *Ici et ailleurs* and *Notre musique*', *Cultural Politics* 10:1 (2014), 72.
43. See especially Edward W. Said, *Orientalism* (New York: Vintage Books, 1979).
44. These new additions to Godard's cinematic canon are largely the result of research performed by the French film historian Nicole Brenez. For a discussion of her role in the project, see Nicole Brenez, 'IFFR Framewoks Master Talk', accessed 14 February 2019, https://www.youtube.com/watch?v=S9PkLYNxO8g.
45. Godard notes how he chose this location for largely personal and practical reasons (such as his friendship with the Tunisian actress Ghalya Lacroix), and that he would have rather filmed in Algeria, because of its stronger historical entanglement with French history. In contrast to French colonialism in Algeria (which began in 1830 and lasted until 1962), Tunisia was only ever a 'protectorate' of France between the years 1881 and 1956, and was given relative autonomy in comparison to that of Algeria. Yet the choice to film in La Marsa, which is located next to the Ancient city of Carthage, could also be linked to the number of references made in the film to Gustave Flaubert's historical novel, *Salammbô* (1862), which was, in part, inspired by the author's travels around north-eastern Tunisia. See Godard, Golotyuk and Derzhitskaya, 'Words Like Ants'.
46. In *The Image Book*, as with all of Godard's late works, literary, cinematic and musical citations and references are identified by a summary list of authors names, with no attempt to distinguish the origin of the text or work in question.
47. Edward W. Said, 'In the Shadow of the West', in *Power, Politics and Culture: Interviews with Edward W. Said*, ed. Gauri Viswanathan (London: Bloomsbury, 2004), 40. The interview was interestingly first published in the journal *Wedge*, in an issue titled 'The Imperialism of Representation/The Representation of Imperialism', that also included a script of Godard and Jean-Pierre Gorin's *Letter to Jane: An Investigation About a Still* (1972), which consists primarily in the analysis of a magazine photograph of Jane Fonda in Vietnam.
48. Said, 'In the Shadow of the West', 40–41.
49. As Godard notes, the film would be ideally shown on a large TV screen, with speakers distant from the screen, so that the spectator is not tempted to naturalise the disjunctive relation between the film's image-track and sound-track: 'What bothers me about the screen, whether it's a TV or a computer, is that the sound goes with the image and we believe what we are seeing.' See Godard, Golotyuk and Derzhitskaya, 'Words Like Ants'.
50. Hito Steyerl, 'In Defence of the Poor Image', in *The Wretched of the Screen* (Berlin: Sternberg Press, 2012), 32
51. Erika Balsom, '*The Image Book* Review: Jean-Luc Godard's Ruminative and Radical Montage', *Sight & Sound* (Jan/Feb 2019), accessed 14 February 2019, https://www.bfi.org.uk/news-opinion/sight-sound-magazine/reviews-recommendations/image-book-jean-luc-godard-ruminative-radical-montage.
52. On the importance of Rougemont's book and the recurring motif of the hand in Godard's late works, see Volker Pantenburg, *Farocki/Godard: Film As Theory* (Amsterdam: Amsterdam University Press, 2015), 217–247.
53. For a recording of the press conference, see 'A (virtual) encounter with Jean-Luc Godard, director of *Le Livre d'image*', accessed 14 February 2019, https://www.festival-cannes.com/en/69-editions/retrospective/2018/actualites/audios/a-virtual-encounter-with-jean-luc-godard-director-of-le-livre-d-image-the-image-book
54. Richard I. Suchenksi, *Projections of Memory: Romanticism, Modernism, and the Aesthetics of Film* (New York: Oxford University Press, 2016), 171.
55. *The Image Book* includes a clip of a sticky piece of nitrate film being unspooled, which is taken from Lucchi and Gianikian's short video about their archival film practice, *Transparence* (1998), and Godard also quotes from their manifesto 'Our Analytical Camera', which was first published in *Trafic* in 1995. For a translation of this text, as well as a number of essays on Lucchi and Gianikia's work, see the special issue of *Found Footage Magazine* 3 (March 2017).
56. Peter Osborne, 'Information, Story, Image: Akram Zaatari's Historical Constructivism', in *The Postconceptual Condition: Critical Essays* (London and New York: Verso, 2018), 156–157.
57. Edward W. Said, *Humanism and Democratic Criticism* (New York: Columbia University Press, 2004), 25.
58. Kracuer, 'Photography', 61–62. This utopian possibility of the photographic archive is what Kracauer famously calls the 'go-broke-game of history'. Ibid., 61.
59. Williams, *Encounters with Godard*, 73–74.
60. Ibid., 56. For a detailed reading of this scene, see Daniel Fairfax, 'Godard the Hegelian', in *A Companion to Jean-Luc Godard*, ed. Conley and Kline, 403–07. On *Allemagne*, see also Pavsek, *The Utopia of Film*, 33–56.
61. An emblematic instance of Godard's non- or anti-translation can be seen in his subtitles for *Film socialisme* (2010), which were created by Godard erasing words and punctuation from the script's English translation and presenting the resulting subtitles with noticeably large gaps between words. As Stuart Kendall notes, figures of translation and non-translation in Godard's films (as well the published scripts for his films) typically serve

a double function: on the one hand, they reflect 'the collapse of communication'; on the other, 'the plurality of the languages and the problem of translation emerge as a theme' that is to be explored. Stuart Kendall, 'Traces of Cinema: Introduction', in Jean-Luc Godard, *Phrases: Six Films*, trans. Stuart Kendall (New York: Contra Munda Press, 2016), xxxvii. For an exploration of issues of translation in relation to *Ici et ailleurs* and *Notre musique*, see Dyer and Mulot, 'Mahmoud Darwish in Film', 70-91.

62. Williams, *Encounters with Godard*, 60.

63. David Cunningham, 'Photography and the Literary Conditions of Surrealism', in *Photography and Literature in the Twentieth Century*, eds. David Cunningham, Andrew Fisher and Sas Mays (Newcastle-upon-Tyne: Cambridge Scholars Press, 2005), 80.

64. Walter Benjamin, *The Origin of Tragic Drama*, trans. John Osborne (London and New York: Verso, 1998), 186.

65. Walter Benjamin, 'Central Park', in *Selected Writings, Volume 4, 1938-1940*, ed. Michael W. Jennings (Cambridge, MA: Harvard University Press, 2003), 190, 173. On the importance of Baudelaire and Baudelaire's notion of correspondences in Godard's late works, see Witt, *Jean-Luc Godard*, 186.

66. See Friedrich Schlegel, *Philosophical Fragments*, trans. Peter Firchow (Minneapolis: University of Minnesota Press), 31-32. For an account of the influence of early German Romanticism on Godard's work, both early and late, see Suchenski, *Projections of Memory*, 153-158. In the video essay, *Soft and Hard: Soft Talk on a Hard Subject Between Two Friends* (1985), made with Miéville, Godard notably connects the Romantic idea of 'projects' to the history of cinema by underlining the shared roots of the words 'projects' and 'projection'. For Godard, as Witt explains, what was distinct about the cinematic projection, in contrast to the small screen of television, was its capacity to afford spectators the opportunity 'to project, lose, and rediscover themselves through films in a way that nurtured the development of a sense of individual and collective identity'. See Witt, *Jean-Luc Godard*, 64.

67. As Nicole Brenez has speculated, Godard may have taken his title from Apollinaire's essay 'The New Spirit and the Poets' (1917), which Brenez gave to Godard while he was in the process of making *The Image Book*, and in which Apollinaire describes the medium of cinema as a 'book of pictures'.

68. See Maurice Blanchot, 'The Absence of the Book', in *The Infinite Conversation*, trans. Susan Hanson (Minneapolis: University of Minnesota Press, 1993), 422-34. On the importance of Blanchot's writings in Godard's late works, see Leslie Hill, '"A Form that Thinks": Godard, Blanchot, Citation', in *For Ever Godard*, eds. Michael Temple, James S. Williams and Michael Witt (London: Black Dog, 2004), 396-415.

69. Theodor W. Adorno, *Minima Moralia: Reflections from Damaged Life*, trans. E. F. N. Jephcott (London: Verso, 2005), 247. As Williams contends, the recurring reference to redemption in *Histoire(s)* seems to point in this direction indicated by Adorno. The portrayal of history in *Histoire(s)*, and later works, moreover, is closely aligned with Adorno's conception of the Holocaust 'as an end point of human civilisation', and history as one 'permanent catastrophe'. Williams, *Encounters with Godard*, 80.

70. On the origins of this phrase, see Witt, *Jean-Luc Godard*, 25.

71. As Witt points out, Godard's definition of the image draws on Sergei Eisenstein's distinction between *obraz* [image] and *izobrazhenie* [depiction], wherein the former designates the product (mental or emotional) of the dynamic interplay between two or more elements. See Witt, *Jean-Luc Godard*, 180. A key reference for Godard since the early 1980s is also Pierre Reverdy's short poem 'L'image' [The Image] (published in 1918 in the Dadaist and Surrealist journal *Nord-Sud*), which defines the image as 'the rapprochement of two more or less separate realities'. For an English translation of Reverdy's poem, which Godard reads in *King Lear*, see Witt, *Jean-Luc Godard*, 180-181. This idea of the image as a poetic and cognitive creation is represented in *The Image Book* by a number of references to Anne-Marie Miéville's 2003 book, *Images en parole* [*Images in Words*].

72. Pavsek, *The Utopia of Film*, 48.

73. See Theodor W. Adorno, 'Parataxis: On Hölderlin's Late Poetry', in *Notes to Literature, Volume 2*, trans. Shierry Weber Nicholsen (New York: Columbia University Press, 1992), 136. In his much-cited reading *Ici et ailleurs*, Deleuze characterises Godard's paratactic and serial mode of construction as grounded in 'the method of AND', disrupting cinema's 'law' of '[f]alse continuity' in favour of a serial concatenation of 'this and then that'. See Gilles Deleuze, *Cinema 2: The Time Image*, trans. Hugh Tomlinson and Robert Galeta (London: Athlone, 1989), 180. In his reading of *Histoire(s)*, Rancière similarly theorises the 'sentence-image' grammar of Godard's videographic montage method in terms of what he calls 'the great parataxis' of modernity. Yet Rancière's comparisons of *Histoire(s)* with the use of paratactic description in Flaubert and Zola, or the 'subject-hopping' of pop culture and advertising, fail to bring out what is significant in Godard's paratactic montage practice. See Jacques Rancière, 'Sentence, Image, History', in *The Future of the Image*, trans. Gregory Elliott (London and New York: Verso, 2007), 33-67.

74. Williams, *Encounters with Godard*, 80. Weiss notes something similar about the intended difficulty of *The Aesthetics of Resistance*, the form and style of which was meant to confront the reader with a form of 'exertion': 'Nothing is made easy for them, just as things weren't made easy for the characters in the novel'. Weiss, Lindner and Rogowski, 'Between Pergamon and Plötzensee', 121.

Critical Theory's contexts of co-operation

Oskar Negt in conversation with Johan F. Hartle

Johan F. Hartle: I want to discuss the possibilities of Critical Theory that you and Alexander Kluge develop in your collective project. To that end, I would like to ask you to reconstruct a few points from your biography. Let's start off by having you describe your path to the Institute for Social Research in Frankfurt and then sketch how your work started out in conjunction with Frankfurt School thinking.*

Oskar Negt: I am currently working on the second volume of my biography and what plays a central role in this is why I gave up my plans to study law in Göttingen and instead take up philosophy and sociology. I connect these two disciplines to the normative side of validity, on the one hand, and the genesis or developmental conditions of norms, on the other. The fact that a student could study philosophy and sociology at the same time was decisive for my decision to go to Frankfurt. My departure from Göttingen was not easy inasmuch as I was content with the lectures I attended in the law school there; Göttingen at that time had one of the most famous law faculties in the world, with Bockelmann doing criminal law and many other renowned professors. But one day a friend asked me: What exactly are you getting your degree in? That's easy, I said: I'm studying law and am, in fact, matriculated at the law school. On the contrary, he said, you don't study law, you're studying legal philosophy. That's something entirely different. I thought about that for about two to three weeks and then said: He's right. I'm not studying to become a tutor who just discusses individual cases. I'm studying legal philosophy. Law did not fulfil my educational dream. On top of that, Frankfurt was already preoccupied with issues like the trade union movement. The city had quite simply so much of what I wanted. The connection between the labour movement and Critical Theory was a reality there because a large portion of IG Metall's brains trust included people who studied in Frankfurt.[1]

Hartle: Of Critical Theory's representatives who have occupied academic positions in the ensuing decades, you are probably the only one who has a strong relationship to the labour movement.

Negt: That's right. But why is that the case? Once again, that has something to do with my family's tradition. My father had been a member of the SPD [Social Democratic Party of Germany] since the workers' and soldiers' councils. He constantly challenged me. He commented on practically every one of the SPD's movements, for example, the Godesberg Programme. It came naturally to me that I would find my friends in Frankfurt among the unionists.

---

* This interview was conducted in Hanover on 27 February 2018 and was published originally as, 'Kooperationszusammenhänge kritischer Theorie: Johan F. Hartle im Gespräch mit Oskar Negt', in *Zeitschrift für kritische Theorie* 46–47 (2018), 145–65. Judith Milz prepared the transcription.

Hartle: How did you experience this at the Goethe University in Frankfurt and the Institute? Just how prevalent were the traditions of the labour movement there? Were you able to rediscover them with Adorno or Horkheimer?

Negt: Attitudes at the Institute were not hostile to unions, but there was an attitude that somehow being part of a social movement – being involved in the tradition of the labour movement – was more ideational. There were no direct political projects of any kind that led from the Frankfurt School to the labour movement.

Hartle: Can you say something about your position in the academic programme there and your relation to Adorno, Horkheimer and Habermas. How did you arrive in this setting?

Negt: You know, so much was based on factors that I am not able to describe in detail. There were, however, two experiences with Adorno that did determine my future path. I was an industrious student but didn't participate in the seminars. I didn't give presentations until I reached a point when I said to myself: I have to somehow show my gratitude using everything that I've accumulated. I agreed to write a protocol for a class on a very difficult text by Kant, namely his 'transcendental schematism'. I worked my way right into the context of that dark chapter and gave my presentation. Adorno was beside himself with joy on account of my protocol, nodded at every other sentence, and at the end of the seminar came to me and said: That was an object lesson in how to write a successful protocol. Protocols played a much larger role in philosophy than reports because they made discernible whether one had understood the text.

The second moment was in the old institute on the other side of the street in Senckenberg. There I gave a lecture on Marx. Adorno's assistant checked it before I gave it. The assistant in question was Habermas. That was my first encounter with him. He gave me the extremely long text back – which, by the way, appeared in thousands of copies[2] – along with a note that Adorno was in agreement that we offer more such lectures on Marx. The point of the story is that I had the feeling that I was actually in line with Frankfurt School thought. An entirely new phase of my studies began at that point.

Later, Habermas came to me one day and said: Do you want to become an assistant? At a point in time when Adorno and Horkheimer each shared a *single* assistant, namely Hermann Schweppenhäuser, it wasn't the case that open positions for assistants were in large supply as was the case a decade later. A very specific kind of cooperation evolved with Habermas, to whom I owe quite a lot. My habilitation was supposed to be about Fichte, but it naturally never came about. Nevertheless, cooperative friendships evolved.

Hartle: You also met Kluge at this time. When was that roughly? And how did this encounter come about? You represented two different contexts.

Negt: For reasons not entirely clear to me, I became an authority when I was in Frankfurt. In other words, I had contact with every group. In 1970, I organised a colloquium at the Juridicum in Frankfurt on legal philosophy. All these people who were politically engaged, like Cohn-Bendit and Joschka Fischer, but who were somewhat unorganised, attended. And there I saw someone who always sat all the way at the back and diligently took notes. One day he approached me and said: May I introduce myself? I'm Alexander Kluge. I said: I know you. You're a friend of Adorno's. I'm surprised that you have the feeling you can learn something from me. We then arranged to meet over dinner and since then we have had this relationship.

Hartle: Does that mean that your own intellectual socialisation and the development of '68 have no shared experiences with Kluge? You met Kluge for the first time two years later?

Negt: That's right. But 1968 played a big role for us because the book project that we collectively pursued was based on a book idea on the specific forms of the public sphere in '68 that I originally proposed to List Verlag. I asked Kluge whether he could imagine writing this book together with me. I was incidentally in a precarious situation because I had already received 2,000 marks for the book, back then an insane amount of money, that I would have had to return if I did not publish with List. And Kluge said that he didn't want to publish it with List but rather Suhrkamp. The decision to write this book came about perhaps two weeks after our first meeting.

Hartle: In this respect, '68 was a preliminary study for Öffentlichkeit und Erfahrung (1972) [*Public Sphere and Experience*, 1993], but the experience of '68 was separate? You had your experience of '68 and Kluge had his?

Negt: The lines were fairly distinct. Kluge was already in Frankfurt back then. I came from Heidelberg, from a political diaspora if you will, which incidentally resulted in me having to give speeches more than I ever had before in my life. Habermas certainly spoke incessantly and he also had a special strategy for speaking. When we debated through the night, he was always determined to support my arguments even when they faded in order not to lose his interlocutor. It was, in other words, a very intense but completely apolitical situation with a view onto the unfolding activities in Frankfurt.

The events of the time didn't initially challenge my political socialisation in this respect. Even the tradition of the labour movement was never called into question for me. On the contrary, shortly before '68 I was an assistant instructor at the Federal Trade Union School in Oberursel. Several unionists were looking within the SDS [Socialist German Student Union] for a deputy head for the School. The bookseller, Josef Lang, asked me whether or not I felt up to working as an assistant there. But it lasted for more than a year and it was also much more than just the job of assistant because the director, Herbert Tulatz, had gone for several years in order to organise unions in Africa. That meant my relationship to the unions preceded all that. As you already suggested at the beginning, it also meant that I was the only one who had an intense, concrete relationship to the labour movement. Back then, unions represented for me the labour movement.

Hartle: At this time there was an intellectual and political conflict with Habermas. You edited the book *Die Linke antwortet Jürgen Habermas* [The Left Answers Habermas] (1969). What circumstances led to this? How do you see this from today's perspective?

Negt: It's a relatively complicated course of events. My intention was to get Habermas out of the line of fire that he started with his concept of 'left-wing fascism', which he himself had applied to the student movement. I had discussed with him that I was editing this book. He wanted to write an afterword. But the book developed more and more into a polemic against Habermas and had already gone so far that it was no longer possible to roll it back. Twenty years later, I apologised for a host of reasons, one of which was the fact that, in the interim, certain contributors were no longer leftist but rather had wandered over to the Right. Uncoupled from the theoretical shifts, my friendship with Habermas remained steadfast. By the way, back then it was possible for a full professor to let an assistant go without further explanation. But Habermas didn't do that. I still believe that he always knew that the trajectories of our scholarship were never very compatible.

Hartle: Where then would you locate the differences?

Negt: He and I talked about that: Habermas takes a leftist position in which the labour movement and labour appear nowhere at all.

Labour and socialist politics

Hartle: Let's linger for a moment longer on Habermas. He published his paradigmatic essay on the distinction between labour and politics, 'Labour and Interaction', in 1968.[3] Your efforts with Kluge to relate the concept of the public sphere back to the concept of production, in other words, to the contexts of labour and experience that belong to the life of production, are an attempt to keep these two strands bound tightly together. This is also your reply to Habermas. Because 'living labour' remains a key concept throughout your theoretical work, perhaps you could say a little more about the trajectories that emerged from this different interpretation of the concept of labour.

Negt: Naturally. Habermas gave me his essay on 'Labour and Interaction'. 'What did you think of it?' he asked. (We addressed one another using the formal *Sie*, which was a good form of protection for such a long-term cooperative relationship.) I said that we represent remarkably different lines of thought and that our relationship had nevertheless endured. Evacuating the concept of labour from interaction and communication is to give up on it politically. Even the way we form our concepts is quite different. I suddenly had the impression that when Habermas spoke about something 'proletarian' it was more an aesthetic category. 'Proletarian' for me was closely associated with an origin story, namely my own history. The story of one's life is always involved in the formation of categories. That also applies to Habermas' middle-class life story.

Hartle: Against this backdrop, how did you conceptually manage to get together with Kluge? You had this experience with Habermas. A certain break with Habermas took place and then two lines started to distinguish themselves more and more. You said that you wanted to write from the perspective of your political experience of '68 as well as the public spheres of '68, and then quite suddenly the agreement with Kluge has you writing a book together with him. Your theoretical impulse and interest were clearly visible, namely to strengthen the concepts of 'living labour' and the 'proletarian' both politically and sociologically in order to grasp the public sphere as a context of production involved in the formation of ways of life. How does Kluge get involved? What were the synergies that suddenly emerged in the first conversations with him?

Negt: When I presented it to Kluge, it was initially the diversity in my concept of labour that instantly fascinated him. Labour is not just wage labour. That means that the rich means of expression for labour must be named if we wish to consider the context of life. We quickly departed from the discursive thought that Habermas imagined. We didn't want discourse but rather literal activities, in the sense of one's own objectivisation as a subject as well as the recognition of people in their objects. That was largely based on Marx's *Paris Manuscripts* with an eye to the dimension of reification as well as the idea that 'the *forming* of the five senses is a labour of the entire history of the world down to the present'.[4]

Hartle: That is also a quotation you comment on explicitly in *Geschichte und Eigensinn* (1981) [*History and Obstinacy* (2014)] and that you use again and again. Does that mean that it was also a fundamental impulse for *Public Sphere and Experience* to think through the history of sensuousness and the constitution of human subjectivity via the history of production contexts?

Negt: I mean the entire substructure of labour, its corporeality. Kluge is an extremely enthusiastic intellectual. When I outlined for him that the substructure goes entirely missing in Habermas and must therefore be filled in, he caught fire. And so we then went on to write these two books. *Public Sphere and Experience* influenced an entire generation with its development of a proletarian public sphere and counter-public sphere because 'proletarian' refers to not just the labour movement but also the substructure. The public sphere stops being a rational form that offers the citizen a liberal platform.

Hartle: Help us readers imagine what went on in your heads, yours and Kluge's. What played a role when you decided to write *Public Sphere and Experience*? There is the backdrop of the *Paris Manuscripts* and the idea that human subjectivity must also be understood according to the history of the relations of production. When looking back from today's perspective, one might say that these ideas of the public sphere or cultural action and the contexts of production go back to Benjamin. You can find it in his essay 'Author as Producer' and, of course, in his 'Work of Art' essay. On the whole, the idea of experience plays a central role. You have stressed that the concept of experience was probably Adorno's central concept.[5] How would you yourself describe the central theoretical impulses that you two were able to quickly agree upon?

Negt: We had to somehow balance out our different origins, which naturally played a big role. But we were careful with how our backgrounds determined our work because the idea of cultivating reason, if I may apply an agricultural concept, presupposes farmworkers: Every person tills their own mental field. But we decided to survey for starters the expanses of the past to discover whether certain answers are better than the ones we ourselves came up with. This theoretical form of agriculture wanted to analyse life contexts as concretely as possible.

If one now considers current political developments, then I can only say how sad it is that so much of what we feared has now come true. When, for example, people's everyday contexts are not worked on, when people don't take their distorted fantasies seriously politically, all the fears of expropriation can add up to the accumulation of a society's raw fears; that then brings people to chase after charlatans and redeemers, as is now the case. That means that the view from below remains crucial.

On this point, another conflict arose that has continued all the way up to Habermas' most recent publication. I challenged him – in my estimation Habermas has a lot of influence – to mention this underside just once and leave out the contractual side of the European context. Lisbon and Schengen are the only things that remain of these agreements. Mention just once the project of labour and refrain from saying that labour's utopias are exhausted. This is a barrier in his work.

Hartle: The concept of labour links you to the tradition of Marxism. There are different Marxist traditions. Another was implemented by Peter von Oertzen at the University of Hanover. There are different discourses, methods and political positions that were carved out in the seventies. Much more than Kluge, you have maintained a relationship to this Marxist spectrum. Looking back now, how would you describe your position? How was your relationship to colleagues at the Socialist Bureau like Frank Deppe, Joachim Hirsch, Wolfgang Streeck? There were extremely different positions within Marxism and nevertheless a collective labour emerged. How do you see your theoretical project within this spectrum?

Negt: My strategic intention with the Socialist Bureau was to create a forum where rapprochement was possible without the pressures of having to become a member or worrying about sectarian exclusions. It was a space for understanding where different positions could bring about something by watching. The concept of 'looking on' [*Zusehen*], which is quite essential for Hegel's dialectic, has once again moved me in recent days. How can someone like Hegel say that the dialectic is looking on at how things develop? How true is that? *Zusehen* also means critically following and commenting on the political development of time. My formulation of 'meta-fractional consciousness' plays a big role for a portion of the Left.[6] In the second volume of my biography, I place a strong emphasis in my RAF speech given at Frankfurt's Opernplatz. It helped illustrate for sympathisers what was wrong and what didn't work, as well as what did work and what socialist politics can really achieve when alliances and associations are organised.

Hartle: If we consider the unique feature of your theoretical work written together with Kluge within the spectrum of Critical Theory, then it possibly consists of the question regarding political organisation and political strategy.

Negt: Hans-Jürgen Krahl was possibly the one exception. He was the only one who dedicated himself to the old Marxist unity of a grand formulation of theory and questions of orientation, the orientation of social movements. Other than him, this hardly existed within Critical Theory. Adorno's 'Marginalia to Theory and Praxis' offers small insights into what he dared to advance regarding organisational questions.[7] Essentially, he left the matter up to others. When you bring into view the unique features of Krahl's thinking, then you see a collective political project whose central concepts – the proletarian public sphere, the counter-public sphere and, later, self-regulation – also accompanied the political development of the seventies and eighties.

Cooperations: self-regulation and Surrealism

Hartle: Your approach to working together remains unique. A cooperative context like yours is an exceptional situation involving an exceptional form of theory. Can you clarify for us how your collaboration with Kluge took shape?

Negt: The images and photographs of our collaboration reveal a mountain of books. We wrote every sentence literally word for word together. Recall the photo reproduced on the front endpaper of the original German edition of *History and Obstinacy* that shows us sitting together at a desk. We had a mountain of literature and manuscripts next to us and dictated our ideas. There were always other people present who took notes. Adorno's secretary, Elfriede Olbrich, was there with *Public Sphere and Experience*. She understood everything, so she refrained from transcribing when we talked nonsense and conversely recorded thoughts that were not dictated. She collaborated. Kluge often started with a sentence that I then continued. That is how it literally took place.

Hartle: How then did you reach an agreement regarding your larger arguments? Did they emerge out of the smaller building blocks of your mosaic? Or did you have a concept in mind that was then translated into or realised as detail work? The concept of the public sphere was already established. You hadn't yet realised the book project for List Verlag that was suddenly supposed to be pursued together with Kluge.

Negt: The question as to how a person manages to write a five hundred-page book is no small feat. You can well imagine that yourself. We had a rule that prevented us from fighting over a

concept or idea for more than ten minutes. If no agreement was reached, then the version first formulated was incorporated into the text. Fights over concepts were less important to us than the constitution of the book's overall context. We never worked together for more than fourteen days to three weeks at a time. We would go our separate ways and then a month later arrange a date to meet again. Some time ago, the German department at Princeton University invited me and Kluge to present on stage how we worked together. For many academics, that must have sounded quite unreal.

Hartle: Let's try and think our way into *History and Obstinacy*. The German original is a huge, 1,300-page project that operates simultaneously on multiple levels. How would you describe today the intention of developing such a large project both theoretical and poetic in nature? The book's argument is based on isomorphisms propped up by the concept of self-regulation. Normally, one would say that empirical social research or psychology have their own domains. With the central concept of self-regulation, you choose both a terminology and a method. You confront image with text and explode every boundary in order to allow this guiding concept to prevail as a poetic principle.

Negt: A specific form of poetics naturally comes from Kluge, but not entirely. Many literary references come from me and many non-literary ones come from Kluge. I can say that writing *History and Obstinacy* was quite pleasurable. In truth, self-regulation was conceptualised as a comprehensive principle. It deals with self-regulation as a psychological category; how single organisms keep themselves balanced using processes of self-regulation. Self-regulation is, however, also a quasi-cosmological principle in the sense that physical processes including the formation of the planets can be understood as the balancing of forces. At the same time, self-regulation is a political concept that describes the balancing of recalcitrant impulses and affects within a community. What brought about this wide-ranging discussion? When you tear down these barriers, a layer becomes visible otherwise hidden from academic discourse.

The concept of self-regulation does recall neo-liberal practices and rules a bit, but it really emerges from the basic idea – this was my experience with educational projects – that when people's fantasies and activities have no place to assemble within the processes of socialisation and the formation of personalities, then certain prejudices and exclusions are ingrained in them. The Glocksee School is an effort to bridge childrearing and education, continuing education, political education.[8]

I believe that it was also important that my biography ran somewhat against the grain of the merits and currents in academia. When I was at the Hegel Congress in Stuttgart in 1981, Habermas and I ate together and I asked him: 'How far along is your book? It should be coming out shortly, right?' Habermas replied: 'Well, you have it easy. Yours is a surrealist book.' He was right in a certain sense. I am actually amazed time and time again that step by step this approach brought me all the way to publishing my collected works.

Materialist theory of education

Hartle: If your intellectual profile runs against the grain of a certain type of academic training, academic philosophy and the academic social sciences (which naturally have been cultivated and stressed in the subsequent development of Critical Theory after Habermas), does that perhaps also relate to a certain type of Critical Theory and critical intellectualism? Would you say, to put it less defensively, that an imperative is hidden in your profile?

Negt: The Glocksee School and my experience with other non-institutional and non-institutionalisable forms of personality formation indeed count among the essential sources of my intellectual activity. This attitude has still other biographical reasons like the aforementioned year when I was an assistant in Oberursel at the German Trade Union's federal school. I had not taken my exams. I was still a student. That unencumberedness allowed me to examine much closer what went under the name of proletariat. When Horkheimer wrote in an early essay on the proletarian fighter, he idealised him. That is the rebellious expression of an entrepreneur's son who could afford to do so. I saw how long it took to turn a normal worker into a fighter. Education [*Bildung*] is required. An upbringing, another word for exemplary learning [*exemplarisches Lernen*], comes about by way of experience. There are, however, sources of obstinacy and they, too, must be taken into consideration. Political training cannot therefore be the sole thing associated with education. There must also be spaces for free forms of socialisation. My experience with the Glocksee School builds on this. When my wife and I had kids, I asked myself: if we go to Hanover because of my professorial appointment, should we hand our kids over to public schools? At that point, my situation turned into a battle for an alternative school.

Hartle: These two aspects of learning – the tradition of workers' education and your efforts to create alternative forms of childrearing and childhood learning – would you describe them as a central impulse for the collaborative work with Kluge? You derived the concept of self-regulation from it. Essentially, Kluge's work on the public sphere in small institutional niches is also an attempt to bring enlightenment or learning into contexts in which they are not a matter of course. Would you say that Negt and Kluge's project is primarily an educational project [*Bildungsprojekt*]?

Negt: Yes. It is an educational project inasmuch as it creates a basis for socialisation that has to do with the stability of democracy, for democracy is the single governmentally organised social order that has to be learned. All other governmental contexts – authoritarian societies, for example – do not make people need more education. They make learning obsolete. In this respect, this also focuses on a prerequisite for democracy. Democracy can't exist if the level of fear is too great or when mental prerequisites don't exist.

Hartle: Traditionally, the concept of learning, which already represents a strong humanistic tradition, presupposes idealistic basic principles. I believe I do you no wrong when I say that the exceptional thing about Negt and Kluge's project was that it wanted to be explicitly materialistic. Perhaps you could say something more about the fault line 'learning and materialism'?

Negt: That can be sketched out in distinction to Habermas' project. In Habermas' discourse, the rational citizen plays the role model of the political. In *Public Sphere and Experience* and in *History and Obstinacy*, the contexts of production and self-regulatory mechanisms take this citizen's place. Self-regulatory mechanisms identify the organism and its corporeal processes. In this respect, the book relies heavily on materialist motives. These differences with Habermas are embodied in a movement. Probably seven or eight years ago when I gave a lecture at the community college in Munich, Habermas appeared with his wife Ute. Afterwards we went to dinner. He said: 'I completely agree with your analysis, but I consider one of your theses completely contrived: the system does not capsize.' And then I said: 'Its stability is a conjecture that departs from presuppositions that we don't yet know. We know not how the system changes.' Habermas captioned the speech he gave on my eightieth birthday with the words 'I underestimated you', and continued by saying that his underestimation consisted in the fact that even the Socratic side of including living conditions is indeed an essential factor for the stability, consensus and inclusion of others. In this respect, my project was seen not only as an educational project but also a socio-theoretical one as well.

But you are right: the collective project with Kluge is only an educational project provided that it is thought of in materialist terms with respect to the superordinate conditions of educational labour and socialisation processes, but also provided that it is understood as a socio-theoretical project. Conversely, it could also be said that the materialist project analysing the social dynamic of capital and labour processes can only be correctly understood when it is also grasped as referring concretely to subjectivation processes and experiences that have to do with the emergence of personalities and the balancing of production contexts.

Politics of the non-identical

Hartle: You have related self-regulation heavily to the developmental-psychological context. The concept is, however, a broader one that describes democratic ways of life. You speak about self-regulation as a principle of communal living in the seventies. Perhaps one could say, because you always emphasised strongly the importance of the council movement and its discussion for '68 and its aftermath, that self-regulation is also a principle for the democratic self-governance [*Selbststeuerung*] of community [*Gemeinwesen*]. Certain forms of political organisation and the institution of the state can be oriented according to principles of self-regulation.

Negt: Yes. The basic requirement that forms the basis of the democratic constitution of our society has to do with the fact that people comprehend the fact that their interests, even individual interests, are not realisable without the inclusion of a social context. Often those who do something willingly are really guided by interests insofar as they relate their social engagement strongly with themselves and don't consider it as a self-evident restoration of certain things to the community. That means that the human being is a social creature. It is not born a political creature. This connection between learning and organisation of social context is so clear to me that I am naturally always glad when I see feedback between socialisation processes and subjectivation as well as general social processes, as well as when these connections are not considered completely unreal. Organising the capacity for resistance, obstinacy and proletarian energies is always then a part of these mental connections when it becomes creative and endows a community with form.

Hartle: The concept of the proletarian acquires in your hands a very unique constitution devoid of substance. This is something you stress later in your television conversations with Kluge. In *History and Obstinacy*, but also in your television conversations with Kluge, it seems that whenever the topic turns to the concept of the proletarian, the non-identical as defined by Adorno is also strongly present. The proletarian and obstinacy are in a certain sense negatively defined.

Negt: Indeed, we use the concept not in terms of any substance but rather as one of characteristics. It is a counter-concept, so to speak, that ignites due to the modes of sociation [*Vergesellschaftung*], a counter-concept for which those social principles responsible for identity formation are central. It constitutes itself by way of exclusions and setting limits. Mobilising exclusions means doing proletarian politics. But the question regarding the non-identical naturally touches on the problem of idealism. For Adorno, the non-identical, not the identical, is the actual material that reason and a person's life contexts work on. Nevertheless, the battle is naturally also waged over the identical. In other words: What am I? What am I expressing? What belongs to me? That ultimately has to do with not only big political questions but also the central question regarding identity during childhood.

Fundamentally, I would say that concepts like 'negative dialectic' delimit themselves from the rattling scaffold of philosophy that Hegel criticised already in his *Phenomenology of Spirit*. It has to do with the simple fact that the world cannot somehow be completely absorbed in the identical. There remains something like – remainder isn't the right word – a block or, as far as I'm concerned, a thing-in-itself. These are different metaphors for what remains outside wherever efforts to integrate and incorporate are detected.

Hartle: There are potentials of obstinacy or the capacity for resistance that are undirected. Some forms of obstinacy and resistance don't lead to emancipation, while others do. Which moments of obstinate development – or obstinate subjective potentials – do you consider to be typical of our age? Where do you locate this distinction 37 years after publishing *History and Obstinacy*?

Negt: Today's situation is linked to a concept that I've used for a while, namely the 'crisis of erosion'.[9] It means that those structures that once produced bonds have loosened. Structural bonds and loyalty get lost, and the fear of loss is naturally tied to obstinacy: I lose something. The subject moves in the direction of a new self-centredness such that the idea of community disappears or frays apart. At this level, emancipatory power gets lost, obstinacy gets constricted, and this ultimately leads to atomisation.

Hartle: From the way you've reconstructed the concept from the title of your book, obstinacy ultimately describes something external. The processes of capital, including labour conditions, constitute types of subjectivities, but then there are the proletarian capacities for resistance and obstinacy that lie outside. A prevalent thesis of our age is that under post-Fordism capital no longer knows exteriority because neoliberal capitalism is capable of incorporating all subjective capacities and potentials. Would you say that this calls into question the model advanced in *History and Obstinacy*? Just how far would you go along with the epochal thesis that capital no longer knows any exteriority?

Negt: The epochal thesis is partially correct. It's correct in the sense that capitalism's potentials are so far-reaching in ways that Marx himself never could have imagined. In the *Communist Manifesto* he used the comparison of a pyramid in order to describe the enormous dynamic of capitalist production.[10] That made a big difference for his argument. That capitalism co-opts, as it were, the total potential of human development including artificial intelligence, etc., that was something I believe Marx could not have imagined by a long shot. He addressed the productive dynamic of capitalism, but not its integrative dynamic. This positive, integrative side of capitalism has self-destructive elements because it doesn't lead to the organisation of life where subjective potentials retain their aims and objectives. That means that dimensions and dynamics of self-optimisation – we can deliberately use this concept in contrast to self-regulation in order to denote the subjective conditions of contemporary capitalism – can be described with the help of a figure that Adorno calls in his essay 'Theory of Half-Education' a kind of 'self-preservation without a self'.[11]

Sociability

Hartle: How are you currently engaged in the analysis of society? What are you working on?

Negt: My lectures from 1972 to 1982 are recorded on 680 hours of tape. The Hans-Böckler Foundation awarded me support to edit them. I would like to condense these lectures that span from Plato to Freud into three volumes under the heading of a political philosophy of sociability [*Gemeinsinn*]. I believe this is acquiring ever-greater significance. In contemporary society, the balanced relationship between the individual and society has simply come undone. There is no dialectic any more but instead disequilibrium. Collective interest no longer arises from the sum of individual interests. Mandeville's maxim 'private vices, public benefits' is mistaken.

Hartle: You now touch upon community and sociability. This reflects your collaborative work with Kluge. The form of collaboration presents cooperation as an essential feature of living labour. You argue in this context that the labour of relationships [*Beziehungsarbeit*] and productive labour cannot be divorced from one another. Kluge's exhibition in the Württembergischen Kunstverein was titled 'Gardens of Cooperation'. Forms of collaboration sprout and proliferate in those gardens. Are these forms of cooperation models for the development of community?

Negt: Kluge relies heavily on cooperation, whereas for me the purpose of cooperation also needs to be considered. Consider the recent volume of the *Alexander Kluge-Jahrbuch* entitled *Stichwort: Kooperation* [Keyword: Cooperation]. Cooperation as it is conceived therein is too abbreviated and under-theorised for my taste. If the dialectic between local and spontaneous forms of cooperation and farther-reaching goals is not considered, then you get a cooperative context that only produces catastrophes. Cooperation as such is not the solution.

Hartle: You've named the determination of aims as a principle that allows cooperation to achieve validity and exemplarity. Let's consider once again the cooperation between you and Kluge, driven by the aim and idea of advancing the project of Critical Theory, and relating it back to

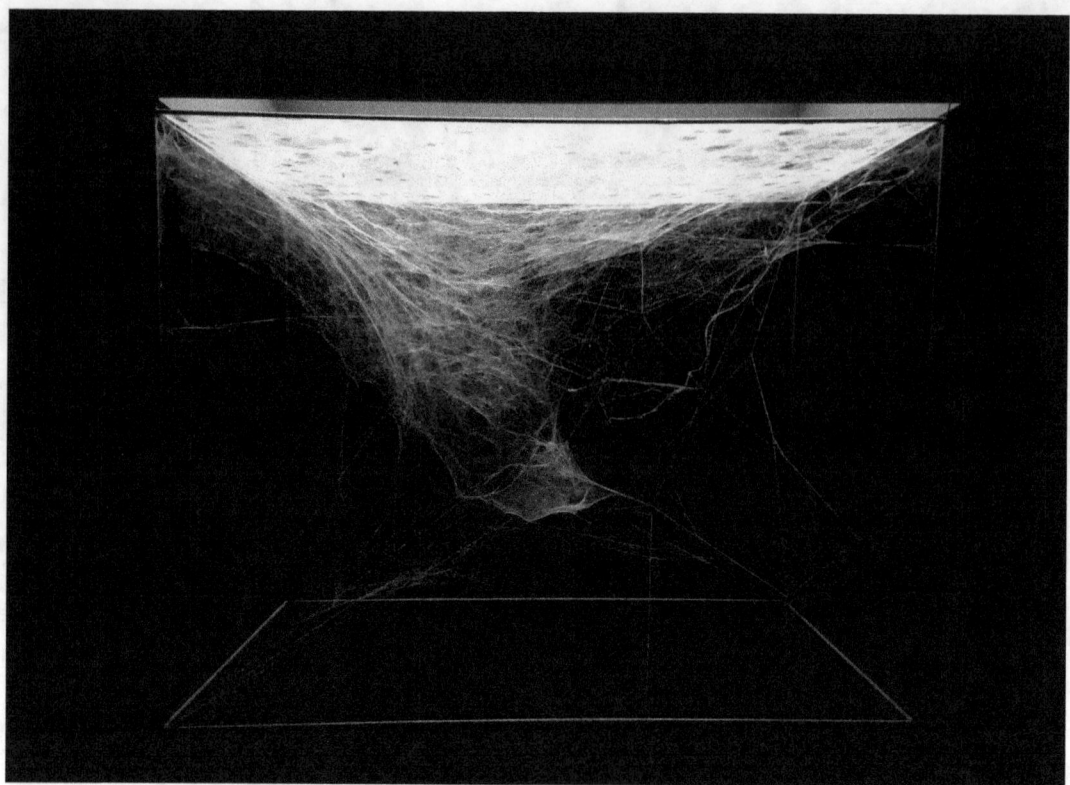

the contexts of experience. This collaboration was an opening up of subjectivity, a form of spontaneous – as Habermas said, surrealist – interaction that bore itself a trace of emancipation. In any case, cooperation has many requirements in order to be able to become a model of emancipation. Which aspects must cooperation include for this to happen?

Negt: For example, the idea of reciprocal help must once again acquire greater validity. In the tradition of the labour movement, forms of self-help are essential. Consider Kropotkin, for example. Unfortunately, all these forms were phased out because they were deemed unsustainable for the revolution. Simultaneously, the central organisational forms of the labour movement, cooperatives and associations, are essential and I am trying to show that in the second volume of my history of sociability. The history of phasing out ideas leads to a false definition of reality. Exclusions are justified with the claim that certain conduct is devoid of reality, which is incorrect. Fantasy still plays a big role, even sociological fantasy. I am quite heartened that my book *Soziologische Phantasie und exemplarisches Lernen* (1968) [Sociological Fantasy and Exemplary Learning] is still acknowledged now and then. I'd like to think that I still hold on to the book's argument about unleashing the creativity of social relationships.

Hartle: In closing I would like to talk a bit about your work's reception. What would you say have been the particularly important waves of reception of your thinking, and not just in the German-speaking world, but also abroad? Who are the important disseminators who have triggered and even channelled the reception of your work?

Negt: Already in *Public Sphere and Experience* the development of a conceptual world emerges in which the bourgeois element no longer plays a dominant role. It occurred to me while studying Kant's lectures that he always delayed his big publications because he had so little time. He was preparing his lectures. The influence of the person who gave lectures in the form of grand arcs was much greater than the influence of his writings. With regard to my own influence here in

Hanover, I can say that in my ten years lecturing I've trained a significant portion of the teachers working here. In other words, effectiveness transpires on different levels.

Hartle: Are there moments beyond this that have been important for the reception within or beyond German-language discussions of your theory of labour penned together with Kluge? The recently published translation of *Geschichte und Eigensinn – History and Obstinacy –* has brought about a new wave of reception.

Negt: I'm naturally happy when we're read and discussed. That goes for every author and naturally for Kluge too, who is now putting on a great many exhibitions. But you are correct: the translation will certainly inspire a new wave of reception and discussion for those readers lacking a strong command of German. Naturally, it will also produce new interpretations. *History and Obstinacy* is currently being inserted into a context along with models of post-Marxism and Western Marxism of the eighties, of which the German reception possibly lost sight. In Germany, the orientation around subjective processes that accompany capital and its processes was hardly to be found in other theoretical models. Our theoretical proposal was unique.

Translated by Richard Langston

Oskar Negt is Emeritus Professor of Sociology at the University of Hanover. Johan F. Hartle is Professor of Political Aesthetics at the Karlsruhe University of Arts and Design.

Notes

1. IG Metall is the major metalworkers' union in Germany, and Europe's largest industrial union.
2. The text was published in 1959 in a pirate edition distributed by the SDS with the title *Über das Verhältnis von Ökonomie und Gesellschaftstheorie bei Marx* [On the Relation of Economic and Social Theory in Marx].
3. Jürgen Habermas, 'Labor and Interaction: Remarks on Hegel's Jena *Philosophy of Mind*', in *Theory and Practice*, trans. John Viertel (Boston: Beacon Press, 1973), 142-69. This article was originally published in *Technik und Wissenschaft als 'Ideologie'* (1969).
4. Karl Marx, *Economic and Philosophic Manuscripts of 1844*, trans. Martin Milligan and Dirk J. Struik, in Karl Marx and Friedrich Engels, *Collected Works*, vol. 3: *Marx and Engels, 1843-1844* (London: Lawrence and Wishart, 1975), 302.
5. Oskar Negt, 'Der Soziologe Adorno', in *Soziologie im Spätkapitalismus: Zur Gesellschaftstheorie Theodor W. Adornos*, ed. Gerhard Schweppenhäuser (Darmstadt: Wissenschaftliche Buchgesellschaft, 1995), 3-26.
6. For a historical overview of Negt's concept of metafractional consciousness', see Oskar Negt, 'Das Sozialistische Büro als Organisationsforum des 'überfraktionellen Bewußtseins', in *Achtundsechzig: Politische Intellektuelle und die Macht* (Göttingen: Steidl Verlag, 1995), 155-9.
7. Theodor W. Adorno, 'Marginalia to Theory and Praxis', in *Critical Models: Interventions and Catchwords*, trans. Henry W. Pickford (New York: Columbia University Press, 2005), 259-78.
8. The Glocksee School is a progressive educational school in Hanover that Negt (along with Thomas Ziehe and Albert Ilien, among others) helped to establish. The school stresses the intrinsic developmental wishes of individual children and attends to a child's own temporal structures as well as the possibility to move freely in space. External disciplinary guidelines (in the sense of a lesson plan or fixation on the classroom) are minimised in the learning process.
9. Negt's use of this concept dates back to the seventies; the first sustained use of the term in his publications can be found in Oskar Negt, *Lebendige Arbeit, enteignete Zeit: Politische und kulturelle Dimensionen des Kampfes um die Arbeit* (Frankfurt am Main: Campus Verlag, 1984), 53-66.
10. See: Karl Marx and Friedrich Engels, *The Manifesto of the Communist Party*, in Karl Marx and Friedrich Engels, *Collected Works*, vol. 6: *Marx and Engels, 1845-1848* (London: Lawrence and Wishart, 1976), 487.
11. Theodor W. Adorno, 'Theorie der Halbbildung', in *Gesammelte Schriften*, vol. 8, *Soziologische Schriften I*, ed. Rolf Tiedemann, (Frankfurt am Main: Suhrkamp Verlag, 2003), 93-121. See, in particular, 115.

Reviews

Exhausting concepts

Pascal Chabot, *Global Burnout*, trans. Aliza Krefetz (London: Bloomsbury, 2018). 144 pp., £96 hb., £23.99 pb., £25 eb., 978 1 50133 438 2 hb., 978 1 50133 447 4 pb., 9 781 501 33439 9 eb.

Philosophers have often described society as being either physically sick or mentally ill, but the diagnoses differ. Metaphors proliferate and medical paradigms shift but neurological and psychological pathologies seem to predominate. For Jean Baudrillard capitalism was hysterical; for Gilles Deleuze and Félix Guattari the schizophrenic was the metonym; whereas Julia Kristeva wondered if 'maladies of the soul' threatended to disappear from contemporary life altogether. More recently, Franco 'Bifo' Beradi and Tiziana Terranova have both paid attention to pathologies of attention; Paulo Virno has identified a mirror of society in mirror neurons; Mark Fisher has perceived connections between capitalism and depression; and Catherine Malabou has described affectless 'new wounded' subjects produced by brain injuries and PTSD.

Yet in spite of the very different psychic outcomes identified in these accounts, the economic, political and technological realities said to both reflect and produce these conditions tend to have some common features: too fast, too busy, too interconnected, too technological, too relentless, too precarious, too stimulating, too intense, too demanding, too vast, too intricate, too bright, too brutal. We are losing sleep, we can't keep up and we can't concentrate on anything any more. What do these shifting psychopathological categories say about the historical moments in which these theories were produced? And what are the differing political implications of the diagnoses?

A recent viral BuzzFeed article by Anne Helen Petersen described millenials (defined as people born between 1981 and 1996) as 'the burnout generation', afflicted by an inability to run simple errands like going to the post office or to finish basic administrative tasks like registering to vote. She connects the phenomenon to the peculiar demands of contemporary working conditions. Though she ascribes it to a specific and implicitly internally homogeneous generation, often the article seems to imply that burnout is actually a universal response to life under capitalism today. Burnout, she claims, is chronic and pervasive: far from a condition linked metaphorically to the contemporary, burnout is the 'contemporary condition … Burnout isn't a place to visit and come back from; it's our permanent residence.'

Despite its philosophical underpinnings, Pascal Chabot's recently translated treatise *Global Burnout* broadly overlaps with Petersen's article: 'Burnout is a disease of civilization', he intones. The pressure to work it harder, make it better, do it faster, makes us weaker. The only things that seem to be diminishing in this account of the contemporary world are the earth's resources and people's leisure time. 'Increasing', 'accelerating', 'evermounting', 'intensifying' – Chabot's adjectives tend to indicate expansion and excess (of speed, of work, of control, of power, of pressure): 'more things, more money, more interactions, more distraction.' In Chabot's account, burnout emerges as a response to a world in which there is too much of everything apart from the time and energy with which to do it.

Although she cites a psychoanalyst who works on 'burnout', Petersen's BuzzFeed piece doesn't outline the term's emergence as a diagnostic category. *Global Burnout*, by contrast, begins by tracing burnout's psychiatric genealogy before excavating its literary pre-history (via a discussion of Graham Greene's 1961 novel *A Burnt Out Case*). As Chabot explains, Herbert J. Freudenberger introduced the term in the 1970s as a way of describing his own experiences as a psychiatrist working with drug addicts at a clinic where the staff were struggling to cope with the long hours and emotional toll of their work.

Although Chabot discusses the 'Maslach Burnout Inventory' test which is used to assess symptoms of burnout, he does not mention that the term is still not included in the *Diagnostic and Statistical Manual of Mental Disorders (DSM),* indicating that it remains more of an informal diagnosis for a wide range of experiences than an official nosological category.

Despite conceding that burnout is a concept 'suffused with considerable ambiguity', Chabot insists that the forms of fatigue associated with it are different from those associated with physical exertion, insomnia, intellectual exhaustion or working long hours. Burnout is also distinct from tiredness or exhaustion. He identifies acedia, a form of mental torpor originally observed among medieval monks, as burnout's antecedent. Acedia was most prevalent among the more fervently religious monks but ultimately resulted in a loss of faith: 'Like the monk who can no longer bear to pray to a God who no longer comforts him, the worker throws up her hands, often in response to a lack of recognition … She has lost faith in herself, but above all, she has lost faith in a system that seems to treat her with contempt.' Tiredness begets disillusionment and what begins as individual discontentment with a specific work environment in which the afflicted person had tried to excel, extends to become a critique the burnt out person eventually levels at society as a whole.

At some points in the book Chabot suggests burnout might afflict any worker striving to adapt to the ever-mounting and impossible-to-meet demands of the neoliberal workplace. While he certainly doesn't think that 'pushing people to their limits in order to extract the maximum profit from their efforts' is good, and even explicitly defines burnout as a symptom of capitalism, these observations tend to be relayed in the smooth sanguine tone of neutral empirical description with none of the jagged anger a more politically engaged account might convey. The discussions of workplace flexibility and precarity here are uncontroversial but more platitudinous than polemical, flitting indiscriminately between classes without grounding the discussion in research pertaining to conditions in specific professions.

After criticising the rigid and segmented schedules imposed on workers, Chabot opines that 'luxuriating in time is one of our greatest occsions of intimacy with ourselves and the world'; but here he seems to imply that people's inability to do so is as much the fault of technology as it is of capitalism. Indeed, the solutions offered by *Global Burnout* occasionally sound like lines from a self-help book: 'yoga, sport, or relaxation – can be highly beneficial', we are advised in a discussion of the Aristotelian notion of 'intuitive equilibrium' and the 'happy medium'. Later he muses phlegmatically that in 'a complex world where we often feel as anonymous as water droplets in a vast ocean, our quest for concrete signs of recognition is altogether understandable', almost echoing the kinds of phrases that might be found on the packaging of scented candles. Lighting a scented candle might be more relaxing than not doing so but it's not going to lead to a transformation in someone's working conditions. Despite identifying material conditions under which people are unable to work less or take it easy, and explicitly stating that people experiencing burnout often castigate themselves for their personal shortcomings rather than blaming the 'social conditions of their work environments', Chabot nonetheless tends to emphasise restoring (individual) balance and harmony rather than changing the (shared) conditions that make people feel burnt out in the first place.

Although he talks about the demands associated with new technologies and sometimes discusses examples of burnout among people in managerial positions in corporate offices, the main victims of burnout in this account are not people who sit all day operating shiny new machines. They are care workers. Burnout may be a new category which Chabot seems to think belongs to the contemporary world, but the kinds of work that he claims produces it are old. Critics of Nick Srnicek and Alex Williams's *Inventing the Future: Postcapitalism and a World Without Work* were quick to point out that the field of social reproduction is one of the most resistant to automation, but that does not seem to be Chabrol's main concern. Despite the book's generalising claims about workplace exhaustion, Chabot explains that burnout originated as a term relating to overworked caregivers and still disproportionately affects people in 'caring professions', whose symptoms sometimes end up reflecting those of the people for whom they are trying to care:

'they were over-worked, perhaps overly idealistic, and certainly over-committed' but eventually became cynical and detached. As in his discussions of other forms of work, Chabot is not very specific about care work. It is unclear, for example, if his analysis includes unwaged work; he gives little consideration of the kinds of people by whom care work is disproportionately performed; he is vague about the relationship between the affective demands of these roles and wage labour; and he does not engage with the large existing feminist literature on these subjects, from social reproduction theory to theories of emotional labour. Instead, Chabot's discussion of care work leads back to a more general discussion of the 'exhaustion of humanism' that emerges from a clash between two distinct but incompatible understandings of progress: 'useful' and 'subtle', with the former connected to scientific and technological progress and capitalist accumulation, the latter to individual well-being.

After considering the 'desire for recognition' at work, Chabot discusses the gendered dimension of burnout (in a separate section from his discussion of care). His main reference here is the psychologist Pascale Molinier's discussions of how working women navigate femininity. His examples are more Sheryl Sandberg than Selma James: 'The challenges [women] face range from determining the implications of stem cell research to trying to stay true to themselves while managing an all-male team.' Chabot is critical of the 'seriousness of the masculine perspective' and celebrates women for wearing bright coloured clothes (*sic*!), ascribing to them the humanist qualities of 'spirit, compassion, imagination' and 'nurturing behaviours' that 'humankind desperately needs'. In this section he does acknowledge that care work is disproportionately performed by women, but although he is quick to point out that compassion is not some innate 'feminine' attribute (almost as if the thought just occurred to him), this does not stop him from waxing lyrical about the 'biological miracle' of motherhood that 'for a woman ... changes everything'.

According to Chabot, the 'fragile human' cannot thrive within a profit-driven society so they burn out, but he consistently identifies capitalism with technological development and proposes as a solution to inequality the resurrection of historical concepts whose oppressive premises he ignores:

If this inequality persists and deepens, technological and economic interests will eventually subsume the interests of the human beings who gave rise to them. This is why a new pact is necessary to protect humanity from its own capacity for self-destruction, just as in the eighteenth century, the idea of a social contract served to defend society from endogenous risks of implosion.

He repeats this call for a renewed social contract towards the end of the book. Conceding that 'the intolerable sensations and perceptions that afflict us constitute a call for changes to our systems of production and consumption', Chabot turns not to Marx but to Hobbes. Burnout 'reflects certain unsustainable values within our society' but rather than burning anything down or considering how burnt out people might struggle to participate in conventional forms of political struggle, Chabot merely advocates 'opening our eyes to our way of life'.

Reading Chabot's account of burnout, I was struck by the assumptions it makes about excess and speed under capitalism. He pays more attention to the experiences that burn people out than he does to the experience of feeling burnt out; he is more interested in the stimulating world than the depleted subjects he claims it produces. He describes burnout as a 'mirror disorder' but is inertia really the mirror image of excess? As a counterpoint I thought of Lisa Baraitser's recent book *Enduring Time* which describes care as 'the arduous temporal practice of maintaining ongoing relations with others and the world.' Baraitser perceives that care is not only about expending energy or working too hard or too compassionately for others:

> To care is never simply a matter of labour or simply a matter of the wish to repair the world. To care is to deal in an ongoing and durational way with affective states that may include the racialized, gendered and imperially imbued ambivalence that seeps into the ways we maintain the lives of others. Care is an arduous temporal practice that entails the maintenance of relations with ourselves and others through histories of oppression that return in the present again and again.

Sometimes things are not fast. Sometimes nothing much happens. Sometimes the demands made on people by capitalism and each other are quiet and ongoing. Sometimes care also contains a violent aspect. Thinking about the temporal aspects of care thematised by Baraitser seems to provide a more promising way of understanding and ameliorating the effects of something as chronic and pervasive-seeming as 'burnout' than Chabot's proposed return to eighteenth-century notions of social contracts.

Hannah Proctor

Insurgent universality

Asad Haider, *Mistaken Identity: Race and Class in the Age of Trump* (London and New York: Verso, 2018). 144pp., £10.99 pb., 978 1 78663 376

In an editorial in the *New York Times* written ten days after the 2016 presidential election, Mark Lilla (Professor of Humanities at Columbia University) challenged the so-called 'Whitelash' thesis, arguing that the reason for Trump's victory wasn't his ability to translate economic insecurity into racism, but rather that the Democratic Party under Hillary Clinton's leadership was itself too focused on identity questions. Identity politics, Lilla argued, were more 'expressive' than 'persuasive,' and, as a consequence, never won elections but often lost them. Lilla's argument, subsequently elaborated in his 2017 book entitled *The Once and Future Liberal: After Identity Politics*, is that liberals within the Democratic Party should spend less time emphasising gender, race, ethnicity or sexual orientation – that is, what *divides* Americans – and more time emphasising the United States' great liberal-democratic institutions – that is, what Americans share *in common*.

This was apparently oblivious to the way in which Trump had actually won the election himself on the basis of a kind of White identity politics (what has been called 'identitarianism'). After all, 53% of White women voted not for the White *woman* but for the *White* ethnonationalist candidate. Nonetheless, since Lilla's op-ed and book, two other notable books have appeared on identity politics in the wake of Trump's election: *Identity*:

The Demand for Dignity and the Politics of Resentment by Francis Fukuyama (author of the once celebrated 'end of history' thesis), and *The Lies That Bind: Rethinking Identity* by the esteemed gay Ghanaian-English philosopher Kwame Anthony Appiah. The former argues that the rise of identity politics is the result of an excessive form of what the Greeks called *thymos* (θυμός) or 'spiritedness' entailing the desire for recognition; the latter shows the fuzzy or imprecise nature of the identity categories that are often taken as immutable givens or essences.

The 2016 election is also the jumping off point for Asad Haider's book, *Mistaken Identity: Race and Class in the Age of Trump*. The book is divided into six short, crisply written chapters. The first offers a genealogy of an identity politics initially theorised as central to a revolutionary transformation of a racist, patriarchal-capitalist order to its recent appropriation by the Democratic Party. Absent a structural critique of capitalism, Haider argues, identity politics ends up taking the bourgeois, heterosexual, White masculinist ideal as normative. This is followed by a chapter that poignantly shows how identity politics has not only become the ideology of the prevailing neo-liberal order, as critics such as Walter Benn Michaels and Adolph Reed Jr. have cogently argued, but also short-circuits genuine movements on the Left seeking to transform it. He provides the example of the counter-productive and occasionally comical debates amongst people of colour on the campus of UC Santa Cruz, where Haider was a graduate student, over the use of the word 'occupy' in reference to protests against the administration which had recently raised tuition fees. He also considers the much more serious political conundrum of the 'Afro-Pessimism' of Frank Wilderson that was to exercise growing influence on #BlackLivesMatter insofar as it refused to reciprocate the solidarity offered to the movement by Palestinian activists. This, I think, is the most important aspect of Haider's argument but one that he fails to develop fully enough.

The third chapter addresses the deep paradox of a tenacious attachment among young activists to the idea of race, in spite of the fact that it has been thoroughly de-mystified as possessing little or no substance in biological terms, while the following chapter is a fascinating reflection on the stand-off between Philip Roth and Amiri Baraka, as well as a reflection on what is, for Haider, the exemplary case of Rachel Dolezal. A White woman who passed for several years as African American and, indeed, played a role in her local chapter of the NAACP, Dolezal is exemplary, Haider argues, precisely because she engages in 'a peculiar introjection of white guilt.'

Chapter five seeks to understand the rise of Trump through Stuart Hall's pioneering work on authoritarian populism as well as Wendy Brown's development of Walter Benjamin's notion of 'Left-wing melancholy' – the full-scale embrace by the Left of its own marginality and failure. Finally, the last chapter develops an alternative that returns to the original spirit of the earliest statement of identity politics by articulating a case for an 'insurgent universality,' based not on an abstract concept of rights-bearers but, rather, on 'particular and concrete individuals – women, the poor, and slaves – and their political and social agency'.

Overall, this is a bracing and valuable contribution *from the Left* to the often vituperative debates swirling around identity politics. Rather than focusing, like Lilla, on the Democratic Party, however, Haider locates its origins in the earlier, pioneering work of the Black lesbian feminist Combahee River Collective. At the same time, Haider articulates a worry about the capacity of identity politics today to serve as the basis for a radical political agenda. In contrast, therefore, to Lilla's rather patronising dismissal, Haider engages in a genuinely immanent critique of identity; that is, he criticises its contemporary *practice* on the basis of its own strongest *theoretical self-understanding*.

Accordingly, Haider defines contemporary identity politics as the 'neutralisation of movements against racial oppression.' This relocates identity politics in a liberal agenda of seeking restitution for victimhood by way of a juridical discourse. Quoting Judith Butler, Haider maintains that 'what we call identity politics is produced by a state which can only allocate recognition and rights to subjects totalised by the particularity that constitutes their plaintiff status.' Contemporary identity politics, in this view, remains fatally trapped within the liberal-bourgeois institutions of the state and its laws.

While Haider's impulse to try to understand the intertwined nature of race and class is correct, it is important to emphasise the way in which race cannot in any straightforward way be understood in terms of Stuart Hall's Althusserian formulation – which Haider himself draws upon – as 'the modality in which class is lived' (the original formulation is from Hall et al.'s pioneering book *Policing the Crisis: Mugging, the State and Law and Order*, published in 1978). In contemporary identity politics, race, gender, ethnicity, sexual orientation and other identities demand recognition and affirmation, and in societies constituted, in part, by the mis-recognition or non-recognition of these identities, this is perfectly understandable and legitimate, to some extent at least. This is especially the case with 'trans' and indigenous identities that have asserted and re-asserted themselves, respectively, in recent years with particular force.

Yet proletarian identity – not unlike the condition of homelessness – cannot be understood in quite the same way. Thought in radical terms, such a form of identity is not simply an empirical sociological category but manifests a form of structural negativity that, as such, demands its own *negation*; just as people who are homeless, far from wanting their homeless condition to be recognised and affirmed, want it to be eliminated through, amongst other things, the provision of adequate housing. Capital cannot properly 'include' the proletariat on the basis of whose un-remunerated surplus labour its own expanded reproduction is premised. In other words, while other identity categories have an interest in recognition and affirmation that, arguably, can be met within capitalism, the proletariat simply cannot. The realisation of proletarian identity is, ultimately, negative rather than affirmative; proletarian 'identity,' unlike most other identities, has an interest in *its own self-dissolution along with that of class society as a whole*.

I would suggest that rather than an individualistic, rights-based model, as Haider argues in invoking Butler, identity politics is based on a particular reified account of experience. Identity politics entails a *proprietary* relation to a reified form of experience – unchanging, fixed, substantive – that can be understood as the possession or property of a given group that is, paradoxically, constituted by that very form of experience. In German the word for authenticity or *Eigentlichkeit* is closely associated with the word for property or *Eigentum*. Identity politics often makes a claim to authenticity and such claims are closely linked to questions of ownership rights. This is why identity politics is often embroiled in questions of 'cultural appropriation.' One suspects that, despite his telling anecdotes, it is far from clear that Haider fully appreciates precisely how deleterious and fractious identity politics can be for Left politics, a glimpse of which we saw in the treatment of the Sanders campaign by Hillary Clinton and her backers at the Democratic National Committee.

Such a proprietary relation to experience is especially well exemplified by Hannah Black's infamous open letter attacking White painter Dana Schutz's painting of Emmett Till, the African-American boy beaten to death by White supremacists for allegedly looking the 'wrong way' at a White woman in 1955, and entitled *Open Casket* (2016), during the Whitney Biennale in 2016. 'The painting,' the letter reiterates several times, 'must go.' Co-signed by some 47 other artists, curators and critics, it demands not only that the painting be removed from the exhibition but also that it actually be *destroyed*. The key reason for this, according to Black, is that Schutz has *no right* to the experience of Black suffering. One immediately wonders whether West German students required a 'right' to Jewish suffering to raise the question of the Holocaust and collective German guilt in the tumultuous years of 1967-77. Why Dana Schutz should be any different is far from clear.

Black's letter is instructive because it makes a truth claim about a particular representation of suffering without carefully attending to the painting's own sensuous particularity (as Zadie Smith precisely does in her response to *Open Casket* in a 2017 article in *Harper's Magazine*). The very premise of the claim confuses ontology with epistemology: that the representation was bereft of truthfulness by virtue of the fact that the race of the artist was simply wrong. The claim has the status of an *a priori* over an *a posteriori*, it is apodictic rather than based on attention to the details of the framing of its subject matter, its composition, use of colour, texture of its brush strokes, and so on. It therefore rules out in advance the possibility of a critical judgment of the work's overall success or failure. The claim, surely, is not simply that the work cannot *succeed* but that it also cannot *fail*. It ought not even be permitted to fail. It rules out in advance Samuel Beckett's claim that art works can fail and they can fail better and they can fail worse.

Artworks, as Benjamin and Adorno both suggested, are constituted by both truth and falsity, and the work of criticism is to draw out their 'truth-content' (*Wahrgehalt*). When they fail better, they fail in such a way that we can learn something from them, including, for example, the conditions of their own (im)possibility. Perhaps, at some level, *all* artworks seeking to express or represent suffering must fail in so far as such artworks remain deeply complicit with the world that produces such suffering in the first place. Surely, it is the role of art criticism to make such judgments about the nature of such failures? Yet Hannah Black moralistically rules out such criticism in advance by advocating the painting's liquidation.

This demand for the work's destruction is the logical conclusion of the radical particularism of identity politics or the idea that identity-based groups are unified by certain experiences that other groups simply have no *right* to. The relationship is one suggestive of property ownership yet a relationship also overdetermined by a sense that the loss of such property entails not just a monetary loss but an ontological one – a loss of being itself. From this perspective, claims or representations made by members of one group about another are not simply to be addressed by judgments, and, therefore, criticisms, because such claims and/or representations constitute hateful and harmful attacks on these very groups. This is also, for example, what came into play in the much-discussed case of Rebecca Tuvel's March 2017 *Hypatia* article on 'trans-racial' identities and the open letter signed by over 800 hundred academics demanding its retraction as opposed to its critical discussion.

If it is true that central to identity politics is a reified account of experience, then a much more promising approach to it, I would suggest, is be found in Frantz Fanon's dynamic understanding of experience. Given that Fanon's work, especially *Black Skin, White Masks*, is so central to identity politics in general, and to Afro-pessimism in particular, (from which in fact the main tropes of Hannah Black's letter seem to be drawn), it is unfortunate that Haider's immanent critique of identity politics remains confined to the U.S. Black radical tradition. Or to put it another way, it is unfortunate that it doesn't seek to engage in an immanent critique of Afro-pessimism's own rather one-sided appropriation of Fanon's thought. In what is surely one of the best accounts of Fanon's thought, *Fanon's Dialectic of Experience* (1997), Ghanaian philosopher Ato Sekyi-Otu argues that it is within a 'dramaturgical' structure that we must seek to understand Fanon's narrative of liberation. 'Thanks to this formal characteristic', he argues, 'Fanon's narrative can give credence to the apprehension of a historical object in its immediate mode of appearance, and yet prepare us for a comprehension of this object – that is to say, a fuller knowledge of its appearance and its conditions of intelligibility.' Attention must be paid, therefore, to the various speech acts that constitute the often contradictory dramaturgical 'stagings' of experience itself.

Through a reading of the *Wretched of the Earth* (rather than *Black Skin, White Masks*), Sekyi-Otu charts the movement of experience beyond the Manichean world constituted by the binary logic of colonialism itself, a logic sedimented in the very architecture and built environment of colonised space as brilliantly represented by Gillo Pontecorvo in *The Battle of Algiers* (1966). Once the armed struggle commences, the colonial world, characterised by an Aristotelian logic of mutual exclusivity, quickly gives way to a more properly dialectical and temporal logic of mediation in which difference between colonised and coloniser is transformed into an internal differentiation of the colonised themselves. The becoming-human of the colonised corresponds, paradoxically, with the dynamic disclosure of difference within the colonised rather than the static and reified difference constituting the Manichean world of the colony.

The immediacy of *identity* based on the supposedly

'natural' fact of race now is fundamentally altered through what Marx called, in the first volume of *Capital*, a transformation in the 'dramatis personae' into *non-identity*; that is, divisions based on social class between a nascent national bourgeoisie, on the one hand, and workers and peasants, on the other, come into view. Sekyi-Otu felicitously calls this the 'dialectical enlightenment' of the post-colonial world, one in which:

> Reason's triumph, the faculty of dialectical disclosure, is in Fanon achieved experientially through a corrosive destruction of the rigidity and simplicity to which a racialised apprehension of the world had reduced everything. Thanks to this 'bitter discovery' of exploitative relations and distributive injustice as intraracial facts, as human, all-too-human possibilities, the nascent postcolonial subject is ready for a veritable political and epistemic reorientation.

What is important to grasp is the centrality of a reified or static understanding of *experience* lying at the heart of identity politics. If contemporary identity politics can be understood as *neo-liberal*, it is because it internalises the logic of the value form at a particularly deep level. This becomes especially clear in the example of Hannah Black where we find precisely what Sekyi-Otu calls the 'rigidity and simplicity to which a racialised apprehension of the world reduced everything.' It is such a 'racialised apprehension' that grounds her demand for the destruction of an artwork.

If the work opens up a world, in Heidegger's sense, then, in demanding *work*-destruction, Black nihilistically demands *world*-destruction – the destruction of the structure of meaning and of sense which the work generates, but also the basis on which that very same work may itself be *criticised*, as exemplified by the oppositional response of Black painter Parker Bright to *Open Casket*. Such world destruction, at the same time, then, profoundly forecloses the possibility of the 'insurgent universality' that Haider champions. Indeed, it forecloses the very possibility of politics as such.

Samir Gandesha

Contemporary Agamben?

Giorgio Agamben, *What Is Philosophy?*, trans. Lorenzo Chiesa (Stanford: Stanford University Press, 2018). 114 pp., $55.00 hb., $18.95 pb., 978 1 50360 220 5 hb., 978 1 50360 221 2 pb.

Giorgio Agamben, *Taste*, trans. Cooper Francis (London and New York: Seagull Books, 2017). 90 pp., £14.99 hb., 978 0 85742 436 5

In seminars with Giorgio Agamben, he frequently expressed his admiration for Walter Benjamin's notion of 'citing without quotation marks'. Although part of a long-standing rhetorical and academic tradition, it is worth bearing this tactic in mind when we read the short preface that Agamben has composed for the five essays collected under the title *What Is Philosophy?* – the title itself already an act of 'citing without quotation marks', insofar as this titular inquiry is indelibly associated with Gilles Deleuze and Félix Guattari's final collaboration. In his preface, Agamben writes that these five texts 'contain an idea of philosophy' that becomes evident 'only to those who read them in a spirit of friendship'. It is this 'spirit of friendship' that is meant to guide our reading. And it demands we encounter what Agamben writes as much as what he alludes to by 'citing without quotation marks'.

What troubles me about this act of reading is that Agamben's primary focus in these texts is what he calls 'the original metaphysical problem of the fracture between the visible and the invisible, or appearance and being.' There is nothing unique in identifying this fracture or even situating it as 'the metaphysical problem' of Western philosophy. But Agamben argues as if this originary fracture – traversing as it does aesthetics, political theory and ethics – is exposed and reckoned with only through his own singular, undeniably erudite, form of philological close reading, which engages only with the founders of 'our' philosophical discourse itself: Plato, Aristotle, etc. Such a focus renders the work of nearly all of Agamben's philosophical peers silent. For instance, he simply ignores Alain Badiou's reconceptualisation of Platonic love in relation to his 'inaesthetics', or Jacques

Rancière's attempt to deal with this fracture through the 'distribution of the sensible'. (To be completely fair, Agamben does acknowledge and then dismiss – in all of a single sentence – Badiou's thesis that 'mathematics is ontology' as yet another misreading of what Plato meant as ontology.) Indeed, the list of contemporary philosophers whose work Agamben engages only through an act of 'citing without quotation marks' is lengthy; even his recourse to a 'spirit of friendship' alludes to Jacques Derrida's *The Politics of Friendship*. This is curious because what Agamben discusses touches so directly on the work of other contemporary philosophers. So much so that it is as if one must keep a virtual set of arguments and positions articulated by these others present as one engages with what Agamben himself has written.

Perhaps Agamben's penchant for 'citing without quotation marks' is overindulged in these shorter texts? Perhaps it asks too much of a reader to engage these texts in such a 'spirit of friendship'? No doubt these issues are exacerbated by translators and publishers desiring to capitalise on Agamben's name by putting out old essays as if they are new publications. This is certainly the case with *Taste*, which was originally written in 1979, as well as the first essay '*Experimentum Vocis*' in *What Is Philosophy?*, which was originally conceived in the 1980s. Yet, even allowing for the belated appearance of these texts in English does not remove the problem created by Agamben's disregard of work by his contemporaries when redressing aesthetics and language. This is especially so when, as he claims, these issues 'extend to all the epistemological statutes of Western culture'. If such is the case, why not create a dialogue with one's 'friends' and not merely ask for an act of reading that would allow us 'to see his limits', a phrase he learned from Martin Heidegger at Le Thor? Of course, even Heidegger himself is rarely cited by Agamben because, as Walter Benjamin said of theology in his own work: 'the blotting pad is related to ink. It is saturated with it. Were one to go by the blotter, however, nothing of what is written would remain.'

I point this out not only because Agamben's philosophy relies so indelibly on Heidegger's 'way to language' and on the manner in which being as such always recedes, preserving itself, but because we must be attentive to the limitations of Agamben's position regarding what philosophy *is*. His argument that philosophy has no unique domain, but takes places across a variety of disciplines and discourses, is far from a revelation at this point. But his insistence that poetry and philosophy are privileged in relation to the ontological category of the 'sayable', the voice that defines the originary limits of ontology, must be closely examined. In the centrepiece of *What Is Philosophy?*, an essay entitled 'On the Sayable and the Idea', Agamben posits:

> It is not the unsayable but the sayable that constitutes the problem philosophy must at each turn confront again. The unsayable is in fact nothing else than a presupposition of language. As soon as there is language, the named thing is presupposed as the non-linguistic or the unrelated with which language has established its relation. This presupposing power is so strong that we imagine the non-linguistic as something unsayable and unrelated, which we somehow try to grasp as such, without realising that in this way we are simply trying to grasp the shadow of language ... I shall try to show that ... the sayable is a non-linguistic but genuinely ontological category. The elimination of the unsayable in language coincides with the exhibition of the sayable as a philosophical task... The truth that is expressed in language – and given that we do not have other ways of expressing it, the truth that is at stake for us as speaking humans – is neither a real fact not an exclusively mental entity, nor a 'world of meanings'; rather, it is an idea, something purely sayable, that radically neutralises the sterile oppositions mental/real, existent/nonexistent, signifier/signified. This – and nothing else – is the object of philosophy and thought.

As we can see from this definitive closing line, Agamben's conclusion is one that divides all of Western philosophy into how each iteration of it deals with language as such, which is for him inconceivable without privileging the human voice. 'Just as the natural life of man is included in politics through its very exclusion in the form of bare life', he writes, 'so human language (which, after all, according to Aristotle, founds the political community) takes place through an exclusion-inclusion of the "bare voice" in the *logos*.' This position motivates him to stage a brief critique of Derridean deconstruction ('founded on an insufficient reading of Aristotle') and Deleuze and vitalism ('the decisive element is clearly not life, but language'), among others. These critiques are not elaborated through any close reading of Derrida or Deleuze, however, but exist precisely as these pithy, dismissive one-liners.

Agamben's philosophy of language centres on

the being-in-language-of-the-non-linguistic, which he terms the *experimentum linguae*, an experience of humanity's opening to language as such. It is for this reason that Agamben hyphenates *onto-logy*, which, for him, signifies the essential link between human being (*onto-*) and language as such (*logos*, speech, reason). He arrives at this position, philosophically, through a rigorous reading of Plato's *Seventh Letter* and through Émile Benveniste's work on linguistics. These works on language and ontology allow Agamben to conclude that 'the semiotic and semantic in language represent two closed worlds between which there is no passage, so there is a hiatus between knowledge of the Other and knowledge of the subject that cannot clearly be bridged.' It is the task of philosophy to allow us to dwell within this 'hiatus', that is, between the semantic and the semiotic, knowledge and aesthetic pleasure. What is at stake politically in the concept of *experimentum linguae* is articulated best in his earlier text *The Coming Community*: 'the era in which we live is also that in which for the first time it is possible for humans to experience their own linguistic being – not this or that content of language, but language itself ... the very fact that one speaks. Contemporary politics is this devastating *experimentum linguae*'. For Agamben, an experience of our very linguistic being is the only potentiality left to us.

Of course, the concept of potentiality is central to Agamben's thought. Drawing on Aristotle's distinction between potentiality and actuality, *dynamis* and *energeia*, he defines potentiality as 'not simply the potential to do this or that but potential to not-do, potentiality not to pass into actuality' (*Potentialities*). In *The Man Without Content* – his definitive statement about aesthetics – Agamben titles a chapter 'Privation Is Like a Face', a phrase from Aristotle's discussion of potentiality. He explains: 'What Aristotle wants to posit is the existence of potentiality: that there is a presence and a face of potentiality. He literally states as much in a passage in the *Physics*: "privation [*sterēsis*] is like a face, a form [*eidos*]".' What Agamben proposes here is that potentiality 'creates its own ontology' by 'emancipating itself from Being and non-Being alike'; potentiality is not merely a matter of will or necessity, it is an experience of the 'hiatus' or 'threshold between Being and non-Being, between sensible and intelligible, between word and thing' which is 'not the colourless abyss of the Nothing but the luminous spiral of the possible' (*Potentialities*). Thus it is the potentiality of aesthetics (the visibility of the Idea, the *eidolon* of being itself) to demarcate this threshold and, ultimately, it is philosophy's ontological-linguistic task to teach us how to dwell within it without regret, desire or hope.

It is this threshold that Agamben investigates throughout his philosophy, especially in his texts on aesthetics, including the short book *Taste*, newly translated for Seagull Books by Cooper Francis. Along with *The Man Without Content*, *Taste* is best read alongside Agamben's essays on the art historian Aby Warburg, his regrettably under-read text on Guy Debord's films, and the short piece 'Judgment Day', which deals with Daguerre and photography. Traversing all of these texts is an argument for 'taste' as 'the problem of the "enigmatic" relation between knowledge and pleasure'. This 'between' is the significant term since Agamben rethinks the potentiality of aesthetics and philosophy in symmetrical terms so as to offer us something beyond what he argues are the missteps of semiotics, psychoanalysis and Marxism – the three fates of critical theory as such. Hence he argues:

> It is perhaps at this point that we are able to grasp the sense of the Greek project for a *philo-sophia*, for a love of knowledge and a knowledge of love, that would be neither knowledge of the signifier nor knowledge of the signified, divination nor science, neither knowledge nor pleasure. So, too, may we now grasp that the concept of taste constitutes an extreme and late incarnation of this very project. For only a knowledge that does not belong either to the subject or the Other but instead is *situated in the fracture that divides them* can claim to have truly 'saved the phenomena' in their pure appearance, without either referring them back to being and an invisible truth or abandoning them to divination as an excessive signifier [emphasis added].

This is Agamben's signature gesture: to construct a philological reading of philosophical discourse in order to reveal our amnesiac relation to the intricacies of how and why these concepts were created; a revelation that is meant to intensify our thinking in the present. The assumption is that it is always a problem of our vantage point in the present that leads to a misreading of the 'foundation' or 'origin' of Western philosophy. Ideally, it is Agamben's aim to read discourse *anamorphically* in order to reveal to us precisely what we've become blind to despite remaining right before our eyes.

Yet the tone of his writing makes one more ready to argue with than to be convinced of his argument. Are we meant to accept that the insight here is unique to his philosophy: 'the fracture of knowledge that Plato leaves as an inheritance to Western culture is, therefore, also a fracture in pleasure ... only by placing oneself upon such a foundation ... will it be possible to formulate in adequate terms the aesthetic problem of taste'? Don't we all find ourselves within this fracture as inheritors of Western metaphysics and thereby of aesthetic discourse itself? Nevertheless, the issue remains that Agamben nowhere addresses the myriad iterations of how to reconcile and/or maintain this 'fracture' that occurs throughout modern and contemporary artistic practice and aesthetic thought. By only returning to some point of origin, and then quite early variations of it (Diderot, Kant), Agamben forecloses on contemporary aesthetic philosophy as such. While insightful in laying bare the opening moves of aesthetics in relation to an ideal of knowledge, Agamben's method is conservative and originalist in that the possible solutions to the problematics he foregrounds are only to be found within the voices of those who initiated it and, subsequently, our misunderstandings of them.

This conservative aspect of Agamben's method also leads to dissatisfaction with the endgame of his philosophy: the 'fracture', 'threshold' or 'hiatus' in which he always desires to place us. While he doesn't address it fully in either *What is Philosophy?* or *Taste*, he has been quite clear elsewhere about the relationship he presupposes between images, history and knowledge as such. 'Historical experience', Agamben writes in the essay 'Difference and Repetition: On Guy Debord's Films', 'is obtained by the image, and the images themselves are charged with history'. He then asks: 'But what is the history involved? Here it must be stressed that it is not a matter of chronological history in the strict sense, but of a messianic history'. It is this concept of messianic time that Agamben appropriates from Benjamin's philosophy of history via a reading of St. Paul that defines the experience of the 'hiatus' he places us in. His essays on aesthetics are unimaginable apart from this messianic perspective. Indeed, Agamben insists that the 'original structure of the work of art' is empty without this messianic endgame wherein 'something must be completed, judged' because 'it must happen here, but in another time; it must leave chronology behind, but without entering some other world'. It is here that his attempt to reconcile Benjamin and Heidegger becomes insupportable. As the art historian Georges Didi-Huberman explains in his remarkable recent book *Survival of the Fireflies*: 'as a reader of Heidegger, Agamben seeks the horizon behind every image ... and that horizon inevitably shapes the metaphysical cosmos, the philosophical system, the juridical corpus or theological dogma'. Hence the 'kingdom's glory' that Agamben discusses in his most recent texts on Judeo-Christian themes. Didi-Huberman is absolutely correct in his claim that Agamben's reliance on the Heideggerean concept of the 'limit' – the very messianic, eschatological limit Derrida never hesitated to remind us to avoid – renders him blind to the subtleties and promise of Benjamin as a philosopher of images and induces him to present a conservative, 'hopeless' vision of contemporary experience.

It is clear that the most insightful and advanced work on aesthetic philosophy is not to be found within Agamben's work (including the forthcoming English translation of *Creation and Anarchy: The Work of Art and the Religion of Capitalism*). Yet he must remain our contemporary, if only for the fact that he remains so untimely. As Agamben puts it in his essay 'What is the Contemporary?', a contemporary is one who 'perceiving the darkness of the present, grasps a light that can never reach its destiny; he is also the one who, dividing and interpolating time, is capable of transforming it and putting it into relation with other times. He is able to "cite it" according to a necessity that does not arise in any way from his will, but from an exigency to which he cannot not respond.' Perhaps it is Agamben's tragic flaw that while giving such poetic voice to the definition of the 'contemporary', he is unable to embody that concept himself. As he imagined, he was unable to see his limit. But we can.

Jae Emerling

The minimus poems

Nathan Brown, *The Limits of Fabrication: Materials Science, Materialist Poetics* (New York: Fordham University Press, 2017). 296pp., £32.00 hb., 978 0 82327 299 0

As its starting point, Nathan Brown's excellent new book *The Limits of Fabrication* asks disarmingly simple questions: how are poems made, and what are poems made of? He takes these questions in the most literal way imaginable: as his subtitle 'Materials Science, Materialist Poetics' implies, he is interested in the nano-particles that constitute the ink of the print, the paper of the page, as well as, conversely, in nano-technology as a form of writing, which Brown shows that it manifestly is. But Brown is also able to scale up, and to work 'literally' in an even more literal manner. A bravura close reading of an Emily Dickinson poem in which Brown shows how the poem semiotically mobilises the diverse pen strokes by which its letters are formed shows just how seriously he takes the substance of the letter, or, as he puts it, the 'subgraphemic dimension of writing operating prior to signification'. Throughout, his study makes salutary use of the path-breaking work on proto-semantics notably pioneered by Steve McCaffery. The two approaches are coherent – just as materials science examines how matter is put together on the nano-scale, so Brown examines how poetry is put together on a scale smaller than the sentence, the word, or even the letter. But that coherence both gives the game away and leads Brown to his most interesting questions of all, because to liken nano-technology to proto-semantic enquiry is to operate by analogy, and therefore not materialistically at all.

Brown is well aware of this, and of its necessity. One of the book's most fascinating aspects is its understanding not only of the ideological weight that 'materialism' is often made to carry, but even more importantly, that 'materialism' itself is not empirically defined. Which is to say that matter cannot dispense with the idea. And therefore, it cannot dispense with poetry.

As Derrida definitively demonstrated, the 'letter' itself is as much an ideality as a material mark, and without this ideality on which the grapheme depends, there can be no 'subgraphemic dimension' at all. This is part of the stakes of one of Brown's most important contentions: that a 'materialist poetics' must do more than simply attend to the well-worn notion of the 'materiality of the signifier', but beyond this, must strive to address the 'manner in which the materiality of language is predicated upon the transformation of "non-language material".' 'Fabrication' in this way also becomes a form of translation, and beyond this, a fascinating means to mobilise the concept of *scale* as a powerful tool for rethinking postwar poetry.

In his Introduction, Brown puts forward three broad goals for his book: to convey to non-scientifically trained readers the importance of materials science for anyone interested in 'structure, form, and fabrication'; to trace 'a tradition of constructivist, nonorganic poetry and poetics from the mid-twentieth century to the early twenty-first century'; and to use the 'intersection of materials science and materialist poetics' to elaborate a 'twenty-first century materialism'. It is the second of these imperatives that lends its structure to the rest of the book, which features chapters based centrally on Charles Olson, Ronald Johnson and Shanxing Wang, along with another jointly examining Christian Bök and Caroline Bergvall.

These are preceded by an important theoretical chapter which establishes much of the grounds for the readings which will follow. Here Brown begins with one of the central points stressed by theorists of nano-technology: that on the nano-scale, the distinction between living and non-living, organic and inorganic, does not obtain. This allows Brown to recalibrate Heidegger's famous distinctions in *The Fundamental Concepts of Metaphysics* between stone, animal and human with relation to *Dasein*, but not along the usual lines: the question here is not what separates human from animal, but rather what partitions the 'inorganic' stone from them both. Brown shows that nanoscale materials science is fabricating materials which while certainly not 'living' are nevertheless not 'worldless' in the manner of Heidegger's stone; rather they 'challenge Heidegger's distinction between modalities of non-living and living being' by virtue of their receptivity and responsiveness to their surrounding environment. For Brown, the implications of this with regard to biopolitics, for example, is not to argue that nano-science has 'created life', but rather to question what defines 'life' as such if inorganic matter can mimic it. Combining these reflections with Jean-Luc's Nancy work on the same Heideggerian questions, Brown proposes the 'inorganic open' as a way beyond the 'biocentrism' of Agamben as well as the anthropocentrism of Heidegger.

Brown's problematisation of the organic/inorganic opposition stands him in very good stead in the subsequent two chapters on Black Mountain poetics, where he is able to significantly remap the terrain by way of his rearticulation of the dominant categories that have tended to chart it heretofore. His chapter on Charles Olson in particular should be required reading for anyone in the field, as here Brown's overlapping theoretical interests coalesce to provide outstanding results. In the bluntest of terms, Brown argues that counter to appearances Olson is a poet of the inorganic, the object and the minimal as much as and sometimes more than the maximalist 'I', which would project its verse outwards from the organic guarantee of life and the vital which is the poet's own breath. To do this he stresses Olson's own idea of 'objectism', and the ways it is informed by Whitehead's rethinking of the object as such. Olson's best readers have always wanted to pressure his too easily overlooked statements in 'Projective Verse' defining 'objectism' as getting rid of the 'lyrical interference of the individual as ego' and asserting 'man is himself an object', but few if any have done so as successfully as Brown. His argument is that rather than assert the rights of life over death (or over the strange undead non-life which Heidegger attributes to the stone), Olson proposes the task of saving the 'object from objectification' – with the object here clearly also including 'man' – by viewing it in terms of Whitehead's views on relationality. For Brown this also differentiates Olson from the Objectivists, for whom the core issues were epistemological and not ontological, as Brown argues they are for Olson. In this view, Olson is no longer primarily the poet of the 'organism, the biological body' but rather that of the 'congery of particles' that Olson mentions in 'In Cold Hell, In Thicket'.

The power of Brown's intervention here is not only theoretical; pragmatically, it opens the way for seeing what was always on display: Olson as a poet of the little, the minimal, the particular in every sense of this word; a major poet not of size and space but rather of scale. Brown is convincing in arguing that often for Olson the body too, as object, is seen in a similar light, *contra* all totalising organicisms: 'a body is a collective rather than a system, an object constituted of and among objects'. He is less so when attempting to read Olson's privileging of the breath along the same lines, arguing that breathing 'manifests the non-coincidence of the body to itself, its participation in an outside'. While this is certainly the case, Brown doesn't convince me that it operates so in Olson's own configuration, where its regulatory function seems closer to the ideological bio-normativity so often attributed to the heart beat. Indeed, inspired by Brown's own work, I would tend to read Olson's embrace in this instance of an organicism which Brown has shown to be recused elsewhere as a symptom of his otherwise materialist desire to explore the *fabrication* of meaningful language out of air – a demonstrable subcurrent running through 'Projective Verse' in many places.

But even if one concludes Olson is more a poet still straining against organicism than one who has definitively broken with it, Brown's argument for the significance of the anti-organicist aspects of Olson's thought certainly holds good in the following chapter on Ronald Johnson and Buckminster Fuller, two other major figures of Black Mountain College. Here Brown decisively intervenes in the opposition between organicist or 'open field' poetics and proceduralist ones, which has dominated work in postwar American poetry to this day. In a fascinating discussion, Brown stresses the importance of the concept of the pattern to both Fuller's thought and the nanoscience which is, in places, explicitly indebted to it, as well as the objectist objection to the pattern on the part of Olson and even more, Creeley. He then turns his attention to Ronald Johnson's *Ark*, a work heavily indebted to Fuller's structural-architectural ideas as well as to Olson. This chapter is at the heart of Brown's entire project, because by showing the ways in which Johnson (and other writers) and nano-scientists are *both* post-Fullerian in fundamental, structural ways, the conflation 'materials science, materialist poetics' finds a historical grounding that goes beyond analogy. Fuller's importance for materials science lies in his isolation of design and pattern as fundamental elements that are also scalable, and as such, 'design' emerges as the core of the 'natural', the latter no longer seen in opposition to technology. From this perspective, Brown shows, a 'nature' poem can be one that, regardless of its subject matter, 'writes the whole qua order, pattern, completion, and design'. The implications of this are quite simply that the rule-bound, architectural, constraint-based work deriving from Black Mountain must properly be seen as no less organicist than, say, the Levertovian poetics to which it is too easily opposed. Or, as Brown puts it in a summary which should significantly reorient work in the field, 'Johnson's fusion of procedural poetics with a commitment to the organic patterning of Nature demonstrates that the real divide in postwar American poetry is not between proceduralism and organic form'.

The implications of this for more recent poetry are explored in the chapter on Christian Bök and Caroline Bergvall. Starting with the importance of crystallography for materials science, Brown has an easy segue into Christian Bök's work *Crystallography*, whose toying with 'crystalline structure' on micro-levels continues the sort of enquiries employed by Johnson, and allows Brown to deploy his proto-semantic reading protocols to excellent effect. Among the most productive of Brown's readings here is his intuition that Bök, like Olson, is very much a poet of the body, but one not focussed on the body's 'facticity' as Olson is, but rather on its 'genericity' by way of the subtraction from it of the organic in favour of the formal model provided by crystal replication. Against this aridity, the superficially similar letter grids of Caroline Bergvall's *Goan Atom* work very differently. In terms of models of replication, we move from the crystal to gene-splicing, and from the subtractive to the performative. Brown suggests that Bergvall's interest in the 'objecthood' of the body is close to Olson in some ways, but they differ massively in Bergvall's queer foregrounding of questions of gender and sex, issues to which Olson was largely blind. One of the most interesting aspects of the section on Bergvall is its attention to her engagement with Hans Bellmer's surrealist dolls. For Bergvall, Bellmer's disarticulation of the female doll's body mirrors her own interest in thinking the 'unfixed' body as well, and again by way of a disarticulation, this time of language. Beyond this, with regard to Brown's larger arguments about objectism, the body and inorganicity, surrealist thought and practice is clearly a very fecund area for further extension of his questions.

Bergvall's feminism also brings explicitly political questions into play for the first time in the book, but it's not until the final chapter that we get to a consideration of what many readers (myself included) might have thought would be a central element of Brown's 'materialist poetics': historical materialism. Brown explores this in his analysis of Shanxing Wang's *Mad Science in the Imperial City*. Wang is in many ways an ideal subject for Brown: born in China, Wang took part in the Tiananmen Square protests before training as a nanoscale engineer in the US, a career he subsequently abandoned for poetry. Starting with Wang's own riff on the old saw 'Think Globally, Act Locally' – 'work nano, think cosmologic' – Brown is able to bring his recurrent concern with scale to bear on the question of global capitalism, as he explores the forms of textual mapping, charting, networking and mourning constituted by *Mad Science*.

Viewing the wildly massive scaling in Wang's slogan as a way of thinking the insertion of the individual subject and its sorrow within history, Brown deploys the Marxist concept of 'real abstraction' as a means to gather together the most important elements of Wang's book. On one level, 'abstraction' enters by way of how *Mad Science* 'attempts a mathematical formalisation of historical processes and an algebraic encoding of subjective experience'; central to Wang's writing project is quite literally to replace the traditional poetic image and its primacy with equations, formulae and diagrams. These now take on the role of the 'concrete' that lyric habitually bestows on objects and images, and Brown does a fine job of theorising this in the context of the modernist suspicion of 'abstraction' in poetry that goes back to Pound. For if Wang's work is in fact concerned with the 'reality' of the 'abstraction' that underlies all capitalist exchange, then the grounding oppositions of Imagism are already surpassed (incidentally, in his Vorticist writings Pound's deployment of the algebraic formula follows analogous logic, though Brown doesn't discuss this). For Brown, then, Wang's embracing of the abstract as itself the matter of poetry enables him to overcome the political limitations of a poetry which would privilege the 'radically particular' (or, the 'nano') at the expense of the totality (the 'cosmos'), while maintaining the former – the particularity of abstraction – itself. Thus, Wang's poetics 'is not only a materialist poetics but also a *historical* materialist poetics because rather than privileging the concrete over the abstract it concerns itself with real abstraction', itself the historically situated realm of the 'mediation between collective history and the singularity of a life'.

As the reading of Wang indicates, while Brown hardly refers to Derrida at all, one of the guiding principles of his book is deconstructive. *The Limits of Fabrication* can be read as a quite systematic deconstruction of several of the most fundamental and indeed limiting oppositions governing work on postwar poetics: concrete/abstract, but also animate/inanimate, organic/inorganic, and, following from the last, organic form/procedural or constraint-based. Brown's work here opens many promising new paths to follow. But it's also important to stress Brown's emphasis on the concept of 'limit' itself, something to which he turns in his conclusion. There, Brown harps on 'fabrication' as artifice, which means it will 'ruin' Heideggerian positings of authenticity, among others: 'My claim is that the essence of both *techne* and *poiesis* is fabrication and that the "human" is inessential, a fabrication'. This 'rigorously *materialist'* (original italics) position leads Brown to conclude on the non-contingent role of accident and error in the history of the invention of the 'new', and one of the great virtues of this book is that, in addition to its theoretical sophistication, it consistently foregrounds the pragmatic moments where texts are constituted, with differing investments in ideal finality, by authors, readers and critics. This itself is a form of materialism, and also, a form of limit. Within a book which, in all its rigour, forces us to think the 'rigorously materialist' as another fabrication itself.

Daniel Katz

Rhythm is rhythm

Janina Wellmann, *The Form of Becoming: Embryology and the Epistemology of Rhythm, 1760-1830*, trans. Kate Sturge (New York: Zone Books, 2017). 424pp., £27.00 hb., 978 1 93540 876 5

Janina Wellmann's ambitious, cross-disciplinary book, first published in German in 2010, sets out to achieve two main aims. First, it attempts to retell and reframe the emergence of a somewhat neglected discourse around rhythm, form and becoming as it appears in the history of science (and embryology specifically) from around the late eighteenth century. Second, it seeks to bring out the broader epistemological implications of this discourse as it emerges from within philosophy, literature, aesthetics and musicology. Wellman organises this project by analysing the emergence of the rhythmic episteme from three perspectives: early German romanticism (in which post-Kantian literary and philosophical critique produce a 'new epistemology of rhythm'); the emergent biological and scientific focus on life and becoming ('biological rhythms'); and the subsequently transformed observational and instructional modes of visuality ('serial iconography').

In contextualising her project, Wellmann argues that, in exploring the rhythmic episteme, her book can help us see how a new epistemology of rhythm and becoming emerged long before critical theories of becoming were employed specifically to destabilise the history of ideas by later nineteenth- and twentieth-century thinkers. So, for example, whilst the young Nietzsche may have sketched out, around 1870, a 'theory of quantitative rhythm' that sought to investigate how the human body is restructured by the rhythmical movement of music and poetry operating upon it, one of Wellman's key arguments is that rhythm thus conceived was an emergent category in the history of ideas much earlier. Other – albeit more speculative – claims to contemporary relevance are that the project may help us to contextualise more historically the radical temporalisations and spatialisations which occur in modern philosophy (epitomised by Derrida's *différance*) or the novel bodily and aesthetic demands of 'new media' also. In a book that already covers so much historical ground, however, it would no doubt be impossible to explore these contemporary derivations of becoming across philosophy and visual culture in any substantial detail. Instead, Wellmann circumvents this issue by carefully delimiting her project to a specific period: 1760 to 1830.

The Form of Becoming traces the emergence of the 'embryological and rhythmic episteme' across those domains of knowledge which became focussed on the 'temporalisation' or 'dynamisation' of observable phenomena from the second half of the eighteenth to the early nineteenth century. One of the key achievements of Wellmann's project is its tracking of the sheer amount of iconographical and conceptual attempts at representing 'rhythm as becoming' from multiple texts in different disciplines. Unsurprisingly, the acknowledgements reference a dazzling range of academic and scientific institutions, across a number of specialisms and territories. Looming over this encyclopaedic landscape, perhaps inevitably, stands Goethe, whose simultaneously literary-scientific obsession with becoming and metamorphosis could be seen to act as a model for the ambitious cross-disciplinary sweep of Wellmann's book itself.

Nonetheless, Wellmann tames a potentially sprawling project by clarifying that the intention is not to identify any single field of knowledge in which the concept of rhythm originated, and she is equally dismissive of any attempt to address 'migrations, adaptations or mutual influence' across disciplines. Rather, the methodological intent is to trace the changing meanings of the concept as they were formed in the experimental systems, research practices and technologies of observation of the period: the 'numerous theatres' attempting to capture rhythm and becoming running simultaneously. This is therefore as much a book about a certain moment in visuality and iconology as it is a history of science or ideas: 'Observation and experiment, text and image, concepts and material objects are all part of this understanding of how a concept is constituted as a category.'

The theory and practice of rhythm became a familiar issue in early twentieth-century modernist aesthetic discourses, particularly in the visual, musical and poetic realms. However its epistemological roots, Wellmann argues, actually lie in the history of science, and the development of embryology more particularly. Embryology, understood as the transformed sense of the relationship between time, rhythm and becoming, is foundational for the critical developments in time and temporality which took hold across human knowledge around 1800 - what Reinhart Koselleck calls the *Sattelzeit* period of European modernity. Wellman makes an explicit connection here by acknowledging Koselleck's studies of the transformation and secularisation of western concepts of temporality in relation to progress, history and culture. However, Wellmann wants to show here not only that rhythm as a concept has a history, but that the impact of temporalisation on the nascent scientific discourse of biological development as becoming – and most specifically embryology – created a wholly new episteme and iconography of form and rhythm.

This striving for the 'form of becoming' manifested itself most immediately in new scientific conceptions of life. Wellmann cites the Haller-Wolf debate of the 1760s, the roots of modern embryology. Swiss naturalist Albrecht von Haller observed that organic life emerges out of pre-formed germ cells, whilst the German physician Caspar Friedrich Wolff argued, based on observation and – more importantly – schematic and visual interpretation, that development is a process of the gradual emergence of forms. Whilst, ultimately, the Wolffian theory of epigenesis dominated and survives in embryological discourse to this day, what is as important here is the employment of new modes of visual interpretation at a certain moment and the novel understanding of rhythm and temporalisation that embryology demanded. The becoming of form emerges as a scientific issue at the level of observation, and so is as much about iconography and visual interpretation as it is about concepts.

STAR WITH AURORA.

To this end, Wellman describes in detail some fascinating observational experiments, revealing their formal particularities and the ways in which each attempt to visualise becoming entailed a transformation of the problem as it moved between concept and image. So, we range from incubated chick eggs (the urtext of embryology) via the knotting of a fishing net (captured for the *Encyclopédie*) to the various choreographies of dancing, fencing and military manoeuvres. These alone make the book fascinating, revealing how seriality and transformation were a formal issue outside of and prior to the emergence of a modernist visual culture.

For Wellman, however, the scientific transformations of the iconography of temporality and becoming manifest themselves in other visual discourses after 1800 largely unconsciously and intermittently. Furthermore, explicit reflection on the development and nature of these connections has been neglected. This is in stark contrast with the plethora of early to mid-modernist cultural discourses around rhythm, which tend to frame it in terms of avant-garde aesthetic reorientations (art nouveau, expressionism, dada, Bauhaus experimentalism) or, sociologically, as the specific articulation of a cultural moment (where for example rhythm signifies a historical response to the demand for 'vitality, order and unity' in the Fascist worldview). Where writers have tried to focus explicitly on rhythm and its mediating role between biology and culture, such as is the case in Ludwig Klage's 1933 *On the Essence of Rhythm*, they have tended to retain a dualism between rhythm as a principle of blind 'life', on the one hand, and meter/cadence as a human act of rationality. By returning to the pre-modernist sources of rhythm as episteme, Wellmann intends to place the origins of this debate a century earlier.

For Wellmann, it is in musicology around 1800 that these theoretical reflections on rhythm become most evident, as the discipline expands into generalised concerns with meter, measure (*Takt*) and accent (*Akzentheorie*) as the keys to an aesthetics of musical form and beauty. Coupled with the physiological disposition of the human as 'rhythmic being', which both romanticism and musicology inherit from contemporary science, a more philosophically systematic account of nature and becoming is revealed. As such, what was new in 1800 was not the musical concept of rhythm itself, but that the changed 'vision of rhythm in both music theory and biology had – unconsciously – reordered knowledge in each domain. Rhythm became understood as the underlying structure of flowing movement, 'development' in both aesthetic and organic meanings of the term. This is important not least because this places rhythm back into its truly multi-disciplinary origins: the category of rhythm for Wellmann indicates a lost unity of cultural and natural thought, which existed before nineteenth-century academic and scientific specialisation split them into separate and distinct spheres.

It will be no surprise to anyone familiar with the all-encompassing cross-disciplinarity of German romanticism that thinkers such as Hölderlin, Schelling, Novalis and the Schlegel brothers play such a crucial role in this story. Romantic conceptions of poetic form and becoming, and their crucial role in re-unifying imagination and understanding, place issues of language, and rhythm and meter, at the centre of poetic theory. It was Klopstock, with his long-term involvement in developing a theory of 'versification' and 'co-expression' of motion and syllables, who paved the way. Poetry might be raised to a form of knowledge in itself, or may even become, in Hölderlin's phrase, a 'better philosophy', and it is the latter who will attempt to marry language as acoustic event with the 'calculable laws' of poetic theory. Issues of literary rhythm, most notably the 'counter-rhythmic rupture' or the caesura, are its most famous moments for Wellmann. Hölderlin's conception of tonal/rhythmic alternation and temporal interruption places him at the heart of contemporary physiological debates on the alternation of matter, wherein the continuing oscillation of organic matter between solid and liquid states is seen as the definitive quality of organic existence itself. The physiology of the body is constituted by transitional matter, ordered according to particular rules. It is the search for these rules of development and transformation which unite romanticism and science at this time, the search for a teleological principle or drive behind 'becoming' itself, which will motivate later contributions to romanticism such as those of Novalis. Wellmann focuses upon August Wilhelm Schlegel's historical exposition of Urlanguage and shows how its emergence from the corporeality of the human being (in his 1795 *Letters on poetry, poetic meter and language*) speculatively extend romantic principles into cultural history itself. In his later Jena lectures on the history of poetic form, art history thus becomes natural and biological history, centred around the understanding of 'humanness' as rhythmical organisation and expression.

With Schelling, the claim became even stronger: rhythm, reconceived systematically via language, philosophy of nature and theories of artistic form, opens up a path to the absolute itself. Music is the art form of the 'informing [*Einbildung*] of unity into multiplicity' as it brings together individual tones and the plurality of their sequences and permutations. Rhythm – which Schelling did not conceive of as a property specific to musical representation alone – is primal to nature and the universe itself, 'pure movement, separated from the object' making visible the original identity of the absolute. Wellmann briefly describes how Schelling's Naturphilosophie fulfils this philosophical task. However, she ultimately stops short of expounding the fuller epistemological and critical implications of this development in the history of ideas. There is, for example, only a passing reference to how Hegel's subsequent *Phenomenology of Spirit* 'overshadowed' Schelling's work at this point.

Perhaps inevitably for such a wide-ranging project, the philosophical considerations are often handled briefly, and, read from a contemporary perspective, may beg more questions than they can possibly answer. The reflections on the inheritance of German romanticism, for example, stop short of any detailed discussion of dialectical philosophy, or any prolonged consideration of how this new episteme may actually have been picked up by other radical or scientifically-minded philosophies of temporality from the mid twentieth century onwards. Overall, one should treat this fascinating project as a philosophically-cognisant and visually-literate history of ideas rather than a work of philosophy per se. It will be up to others to capitalise on its historical foundations, particularly the multidisciplinary connections it makes and the close visual analysis it offers of early iconographical experiments in capturing becoming.

Nick Lambrianou

Kojève's death

Jeff Love, *The Black Circle: A Life of Alexandre Kojève* (New York: Columbia University Press, 2018). 376pp, £30.00 hb., 978 0 23118 656 8

In the notebooks Alexandre Kojève wrote on his way to Germany, he sketched a structure of all relevant fields of knowledge, with each field labelled 'bolshevism in …': 'politics', 'religion', and so on. This is a particularly interesting series of notes for Kojève to have written, given that he was himself heading from Soviet Russia to Germany to pursue his intellectual path. Evidently Kojève attributed a central importance to the revolutionary events in Russia. Yet, it is difficult to ascertain from this outline whether he saw bolshevism as particularly relevant to his own intellectual development as someone of Russian origin, or took bolshevism as a phenomenon of world-historical significance, or whether, indeed, he had totally different aims. The inscrutability of Kojève's relationship to Lenin's leadership certainly seems apparent in the fact that he was not able to identify in his notebooks a theorist for 'bolshevism in politics'. (It seems that Kojève did not intend to take up that role for himself, since the last entry in his scheme was 'bolshevism in philosophy = me'.)

Later in life, Kojève declared himself to have already been a convinced revolutionary by the time he left Russia. Yet, while it is clear that Russia played a central role in the early Kojève's stance towards his own time, it remains difficult to discern his specific position towards the revolution. It is particularly surprising, then, that most of the secondary literature on Kojève's work has paid little if any attention to his Russian context, especially given his later propensity to refer to himself, according to Raymond Aron, as a 'Stalinist of strict observance'. Similarly, little attention has been paid either to his upbringing in Russia prior to the revolution, nor to his regular contacts with some prominent figures in the Russian diaspora. Jeff Love's new book *The Black Circle: A Life of Alexandre Kojève* is welcome, then, in so far as it promises to begin the work of engaging with a key aspect of Kojève's Russian background and influences, namely his interest in Russian literature and theology. While this limited scope has its drawbacks, there is little doubt that several of the figures to which Love refers possessed a considerable importance for Kojève. However, the Russian context of *The Black Circle* is not as clear-cut as one might assume. As such, Love's book also promises to become a controversial one.

The subtitle of the book is *A life of Alexandre Kojève*, but, in fact, there is little discussion of Kojève's own lifetime. (Marco Filoni has already provided what is likely to remain, due to the reduced availability of sources, Kojève's definitive intellectual biography). Indeed, even Love's discussion of Kojève's theoretical life devotes far more attention to death and suicide than it does to any notion of life. The main title of the book is taken from a painting by Malevich that, as far as we know, Kojève never laid eyes on. As we shall see, this is the most telling aspect of Love's narrative: that it unfolds outside of Kojève's own gaze.

Despite this, the book is organised as if Kojève's Russian context was at its centre: it is divided into three sections, the first of which is entitled 'Russian Contexts', with the following two entitled 'The Hegel Lectures' and 'The Later Writings', respectively. The last two sections are followed by an epilogue called 'The Grand inquisitor', alluding to Dostoevsky. While this arrangement suggests some sort of dialectical structure, the sections remain significantly unconnected. In fact, the book presents two disjointed narratives: the first advances Love's reading of some Russian authors (Dostoevsky, Soloviev and Fedorov), while the second focuses on Kojève's works, beginning with a presentation of his early works, which are mostly reduced to the seminar on Hegel, followed by his 'later works', a category under which Love subsumes anything that Kojève wrote after the Hegel seminar. Yet, from the early, more draft-like writings to the later, more systematic ones, Love fails to recognise any change across Kojève's oeuvre. Instead, Love argues, the later writings are nothing but a 'painstaking development' of the earlier work.

Kojève's path towards philosophy was significantly influenced by his early formal education. Like most other intellectuals educated in imperial Russia, no explicit engagement with philosophy was provided, and it was through Russian literature, particularly Dostoevsky, that philosophical ideas were first presented. (Levinas recounted, for example, that this was the case for his education too). There is little doubt that Dostoevsky's influence on Kojève was paramount. However, this is never properly explored in *The Black Circle*; instead, there are mere extrapolations of ideal types taken from Dostoevsky's books – for example, the tension between theory and practice in the man from the underground, or the relation between suicide and theory in Kirillov - that are later associated with Kojève. No reference is made to Dostoevsky's legacy or the various interpretations of his work. Kojève's own references to the novelist are equally ignored. Love merely acknowledges in two footnotes that Kojève's biographers – Marco Filoni and Dominique Auffret – have already established the relevance of Dostoevsky for Kojève's work.

Love's analysis of Vladimir Soloviev, on whom Kojève wrote his thesis and published a few articles, is undertaken in a similar manner. Love presents Soloviev's conception of Sophia and the Godman, but there is no discussion of Kojève's own writings on Soloviev. In addition, the context in which Kojève wrote and published on Soloviev is totally ignored. It is irrelevant for Love that the discussion of Soloviev's Sophia was of central importance for the Russian diaspora in Paris, including Lossky, Berdyaev and Bulgakov, with which Kojève is known to have been in contact when he published his two French articles on Soloviev. Similarly, in discussing Fedorov, the last Russian reference in his book, Love offers no explanation for his influence on Kojève, and his inclusion seems to merely advance one further ideal type, namely, the removal of death from human life and the overcoming of the dependence on biology. Certainly Kojève dwells extensively on death, but the inclusion of Fedorov is only justified once the Russian context has been reduced to a debate about death. What at first sight may seem mere methodological inconsistencies in *The Black Circle* later become the basis for Love's arguments. The ideal types provide the foundations for the narrative under which Kojève is read, and Kojève's dialogues and more layered positions are repeatedly set aside in order to restate the centrality of Love's own concerns.

Love's interpretation of Kojève's own work is slightly different. Here he does break some new ground. Unlike the majority of Kojève's twentieth-century readers, Love does not restrict his attention to the Hegel seminar, dedicating some consideration to the *Outline of a Phenomenology of Right*, as well as to the books Kojève wrote during his work as a French bureaucrat. Even when Love's analysis turns to the Hegel seminar, he draws out some of the crucial steps that are usually overlooked or ignored, particularly in the Anglophone world, where the book that resulted from the seminar was only partially translated, and where the debate with Leo Strauss has guided most interpretations. Here Love sheds light on Kojève's approach to death and focuses his interpretation through Kojève's notion of Wisdom as the basis for an overcoming of the distance between theory and practice.

(This section of the Hegel lectures is available in the English translation, but the influence of Soloviev's Sophia, as well as its importance for the debate concerning the end of history, make it more relevant than has previously been recognised.) This is no small feat in the interpretation of an author who is so often remembered only for his presentation of Hegel's 'master-slave dialectic' and the end of history thesis. No doubt the increased availability of many of Kojève's previously unpublished texts has made this shift of emphasis easier, but realising the promise of these texts is only slowly gaining pace. The problem is, however, that Love does not perform this shift in order to provide any in-depth, philological or conceptual analysis of Kojève's proposals. Instead, Love redirects the attention to these other elements in order to construct a new, overarching narrative about Kojève's works, in which Kojève is presented as the introducer of an as-yet-unexamined criticism of the modern, free, historical individual.

According to Love, Kojève's criticism of individualism was the starting point of his reading of Hegel. The centrality of death in Kojève's reading of the master-slave dialectic would here be the most radical critique of individualism. That is, if the individual is to be perceived as totally free, it must be equally free from death. Love engages elsewhere with other elements of Kojève's criticism of individualism, but they all end up returning to death, as he reduces every action other than suicide to a form of animal self-preservation. In fact, the last paragraph of *The Black Circle* before the epilogue presents Kojève as an open apologist of suicide. From this perspective, Kojève's focus on the master-slave dialectic should be perceived not so much as a philosophical engagement with Hegel, but as the starting point from which to narrate the history of the abandonment of human subservience to preservation. Assuming that Kojève is able to overcome this submission to the power of death, the human form that is left is no longer a self-asserting being that takes its conservation as its ultimate goal. Yet the main problem with Love's analysis is that once he establishes the relation to death as that element which separates human from animal, he forces Kojève into the schema of ideal types he presented in the section on the Russian context. According to this point of view, Kojève would either have to defend a Fedorovian overcoming of the biological determinants of human life (i.e. achieving eternal life), or a Dostoevskian/Kirillovian refusal of the subjection to biological death (i.e. suicide).

This criticism of individualism that is attributed to Kojève would simultaneously avoid the pitfalls of liberal individualism and communist collectivism. But, while it is relevant to recognise this contribution of Kojève, one can find plenty of other parallel projects in the French culture of the time, from Georges Bataille's *Acéphale* to Emmanuel Mounier's personalism. Love neither relates Kojève to the pervasive criticisms of liberal individualism during the period, nor does he delineate those ideologies that Kojève would be opposing. Even without following a historicist path, it would be relevant to inquire as to how Kojève followed such a course without falling into the fascist trap that became so dominant in the interwar period. However, not even in Love's presentation of Kojève's work as an open polemic against Heidegger is there any reference to such debates.

Love is correct in stating that several of Kojève's works stand as a direct response to Heidegger. In 1931, Kojève wrote a book on atheism (recently translated into English by Love himself) whose terms are clearly in dialogue with Heidegger's *Being and Time*, and Kojève spent the rest of the 1930s writing book reviews that presented Heideggerian phenomenology as the most promising branch of contemporary German philosophy. It is true that in the introduction to his 'Introduction to the System of Knowledge', Kojève says that Heidegger took a wrong turn, but he still acknowledges the influence of the 'ex-Heidegger'. Most importantly, the appendix to Kojève's seminar on death – to which Love rightly devotes considerable attention (but over-biologising it and therefore missing Kojève's point) – is a clear dialogue with Heidegger.

The briefest way to indicate how Love misses Kojève's point on death – by associating it with a need to commit suicide – is to look at Kojève's analysis of Kandinsky's work; a text that Love does not analyse. In Kojève's approach to Kandinsky's 'concrete art', as he called it, Kojève claimed that it was the first to fully overcome the attempt to transcribe the given into art. This would eliminate the unavoidable shortcoming of an art that would try to be wholly faithful to what it represents, abstracting from what constitutes it: its life. Only once art is assumed to be this death, as the removal of life from the given, can art become fully concrete and produce artworks that retain their full value only in and through the artwork, therefore embracing an attributelessness through abandoning the given as its object. The main argument of *The Black Circle* remains at the abstract level (i.e. biology), without stepping into the concrete (i.e. discourse). As a result, the contradictions that Love explores in Kojève's work miss their target. To focus on the actual contradictions in Kojève's texts would require, not Love's abstractions, but a concrete presentation of Kojève's ideas.

Unlike Kojève's own book reviews, I will not finish this one by arguing that Love's book should not be read. Instead, I will conclude by cautioning the reader not to expect to find in Love a dialogue with either Kojève or the history of Russian or twentieth-century thought, but rather a contentious use of Kojève to construct a contemporary argument against individualism. To properly engage the latter would require a much more refined reading than I have provided here, showing how it is current political debates that ultimately inform *The Black Circle*'s account of Kojève.

Jorge Varela

How can a word be bad?

David Sosa (ed.) *Bad Words: Philosophical Perspectives on Slurs* (Oxford: Oxford University Press, 2018). 256pp., $60 hb., 978 01 98758 655.

'Slurs' - understood here to be particular words designed by convention to derogate targeted individuals or groups - are a puzzling category of speech, which raise a variety of philosophical questions pertaining to their mechanics, meaning, use and moral/political effects. They constitute a particular sort of speech act – slurring words *do something*, namely, harm individuals or groups in particular ways. David Sosa's collection, *Bad Words*, brings together leading voices in the philosophy of language in an effort to begin to solve some important puzzles: in particular, the question 'How can a word be *bad*?' (and consequently, 'How can slurs be *bad words*?').

The first chapter by Luvell Anderson, 'Calling, Addressing, and Appropriation', offers an account of the difference between Black and non-Black uses of 'the N-word', and specifically, how it can be the case that Black uses of the word can be non-derogatory in some instances. Dominant understandings of slurs, Anderson contends, are unable to account for the non-derogatory use, and why it is restricted to certain linguistic users (i.e., why it can only be non-derogatory when uttered by certain people). With the important caveat that acceptance of in-group uses of 'the N-word' is far from universal amongst Black people, it is nevertheless the case that there are members of the Black community who see the term as, in some contexts, an empowering expression of camaraderie, relatively autonomous from White misuse. After surveying three possible answers to this puzzle, and identifying shortcomings of each, Anderson draws on the concepts of *speech communities* and *communities of practice* to develop a distinction between *calling* and *addressing*, which he contends has the explanatory power to make sense of the specific illocutionary act undertaken by in-group members, and which allows for neutral or even endearing uses of the term.

Though Anderson restricts his analysis to an explanation of only one slur (and the appropriate contexts for its non-derogatory use), his argument has the potential for broader application than this one particular case. For example, his theory might be adaptable to cover in-group uses of other slurs, including, perhaps, non-derogatory uses of 'queer', 'butch', 'faggot' or 'dyke' among members of the LGBTQ+ community. To *address* a fellow in-group member as a 'dyke' might carry the exact opposite valence as when an out-group member *calls* that same person a 'dyke', where the former has a potentially positive (but at least neutral) connotation and the latter likely has a negative one. Overall, Anderson makes a compelling case that one must have the proper standing to perform certain illocutionary acts (i.e., must be part of the relevant *community of practice*), which has additional potential applications not taken up here.

Elisabeth Camp, in her 'Dual Act Analysis of Slurs', contends that the use of a slur effectively performs two separate speech acts, which serve two distinct but co-ordinated communicative roles: a truth-conditional *predication* of group membership and an *endorsement* of a derogating perspective of that group. Against the assumption that the predication of group membership is the primary function of slurs, and the endorsement of the derogating perspective is merely supplementary or secondary, Camp argues that the degree of centrality of either is contextually variable. In other words, slurs involve two distinct speech acts, and the prevalence of either depends heavily on contextual facts – we should not assume that one (i.e., predication of group membership) is always primary.

Kent Bach similarly proposes that slurs have two separate functions, though he argues against the commonly held notion that one aspect is descriptive and the other expressive (as 'hybrid expressivism' would have it). Rather, Bach defends a view which he calls 'loaded descriptivism', for which both components of the meaning of a slur can be properly understood as descriptive. Slurs, Bach argues, do indeed express contempt (or some such attitude), but that attitude is only expressed derivatively. Bach's account holds that what makes slurs unique from their neutral counterpart terms is not the attitude expressed, but rather, that slurs have *additional* descriptive content. More clearly, slurs do more than simply categorize people into a group (i.e., what the neutral counterpart term does), but also attribute some negative evaluation to the target in virtue of their membership in a particular group, and this attribution is inherently descriptive, not expressive.

In 'Slurs, Dehumanization, and the Expression of Contempt', Robin Jeshion moves the focus away from pure semantic analysis and takes up the important moral dimension of slurs – a rare contribution to the overall collection in this regard. In particular, Jeshion focuses on the power of slurs to *dehumanize* targets, and argues that any useful theory of slurs must explain *how* it is that slurs have this dehumanizing effect. Drawing on some powerful first-person testimonies, Jeshion argues that slurs have not two, but three distinct semantic functions, and furthermore, that attention to all three is the only way to have a conception of slurs that can account for their dehumanizing consequences. The three semantic components of slurs are: 1) the group-designating component, by which slurs designate the same group membership that the neutral counterpart does; 2) the expressivist component, by which the speaker expresses contempt for the target on account of the designated group membership; and 3) the identifying component, by which the speaker classifies the target in a way that aims to encapsulate *what the target is,* thereby defining the target's social identity. By way of the third semantic component of slurs, speakers regard the slur's target contemptuously on the basis of the target's *identity qua person.*

In order to flesh this out fully, Jeshion enters into terrain that the other contributors' generally try to avoid, namely, a foray into the moral psychology of contempt. She convincingly argues that this third part of the semantics of slurs (that is, the identifying component) semantically encodes one aspect of the nature of contempt, namely, that contempt involves taking those properties that are the basis for the contemptuous regard as fundamental to the target's identity as a person. Importantly, insofar as contempt is an affective attitude, it need not be consciously or explicitly recognized or endorsed by its possessor: 'One may regard someone with contempt while being blind to one's contempt'. For this reason, her analysis of slurs as encoding contempt (where that contemptuous regard might be invisible or unconscious)

goes a long way toward explaining why slurs are so socially powerful and morally insidious – the invisibility of the contempt encoded in them can drive other phenomena, such as implicit bias and microaggressions, which reflect contemptuous regard (that is, ranking another as low in worth, underserving of full respect, and so on). Furthermore, insofar as contempt inspires the 'reciprocal emotion' of shame, those who are the subject of contempt are also likely to experience shame; this sense of shame is particularly destructive, as it leads to negative self-evaluation, and ultimately social exclusion and alienation. Thus, Jeshion's account of slurs helps us to make sense of how slurs can inspire contemptuous feelings about the target by others, but also negative self-evaluations by the targets themselves. On both fronts, the deep moral significance of slurs becomes readily obvious.

Adding an analysis sensitive to social identity and historical context (in ways many of the pure semantic theories are not), Ernie Lepore and Matthew Stone highlight the particular interpretive strategies involved in interpreting slurring terms, arguing (contra common practice in philosophy and linguistics) that there is no possible *general account* of the interpretation of slur terms: their interpretation is open-ended and involves social and historical contexts. One interesting dimension of their chapter is the role of one's perspective (or, standpoint) in interpreting the tone of slurs. They note that 'powerful people must be very skeptical about their intuitions about the tone of slurs that target others. Their experience may be far removed from the factors that really matter'. This is important because, on their view, it is the tone of a slur that influences how hearers are made to think about targets. Thus, different hearers, in light of their social and epistemic standing, are likely to interpret the target of slurs differently, insofar as they are likely to interpret the tone of the slur directed at them differently.

The question of how slurs give rise to offense is taken up in Mark Richard's contribution, which does an interesting job of articulating why slurs can cause offense even when the speaker does not intend to do so (i.e., when the speaker intends to use the slur in some neutral way). Richard argues that speakers are often responsible for the negative impacts of their speech, even when they mean no harm. Speakers (often speaking publicly) cannot control in what register and as a part of what group they are taken to speak, and as such, they have a responsibility to anticipate how they can be, or likely will be, taken up. If they have reason to believe that they will be interpreted as using a term slurringly, or of being a member of a group that does so, they have reason to avoid the term (especially when there is a more neutral counterpart available to them). To fail to do so amounts to a sort of linguistic negligence. In the final entry of the collection, Laurence R. Horn examines the phenomenon of taboo avoidance, and the process of shifting meanings from taboo to acceptable (or negative to positive), arguing that this is part of the story when slurs are reclaimed to take on new, positive meanings despite histories of being taboo. His analysis offers interesting historical insight into why some words become (and cease to be) regarded as 'taboo'.

Overall, Sosa has offered an insightful overview of thought-provoking philosophical work on slurs, although it would have been good to see a better balance between more technical analyses of the semantics of slurs and moral/political analyses of the social significance of slurs. Whilst the former is critically important (and indeed, necessary if we want to understand what particular slurring words *mean* – an essential piece of understanding *how* they cause harm), too heavy a focus on semantics in a collection on slurs is limited. In the particular social and political moment in which we find ourselves, one in which 'speech' itself is at the core of particularly polarised social and political debates, more engagement is needed with *why* we ought to care about slurs (beyond their being semantically puzzling). Understanding slurs – both their semantic functioning and their social and political force – is a complex philosophical challenge, but an intensely important and worthwhile one. As Elisabeth Camp aptly puts it, 'slurs are so infuriating in part because they are so viscerally and socially potent while also being so representationally and evaluatively slippery.'

Heather Stewart

Tangled up in metaphor

Stefanie R. Fishel, *The Microbial State: Global Thriving and the Body Politic* (Minneapolis: University of Minnesota Press, 2017). 144pp. £86.00 hb., £21.00 pb., 978 1 51790 012 0 hb., 978 1 51790 013 7 pb.

Taking to task the metaphor of the body politic that she claims is central to the concept of the state in International Relations (IR), Stefanie Fishel uses posthuman and new materialist theories, along with new developments in the life sciences (in particular metagenomics), to argue that the use of this metaphor needs to learn from *real* material bodies and their relations. Bodies, she argues, are always in dense entanglements with other communities and forms of life, particularly bacteria as well as microbes of the wider biosphere. *The Microbial State* thus seeks to develop metaphors of the body politic that reflect these deep entanglements. We require, Fishel argues, different metaphors to those characteristic of an exclusionary, inside/outside, medical or war-like model in order to move instead toward a view of bodies as fully embedded in our worlds with myriad connections.

As she makes clear in her opening chapters, International Relations in particular needs a bigger vocabulary: 'new words for a world facing novel challenges'. Metaphors are the focus of extending this vocabulary in *The Microbial State*, with these seen as themselves actants in the political realm, 'forming relations, developing meanings, and shedding light on the discursive and material foundations of the political process'. Too often, we are told, the use of metaphor in political practices is one that reduces complexity and tensions down to choices 'between two supposed opposites.' This is developed, most interestingly, in subsequent chapters through an argument that such binaries can be challenged by drawing on recent work in metagenomics and in the life sciences on bacteria and viruses.

Fishel's aim is to take insights from the Human Microbial Project, the Committee on Metagenomics and the *Ending the War Metaphor* report from the Forum of Microbial Threats initiated by the Institute of Medicine, along with other research that suggests that people are indeed more than 'human', made up as they are of symbiotic relations with a whole plethora of bacteria without which we would not be able to live. The same goes for nearly all forms of animals which have symbiotic relations with bacteria in their guts (a possible exception being the wood-eating marine crustaceans known as gribbles). Fishel takes recent work on people's microbial kin further here, arguing that with the exception of policies around pathogenic viruses and bacteria, microbes rarely register as objects important to politics. She suggests that it is time they did. Her aim is then to apply these insights to the discipline of IR and beyond this to develop 'new designs for global thriving: to generate analogies for bodies to thrive in entangled communities and politics'. It is a bold aim, and one that can – in places – seem somewhat peculiar. At times the argument convinces. Nonetheless, Fishel's approach is not without its problems, particularly in terms of its principal focus on metaphors.

Throughout the twentieth century, and back in to the nineteenth, there have been wars on viruses, pathogens, bacteria and more – this is the war metaphor that is so widespread in discussions of health and which the Forum of Microbial Threats has sought to challenge. These wars have been fought in modern western homes, on toilet seats, in human bodies, in seeking to render industrial chicken or beef farm facilities biosecure, in pathogen control policies in colonial east Africa around the tsetse fly (as detailed by Clapperton Chakanetsa Mavhunga), and so on. Indeed, possible examples are profuse and are to be found in virtually all terrestrial spaces. There have been some major benefits, at least for some, to this biopolitics focused on what have come to be known as germs, pathogens and viruses. But as many environmentalists have been arguing for some time, there are also a whole raft of consequences following from these war-like attempts to wipe out viruses and germs, and an enormous industry services and creates desires for extinguishing germs and viruses as if they are simply things needing eradication. This approach to simplifying systems by removing other species can be seen in a whole series of activities such as in industrial plantation agriculture, and other examples of stripped-down ecosystems.

In recent years, all kinds of rewilding projects have been developed in various landscapes, especially in developed countries, to seek to restore species exterminated or removed by people, such as goshawks and beavers in Britain. The geographer Jamie Lorimer has recently written of how another 'rewilding' has been taking place, focused much more on bodies, specifically the rewilding of people's guts with all kinds of probiotics aimed at diversifying the microbial communities that are increasingly seen as important to people's health, whilst a small number of people seek to infect themselves with helminths or worms as a way of addressing auto-immune diseases.

New research on the gut and its flora, and its influence on immunological systems, inspires a widening of the notion of the human to include communities that co-produce bodies, and by extension, for Fishel, which serve to complicate the state-as-person metaphor relied upon in International Relations. A good deal of focus is placed here on the immune system and on recharacterising this from being seen simply as a defence against invading organisms to being seen as something that is formed by complex processes of a body living in relation to communities. For example, according to some, parasites like those aforementioned intestinal worms are often important in helping the immune system develop.

Fishel's biopolitical project seeks to extend this kind of thinking about the immune system, as something much more than just a line of defence, from the body to the State as a way of challenging the exclusionary state's presentation of outsiders as potential contaminants and threats.

> Conceptually, metagenomics implies that the human body as a communal gene pool, and its self-extending symbioses are highly adaptive and robust against environmental perturbation and dynamic self-sustaining and self-repairing processes. Metaphorical framings built from these understandings of microbial communities aid in bringing system-based understandings of complex processes to the international realm. Many problems that the state in its current form has been unable to address – warming oceans, pandemics, climate change, flows of immigrants and migrants – may be easier to address.

This is a big claim about the effects of changed metaphorical framings, though it is one that seems to be mostly evacuated of political discussion, despite the call for more of a politics based around microbes. Such lack of an actual politics is, of course, one of the most oft-repeated criticisms of new materialism. More specifically, a crucial question here would be: how exactly do metaphorical framings change, and to what degree do dominant metaphorical framings emerge out of differing political positions?

This is where Fishel's approach can seem altogether too woolly, with a tendency to evade the complex political reasons why states consistently refuse to engage with the aforementioned 'novel challenges'. New metaphorical framings may indeed help with systems-based understandings but in *The Microbial State* we mostly get metaphors and approaches taken from the sciences that are then to be applied to the social, revamped as an extended social of actor-network forms. Fishel argues that metaphorical framings are crucial in the ways stuff gets done, or we might say the way in which people and things get stuffed. But if metaphorical framings are doing work, it is only some of the work and we need more than a simple call to change these. Otherwise, Fishel's claims begin to sound rather too much like the old environmentalist refrain that all we need for radical change is to change our 'values' and ways of perceiving the world. As we have seen with environmental issues, socio-ecological metaphors and ways of framing problems can change, but often political economic goals remain much the same, based on social-ecological exploitation and short-term profit.

This book seems to emerge out of health problems that Fishel experienced, fuelling a desire to change how International Relations frames the world it seeks to understand. Once the book gets through the usual materialist justifications for such reframings, it becomes an interesting attempt to work with potential changes in our metaphors. But it always feels like it needs more politics than the call for such changes can itself provide.

Chris Wilbert

Lucid dreaming

Alfie Bown, *The Playstation Dreamworld* (Cambridge: Polity Press, 2017). 140pp., £40.00 hb., £9.99 pb., 978 1 50951 802 9 hb., 978 1 50951 803 6 pb.

We are fast approaching a point where one third of the global population will play video games on a regular basis. As such, video gaming ought to become a serious object of philosophy, not least because of its impact on players' perception. It is this that frames the central argument of Alfie Bown's *The Playstation Dreamworld*, a book that makes the 'gamer' – that most contemporary of subjects – both the analysand and actor of twenty-first century life.

The power of video games in shaping our vision is not lost on the Right, as demonstrated by Steve Bannon's courtship of gaming communities during his time as executive chair of Breitbart, nor on the US military, which since 2002 has produced *America's Army*, a free-to-download game that allows potential recruits to explore the realm of battle training alongside other online players. Indeed, the world's most belligerent fighting force seems so convinced of gaming's potential that in November 2018 they announced the formation of an official US Army e-sports team. What should cause concern here is, however, not so much the notion that soldiers might make good e-sports players, but that the US Army sees the potential for backwards compatibility: gamers can make good soldiers. This does not mean that in the battle against the military industrial complex all is lost; Bown closes the first of six chapters – divided into a 'tutorial', three 'levels' and 'bonus features' – by effectively stating that if video gaming might be the worst thing that ends up ever happening to us, it could equally turn out to be the best. However, the outcome, for Bown, depends on a psychoanalytical reading of the position of the gamer in relation to the gaming 'dreamworld'.

Employing an array of examples from the history of gaming and film – including *Angry Birds*, *Candy Crush*, *Farmville*, *The Matrix*, *Papers, Please*, *Stardew Valley*, *Westworld*, *World of Warcraft* and *Zelda* – Bown argues that the task for the gamer is to turn the inner dreamworld outwards. In this way, she or he can avoid the dreamworld of the other (corporation or government) being turned inwards on them via the gaming interface. Here, Bown makes a nod to McKenzie Wark's *Gamer Theory* (2006), arguing that the development of, for example, virtual or artificial reality means that 'it is less a question of games becoming like reality but of reality becoming like games.' Of course this notion of a reality dictated by the digital realm of video games causes alarm; and perhaps rightly so. The condensation within video gaming of just about everything negative in society – including misogyny, racial stereotyping, violence, competition, prioritisation of material gain over self-development, and so on – leads to a saturation point, which if ported back into the real world might seem to threaten a descent into barbarity. This fear grows if we consider the scope of new technology for controlling the movements of people. Artificial reality games such as *Pokemon GO* – whereby a smartphone interface superimposes digital forms over the real world – serve, Bown continues, to regulate our space as part of Google's 'interest in the organisation of desires.' *Pokemon GO* must be seen in this respect as part of the wider Google project, a side effect of its desire not just to map the world geographically, but to manipulate us within it. Subconscious desire is not so much fulfilled by technology as it is shaped by it. As such, any slide into savagery will not likely come from the street upwards but be imposed, in line with the dominant history of the twentieth century, from the top down via a media industry that is increasingly focused on the production of ever more absorbing video games. Google's founding motto was 'don't be evil'. But this has always appeared a strange form of reverse psychology; amoral at best, oddly sarcastic at worst.

Referencing Jane McGonigal's 2010 book *Reality is Broken*, Bown counters the latter's argument that games such as *World of Warcraft* act simply to engage the gamer in a kind of 'blissful productivity' by asserting that the replication of real world capitalist goals and violent competition only serve to shore up the capitalist cause. In short, if games can tell us how to behave, they can tell us how to *behave badly*, and this can make them a powerful ideological tool for the creation of specific forms of subjectivity. Drawing on Althusser's theory of 'interpellation', Bown argues that subjects are bound into particular behaviours by games. This is certainly worrying in the case of war games such as *Medal of Honor: Warfighter*, which not only replicate the experience of the 'war on terror' but involve the player in it. However, one must be careful in choosing such sensational examples. While the proximity of gaming to the military-industrial complex may be cause for concern, its plodding infiltration into everyday life is perhaps more significant in terms of the overall political influence gaming might wield.

Indeed, Bown sees an obfuscated connection between gaming and capitalist ideology working on every level. For example, the seemingly innocuous distraction of a game such as *Candy Crush* – a puzzle-matching game developed for Facebook in 2012 – actually underlines the seriousness of capital, as play reinforces the sense that something more important needs doing (i.e. 'working'). Similarly, while the farming simulator *Stardew Valley*, released for PC in 2016, encourages a conscientious and almost mundane self-sufficiency, its anti-globalism risks teetering over into a kind of *volkisch* yet entrepreneurial rejection of internationalism.

Ultimately, all roads lead to capital. Even when one thinks one is enacting some counter-cultural form of gameplay, this invariably rebounds, thereby reinforcing, Bown asserts, the central tenet of Mark Fisher's *Capitalist Realism*: that 'there is no alternative'. As familiar and unfulfilling as this point may be by now for readers of contemporary theory, it serves to remind us of the inexorable link between psychology and material conditions, a point central to Fisher's own body of writings. In lieu of any direct citation of Marx, other than a paraphrasing of Groucho in the first chapter, Fisher's mention in *The Playstation Dreamworld* is the link that drives home the fundamentally political nature of Bown's project.

From here it is argued – however cautiously – that gaming may just be able to help the Left find a way out of its impasse, for two principal reasons. The first appears entirely pragmatic: given the exponential growth of the gaming community, any change to the societal structure will have to involve gaming. The second is more nuanced and revolves around gaming's innate affinity with human psychology in so far as video games 'are not a text to be read but a dream to be dreamt.' In a dream, unlike a book or movie, the individual dreamer experiences 'desires, anxieties, passions, and affects', yet they are also generally governed, to some greater or lesser extent, by the wishes of an external actor. The truth is that games operate us more than we operate them. Whilst this appears to present a limitation to political agency, Bown argues that it also offers an opportunity to consider the gamer, and not the game, as the analysand. As such, it may be possible to coax and guide the gamer to take on personal and social responsibility, provided she or he is accompanied by a worthy analyst.

The Playstation Dreamworld undertakes no extensive analysis of gamers, though the groundwork is laid for this via a consideration of Freud's and Lacan's characterisation of the dream as the 'disguised fulfillment of a repressed, infantile *wish*', or, in the case of Lacan, a repressed *drive*. In understanding the importance of this practice of analysis, two passages in the book are crucial. First, early in 'Level 2', Bown quotes Freud from the *Censorship of Dreams*, writing that 'dreams are things which get rid of psychological stimuli disturbing to sleep, by method of hallucinatory satisfaction' – in which case we need to enquire as to what are the 'disturbing stimuli'

relative to waking experience which gaming 'gets rid of'. Several pages later Bown responds to this question by stating that videogames are the experience of someone else's dream *as one's own*. Put simply, the video game has the capacity to instill the drives of another, disguised as our own wishes. While the same could be said for dreaming, gaming uniquely makes us feel in control of our environment and is therefore particularly effective not only in instilling political viewpoints but in preempting them. As such the 'disturbing stimuli' replaced by the hallucination instilled by gaming is none other than our resistance to a given ideological program, as we make it our own.

As this point – in 'Level 2', so halfway through the book's theoretical gameplay – we are left at an impasse familiar to media theory: namely, we can identify what is happening but are without an adequate course of action to do anything about it. We know the media is run by elite forces in order to influence us, but, if we are being influenced, is it really likely that we will succeed in developing some incisive response? Yet, in this case, due to the particular configuration of gaming and psychology, Bown doesn't really need to deliver a knockout blow, for if gaming is a dreamworld and the gamer is a voyager, the analyst need only provide the gamer with the skills to recognise the dream for what it is. As Bown points out in Level 3, the awareness of the existence of a mechanism for constructing gamers' desires may be enough to lift the veil on what he terms 'the desire revolution'. In psychology, naming a mental illness goes part way to solving it. This would appear to be the strategy which *The Playstation Dreamworld* favours.

Later on in Level 3, Bown refers to the famous choice presented to Neo in *The Matrix* between a red and a blue pill. The former reveals 'the painful truth of reality', while the latter will leave him 'within the blissful ignorance of illusion'. Bown goes on to recall Slavoj Žižek's proposed third choice: a pill that would enable – to quote the Slovenian philosopher – a perception of 'the reality in illusion itself'. It is this eyes-wide-open approach that Bown recommends in analysis of the problems confronting the gamer, and wider society today. It appears less as an attempt to convince the reader of gaming's revolutionary potential than an argument for the consideration of the gaming subject as both object of reflection and serious political player.

Mike Watson

Companion for a damaged world

Jeffrey Jerome Cohen and Lowell Duckert, eds, *Veer Ecology: Companion for Environmental Thinking* (Minneapolis; London: University Of Minnesota Press, 2017). 536pp., £83.72 hb., £20.93 pb., 978 1 5179 0076 2 hb., 978 1 51790 077 9 pb.

The resource depletion, environmental degradation and global climate change that characterise our present time warrant an urgent questioning of the ways that we frame our interactions with the world. Such evidence of ecological damage demands of us the development of positive alternatives regarding how we engage with our environment. This can best be undertaken with transdisciplinary thinking that momentarily slows down and resists temptations to hastily instrumentalise knowledge. The strength of *Veer Ecology: A Companion for Environmental Thinking* is its proposition that, when we consider verbs in association with the environment, we should extend our thinking beyond describing the work that we can do to help the environment with words like *reduce, recycle, conserve* and *protect*. Instead, we might shift the focus to ourselves in an attempt to understand how our self-conceptualisation informs our environmental engagement.

To this end, the contributors to Jeffrey Jerome Cohen and Lowell Duckert's collection consider words like *environ, curl, obsolesce* and *power down*, which they commonly relate to the verb chosen as the overarching theme of the book: *veer*. This task has a preventative aspect to it, because it seeks to harness a potential to restrict causing further environmental damage by improving our relations with the world. At the same time, it can also help us learn to flourish in the world that we have inherited. Prompted by Donna Haraway's conception of companionship, whose etymological excavation of the word conjures up an image of breaking bread at a table, together

the authors encourage readers to embrace theoretical messiness in order to gain perspective, by slowing down, contemplating and playing. Moments of obscurity and lack of perspective occasionally mark the book, whose promise is significantly greater than its provision, yet the companion is nonetheless noteworthy for the type of thinking and ways of being that it instigates.

The central verb chosen to bind the work together, *veer*, is drawn from Nicholas Royle's book, *Veering: A Theory of Literature* (2011), and denotes a movement of transportation towards the unexpected. As the editors explain, to veer 'is to gather *(anthologise)* unlikely but passionate companions, and in that sudden community to hope ... [T]o veer is to enlarge, to break closed circles into spirals, to collect for a while, to dwell in revolution'. The book is consequently presented as an anthology of reflections on verbs that are intended to awaken our imaginations and cultivate a way of thinking that encourages us to 'contemplate more in order to act better'. The editors describe the multifarious possibilities brought about when we 'turn back to forge ahead'; something which is often done, throughout the book, against a literary backdrop. Vin Nardizzi's 'Environ', for example, turns back to reveal the violent history of the word *environment*, which he shows is represented as a dangerous force, used to denote matters of security and militarism, or the bestowal of a curse, in the writings of Christopher Marlowe, William Shakespeare, Sir Philip Sidney and Mary Sidney, Countess of Pembroke. This leads him to argue that, in the sixteenth century, acts of environing can persist as hazardous enterprises, as they do today, though he neglects to explicate the full contemporary resonance of this. In her essay 'Curl', Lara Farina similarly embodies an ecocritical response to the task, looking to representations of the vegetal world in the works of Ursula Le Guin in a way that would de-centre the human.

Taken together, the essays encourage new ways of thinking that can spur action where it is needed and hesitancy where action has hitherto taken precedence, so exacerbating damage. Margaret Ronda's poignant essay 'Obsolesce' encourages a historically and culturally situated examination of an increasingly significant ecological problem contributing to the Anthropocene. Her piece examining e-waste offers an example of the kind of connective and nuanced analysis that is required today and traces the problematic circulation of discarded laptops, tablets and cell phones that reverse the global itinerary of commodity production, returning to countries like China, India, Nigeria and Ghana where materials were originally sourced, causing havoc. Highlighting consequences of lack of care and infrastructure concerning e-waste, she sheds light on the economies of informal workers, including children, created in cities like Accra and Lagos, where people scavenge in dumps for material to sell to local scrap markets.

In doing so, Ronda also sheds light on a conspiracy of blindness generated by market stratagems that serve to maintain these socioecological activities, drawing connections between the problems of e-waste and the postwar economic growth that became an increasingly central organising principle of commodity production in the global economy by the late twentieth century. She examines how consumers were deterred from reusing goods that were 'legally dead' as a consequence of the thought of the economist Bernard London. According to Ronda, in 1932, London argued for the addition of expiration dates to products, initiating a mainstream culture of disposability that led to the manufacturing of products intended for limited use only, and designed to break down or lose functionality. By the early 1950s, she notes, the industrial designer Brooks Stevens could claim that our whole economy is built on planned obsolescence, and that 'we make good products, we induce people to buy them, and then next year we deliberately introduce something that will make those products old fashioned, out of date, obsolete.' Stevens' claim is instantly recognisable today with regard to electronic goods, as Ronda succeeds in showing.

The strength of Ronda's essay is not to be found in a suggestion that we might ourselves 'obsolesce', which is a direction that other authors follow but which appears to be resisted here. Instead it is the importance of the point illustrated throughout, evoked through her meditation on obsolescence, that there remain insufficient ecologically-sound means of disposal for products that are rendered obsolete in a culturally, economic and sociologically embedded process, and there remains a lack of thought directed to addressing this issue.

Profitably read in conjunction with this is Jesse Oak Taylor's 'Globalise', which contains a comprehensive overview of three signal years, 1610, 1784 and 1945, each proposed as a candidate for the *golden spike* defining the origin of the Anthropocene. In Taylor's essay, he suggests that globalising our thinking, acting and seeing enables us to reimagine our modes of dwelling, and both he and Ronda demonstrate the requirement for a re-contextualisation of our position within an increasingly complex web of life that moves beyond the one-dimensional thinking that contributed to our current state of damage.

Joseph Campano's piece 'Power Down' examines the blackout that struck America's East Coast including New York City in 1965, and which recurred in New York in 1977, reflecting on the forms of community and mutual care that arise when energy is in abeyance. Campano's essay reads as a meditation on Adorno's concern about our lack of free time and an attempt to transform the sense of exhaustion that may derive from this into something positive. Campano describes his chosen phrase as a suggestion that, in addition to powering down our electronic devices, we might comparably monitor our affective states, and respond to sociological and ecological crises with an *aesthetics of exhaustion* in the place of fear, panic, anger or false empowerment.

As with other essays in the volume, the attempt to compact what needs to be a complex resolution to a complex crisis into the form of a soundbite can render the text obscure and diminishes some of the more interesting points raised, such as the relationship between vulnerability and collective precarity. Brian Thill's 'Shade', where he contends that we should fracture the spectacle's prominent connection with ecological thought, seems wrong-footed in this respect, and although one can recognise that he is suggesting that we do not rely on shocking images to prompt action that is already our responsibility, his means of expression detracts power from his point.

Veer Ecology is a valuable contribution to efforts to make sense of the extraordinary transitions put in place by drastic environmental change. Whilst its strength lies in the willingness displayed by the authors to re-examine the groundwork of our thinking, the book fails to take fully the opportunity to consider in detail the overlooked societies which are most likely to be affected by rich countries' actions yet whose plight often remains hidden from their view. Examples of such valuable global thinking, which show how ecology and policy might intertwine, shine through when they appear, such as in Ronda's essay.

Additionally, the commitment to Royle's term *veer* and the necessity to commit to providing a verb that changes the way we conduct ourselves has the effect of limiting the content of some essays and extending themes in others whose purposes can be elusive, such as the word play with references to the *whirled* in Tim Ingold's contribution. If chosen terms were used more as springboards, they might have been less restrictive.

It would be beneficial, in this regard, to read *Veer Ecology* in conjunction with other contemporary thinkers whose strengths supplement some of the book's weaknesses, such as Donna Haraway or the geologist and writer Jan Zalasiewicz. This would help us to extend and develop the notion introduced early on that the way we tell stories, the narratives that we consider ourselves through, are reflected in our engagement with the world around us, and therefore deserve careful attention on the part of any environmental thinking.

Alice Gibson

www.ingramcontent.com/pod-product-compliance
Lightning Source LLC
Chambersburg PA
CBHW081101070526
44583CB00019B/2516